U.S. Protectionism and the World Debt Crisis

U.S. Protectionism and the World Debt Crisis

Edward John Ray

Q

QUORUM BOOKS

New York • Westport, Connecticut • London

Library of Congress Cataloging-in-Publication Data

Ray, Edward J. (Edward John)
    U.S. protectionism and the world debt crisis / Edward John Ray.
      p. cm.
    Bibliography: p.
    Includes index.
    ISBN 0-89930-367-6 (alk. paper)
    1. Protectionism—United States. 2. United States—Commercial
policy. 3. Debts, External—Developing countries. I. Title.
II. Title: United States protectionism and the world debt crisis.
HF1756.R28   1989
382.7'3'0973—dc19   89-3774

British Library Cataloguing-in-Publication Data is available.

Library of Congress Catalog Card Number: 89-3774
ISBN: 0-89930-367-6

First published in 1989 by Quorum Books

Greenwood Press, Inc.
88 Post Road West, Westport, Connecticut 06881

Printed in the United States of America

The paper used in this book complies with the
Permanent Paper Standard issued by the National
Information Standards Organization (Z39.48-1984).

10 9 8 7 6 5 4 3 2 1

Copyright Acknowledgments

The material developed in Chapters 1 and 2 represents an expanded version of Edward John
Ray, "Changing Patterns of Protectionism: The Fall in Tariffs and the Rise in Non-Tariff
Barriers," *Northwestern Journal of International Law and Business* 8, no. 2 (Fall 1987), pp.
286-327 (copyright 1988). The material contained in Tables 3 through 9 is taken from tables
in two publications of the International Monetary Fund, *World Economic Outlook*, April
1987, and *International Capital Markets* (December 1986). The specific references to those
publications are listed on the tables themselves.

To Beth

Contents

Figures

Tables

Preface

The idea for this book arose from two coincidental events. First, in early 1987 I was approached by John H. Ehrlich, then editor-in-chief of the *Northwestern Journal of International Law and Business*, about the possibility of preparing a paper summarizing the literature on the political economy of protectionism as part of a symposium for the fall 1987 issue. Then, in the early autumn of 1987, Liliane H. Miller, acquisitions editor at Quorum Books, contacted me after having read my recently published paper on U.S. preferential trade arrangements with developing countries. She inquired about the possibility of my preparing a longer manuscript dealing broadly with protectionist issues and focused on the implications for developing countries.

The coincidence of having just finished a summary of the protectionist literature and having authored several pieces dealing with trade and developing countries led me to conclude that 1987 was as good a time for me to prepare a book-length manuscript on the subject as it would ever be. Hopefully, the reader will find the book as timely to read as I found it timely to write.

Since the first two chapters build upon the material published in the *Northwestern Journal of International Law and Business*, I owe the editorial staff special thanks beyond the simple copyright acknowledgment given eariler. The editorial staff of the journal made important contributions to the presentation of ideas expressed in the earlier publication. The expansion of the general analytical approach embodied in the book benefitted from the editorial process for the journal, especially concerning points that could be expanded and clarified.

I am indebted to Bob Baldwin for his many years and many kinds of encouragement for my work on protectionism and for being too busy to write the survey paper for *Northwestern*. Obviously, I would not have ventured into book-writing territory without the encouragement of Liliane Miller.

As will be abundantly clear to the reader, Bennett D. Baack and Howard P. Marvel, with whom I have co-authored papers on trade and protectionism, have contribued substantially to the development of ideas presented in the book. There are also many colleagues, editors and anonymous referees for journals around the world who have helped me to get my story straight over the years. Johannes Denekamp and Dan Evans provided valuable research assistance for a number of my earlier works in this area as well as for the preparation of this manuscript. Finally, my thanks go to Linda Lewis, who is both an excellent typist and interpreter of my sometimes garbled instructions for preparing the original manuscript.

U.S. Protectionism
and the
World Debt Crisis

Introduction

Chapter 1 outlines the course of inquiry to be followed in succeeding chapters after reviewing the analytical framework that is at the center of this study. In particular, we will review earlier work by George Stigler, Sam Peltzman, Gary Becker, Howard Marvel and Edward John Ray that adapts Stigler's original analysis of the capture theory of regulation to the subject of regulation of international trade. The framework we will outline combines two different strands of the literature on the political economy of protectionism. In brief, we will argue that policy is the product of a weighted consensus of constituent demands that remains stable and predictable over time unless those weights are disturbed by substantial and persistent shifts in the underlying political and/or economic interests of the parties vying for political favors.

The discussions that follow in Chapters 2 through 8 will review U.S. trade policy throughout the post-World War II period with a particular emphasis on how that policy has affected developing countries. The empirical evidence on the impact of preferential trade agreements on U.S. imports of manufactured goods will focus on the seven leading market debtor nations (Argentina, Brazil, Indonesia, Korea, Mexico, Philippines and Venezuela). The theme throughout the book is whether or not U.S. trade concessions to developing countries in general and to these seven in particular contribute positively to their efforts to meet their debt obligations.

Beginning with the formation of General Agreement on Tariffs and Trade (GATT) after World War II, the United States in conjunction with other industrial nations embarked on an ambitious effort to liberalize international trade on a multilateral basis. Through successive rounds of negotiations, tariff rates have been reduced substantially among the industrial nations, and progress has been made in defining codes of conduct for the use of nontariff trade barriers (NTBs).

Chapter 2 reviews the changes in tariffs and NTBs that have been implemented under the auspices of the GATT from the end of World War II to the full implementation of the Kennedy Round tariff cuts in 1972. We will focus on the post-Kennedy Round structure of tariffs in the United States and the other leading industrial countries and its implications for the efforts of developing countries to export manufactured goods to the industrial economies. In the process we will illustrate the relevance of the analytical framework outlined in Chapter 1 in understanding the system of tariffs and NTBs that emerged by the mid-1970s. In substance the chapter will be an expanded version of an earlier paper by Ray and Marvel (1984). The chapter will clarify the context within which preferential trade agreements emerged.

Chapter 3 expands upon earlier work on the U.S. Generalized System of Preferences (GSP) presented in Ray (1987). In particular, the chapter contains an in-depth analysis of the GSP agreement adopted in 1975. The focus for that analysis is the extent to which the agreement was responsive to the demand of developing countries for more open access to the U.S. market for their exports of manufactured goods. In addition, we will assess the relevance of the analytical framework developed in Chapter 1 in forecasting which industry interest groups within the United States and in the developing countries would win and which would lose from such an agreement.

The purpose of Chapter 4 is twofold. First, it reviews the status of the world debt problem in 1987, focusing on the seven countries with the largest market external debt positions: Argentina, Brazil, Indonesia, Korea, Mexico, Philippines and Venezuela. We will review arguments about the causes of the debt crisis and proposed solutions with particular emphasis on the relevance of that literature to the seven debtor countries. Second, in anticipation of later chapters, we will review domestic and international economic conditions for each of the seven with a view toward assessing the extent to which expanding exports of manufactured goods to the United States could play a significant role in assisting each country in meeting its external debt obligations.

The GSP was revised and renewed in October, 1984. Chapter 5 will include an analysis of the new bill, comparing and contrasting its content with that of the original 1975 bill. The focus of that analysis and comparative study will be whether the new bill is more or less responsive to the needs of the manufacturing exporting interests of the developing countries in general and the seven in particular. From an analytical standpoint we will be interested in explaining differences in the two bills on the basis of changed economic and political conditions in the United States between 1975 and 1985.

Chapter 6 is primarily an empirical piece. Using U.S. import data from 1985 and 1986, it will complement the analysis in Chapter 5 by providing an empirical analysis of the characteristics of GSP imports into the United States during the first two years of the revised agreement (1985-1986). Pooling time-series and cross-sectional data will allow us to assess the differential effects of the new legislation for developing countries in general and for the severely indebted seven in particular.

The preferential trade aspects of the Caribbean Basin initiative (CBI), adopted in 1983 and implemented in 1984, are interesting to study in relation to the new GSP legislation for two reasons. First, since the CBI was adopted shortly before the renewal of the GSP, it is worth probing whether or not the successful passage of the CBI legislation influenced the content of the 1985 GSP bill. Second, to the extent that the CBI remains more liberal than the revised GSP, we will be able to provide evidence regarding the impact of political shocks on economic legislation. The CBI remained on the shelf until the Grenada invasion and the subsequent upsurge in interest in the political future of the Caribbean gave the Reagan administration the support it needed to get the CBI through Congress. In addition to providing an analysis of the similarities and differences in the actual bills, we will review empirical evidence on the characteristics of manufactured imports into the United States under the auspices of the CBI that can be compared with the GSP findings of Chapter 6.

The final chapter of the book has three major themes. First, we will sum up the implications of the preceding chapters with respect to the issue of whether or not the current GSP legislation can play a significant role in providing severely indebted nations with the kind of access they need to U.S. markets for their manufactured exports to alleviate their debt burden. Second, following the discussion of the role of political crisis in changing the content of preferential trade legislation in Chapter 7, we will assess the likelihood that political shocks in the major debtor nations could generate significant revisions in the existing GSP. Finally, we will discuss the relevance of these preferential trade agreements to the central role that GATT has played in world trade negotiations in the last forty years. Specifically, we will explore the question of whether preferential agreements like the GSP and the CBI undermine the historical commitment to multilateral negotiations as the dominant means to liberalize international trade.

REFERENCES

Ray, Edward John. "The Impact of Special Interests on Preferential Tariff Concessions by the United States." *Review of Economics and Statistics* 69, no. 2 (May 1987): 187-93.

Ray, Edward John, and Marvel, Howard P. "The Pattern of Protection in the Industrialized World." *Review of Economics and Statistics* 66, no. 3 (August 1984): 452-58.

1

An Analysis of Protectionism in the United States

This book provides an analysis of U.S. preferential trade agreements with developing countries and relates those agreements to the current international debt problems of developing countries. The organization of the book is reflected in the contents and does not require repeating here. Instead, we will outline the importance of the issues to be discussed, the significance of the empirical evidence assembled and the timeliness of the study.

A number of empirical studies have been published in recent years that clarify the extent to which the pattern of protection within a given country can be predicted based on simple models of the political economy of trade regulation. Papers like Marvel and Ray (1983), Ray and Marvel (1984) and Ray (1987a) have progressively sharpened our focus on the impact of protectionist measures in the United States and other industrial countries on the ability of developing nations to export manufactured goods to industrialized nations. The papers by Marvel and Ray have applied the Stigler-Peltzman-Becker analysis on the regulation of industry to the regulation of international trade by means of tariffs and nontariff trade barriers (NTBs). In this chapter, we will provide a fuller explanation of that model that will serve as a backdrop for the empirical work of subsequent chapters.

The book provides a detailed discussion of the economic implications of both the initial and revised versions of the Generalized System of Preferences, (GSP) first adopted in 1975 and revised and renewed in late 1984. Those discussions are timely in three respects. First we will compare and contrast the actual pieces of legislation within the context of the model developed in this chapter. Furthermore, the discussion will be focused on the relevance of both GSP documents to those developing countries that currently have the greatest external debts with respect to private lenders: Argentina, Brazil, Indonesia, Korea, Mexico, the Phillippines and Venezuela.

Second, by using 1985 and 1986 data on U.S. imports of manufactured goods, we will provide original evidence on the characteristics of manufactured imports from developing countries in general and from the heavily indebted nations in particular. By reviewing the data for both years we will be able to assess whether or not the two pieces of legislation contributed positively to the possibility that debtor nations could meet their debt payments in part through expanded manufactured goods exports to the United States. We will also be able to provide the first tangible evidence of whether the revised GSP is more or less promising in that regard.

While there has been a great deal of discussion of debt forgiveness, concessionary credits and other means for alleviating the international debt crisis, there has been very little discussion of the role played by protectionism in the industrialized countries and preferential trade agreements between the industrialized countries and the debtor developing nations. Chapter 4 will provide a discussion of the world debt crisis that puts the trade issue in perspective. That discussion will focus on the seven major borrowers from private institutions.

However, it is worth noting here why the relationship between manufactured exports to the industrialized countries is an important element in the world debt story. In simple terms, like Blanche Dubois in *A Streetcar Named Desire*, nations cannot get by in life depending upon the kindnesses of strangers. Regardless of how much assistance the developing countries obtain in meeting their current debt obligations, they face great difficulties in attracting new investment funds. Our focus on the major debtors to foreign private lenders is intentional. In order to get back on the track of economic progress, those nations must not only resolve their current debt problems but also establish themselves as attractive markets for foreign investors in the future.

That kind of long-term financial health requires some proof that debt crises will not be a recurring problem and that creditors can expect to get paid. Part of the process of both resolving the current debt problems that developing countries face and reducing fears of a recurrence will be for those developing nations to demonstrate a substantial ability to export manufactures to the United States and other industrialized countries. Net export earnings from manufactured goods sales in the industrialized countries are needed to retire current hard-currency debt obligations and to provide confidence in the stability of developing countries' currency values. Stable currency values will be part of the formula for reducing capital flight and encouraging foreign capital investment in the future in countries that are heavily in debt today.

The need for monetary and fiscal reforms in many debtor nations is obvious and crucial. However, those aspects of the debtor-nation problem are beyond the scope of this study. Instead, we will focus on the role that healthy export earnings can play in promoting a market solution to the debt problem and providing confidence that the debt crisis will not recur. How relevant the role of export earnings from manufactured goods will be in promoting long-term economic progress in developing countries will depend in part on protectionist policies in the United States and other industrialized nations. That is the linkage that we want to analyze.

The third feature of the book is that it will provide an analysis of newer programs such as the Caribbean Basin Initiative (CBI) and the United States-Canada Free Trade Agreement that have implications for the future course of world trade including patterns of trade between the United States and developing countries. Within the context of that discussion in Chapter 8 we will assess the role that political crises in debtor nations might play in reshaping the GSP and other preferential trade agreements in the future.

Chapter 8 also contains a discussion of the relationship between the emergence of special preferential trade arrangements between industrialized and developing countries in the last fifteen years and the apparent decline in optimism about the current Uruguay Round of trade talks in Geneva. Those talks are aimed at continuing the trend of the last forty years of trade liberalization on a multilateral basis under the auspices of GATT.

As this brief description suggests, this book should appeal to a number of audiences. Professional economists and policymakers might benefit from an opportunity to learn about the broad implications of trade legislation for the debt problems that they have had an opportunity to consider from narrower or simply different perspectives.

The book should appeal to academic economists and political scientists interested in further analytical and empirical work on the characteristics and consequences of U.S. protectionism. The book includes a considerable amount of empirical work that has not been published to date.

Finally, the focus of the book should make it attractive as a supplementary reading for advanced undergraduate and graduate courses in international trade, economic development, international business and/or international political economy. There is, in fact, nothing in the basic analytics of this chapter that could not be applied to other areas of policy analysis that involve the interactions of domestic special interests and national political and economic objectives.

The basic thrust of our analysis is that trade policy is the product of our collective pursuit of national political objectives tempered by the influences of economic special interest groups. For example, in the late nineteenth century the United States built a world-class navy during peacetime in order to assume the role of a major player in international political affairs. Major manufacturing sectors within the country including steel and textiles emerged during that same period as serious competitors in world markets. That combination of national ambitions and industry-level economic interests played a critical role in explaining the shift in U.S. trade policy away from highly protective tariffs toward freer trade at the turn of the last century.[1] In the late twentieth century we face changed political and economic fortunes that threaten to end four decades of commitment by the United States to trade liberalization. We will review the recent political and economic changes that have affected U.S. trade policy and provide an analytical framework within which we can explain changes in trade policies as well as anticipate the course that international trade relations will follow for the foreseeable future. With generous reference to the vast literature on the political economy of trade restrictions, we will explain the shift in protectionism from tariff to nontariff trade barriers that has been occurring throughout the last two decades. The relative shift from tariffs to NTBs in industrialized countries represents a grave threat to competitive exports of manufactured goods from developing to industrialized countries including the United States.

There are a number of useful surveys of the literature regarding U.S. trade policies in the postwar period, including Baldwin (1976b, 1984, 1986a), Kaempfer (1987) and Marks (1987). There are also numerous studies of the determinants of trade restrictions within individual countries such as Baack and Ray (1983), Caves (1976), Caves and Jones (1977), Cheh (1974, 1976), Deardorff and Stern (1979), Fieleke (1971), Helleiner (1977), Marvel (1980), Marvel and Ray (1983, 1987), Pincus (1975), Pugel and Walter (1985), Ray (1981a), Riedel (1977), Stern (1964), Stone (1978), Taussig (1931) and Tosini and Tower (1987) and of the determinants of trade restrictions among trading partners, with particular emphasis on those between industrialized and developing countries: Balassa (1967), Balassa and Associates (1971), Bhagwati (1982), Clark (1987), Deardorff and Stern (1985), Grossman (1982), Krugman (1983), Ray (1974, 1981b, 1987a, 1987b), Ray and Marvel (1984) and Verreydt and Waelbroeck (1982).

Along quite different lines, a number of interesting papers have speculated about changes that might be made in the mechanisms used to determine trade policies both within the United States and for the GATT members that would encourage a continuation of the trend toward trade liberalization of the last forty years. Examples of those papers would include: Arendt (1987), Baldwin (1986b), Goldstein and Krasner (1984), Snape (1987) and Wihlborg (1987).

While this chapter and the next one will each touch upon many of the points raised in this literature, it will not entail detailed explanations of arguments or of empirical findings. Readers interested in such details should refer to the original works. Here we will concentrate on defining an analytical framework that can explain how the efforts of special interest groups interact with overriding domestic political concerns and foreign policy objectives of a country to influence the overall structure of trade regulations within that country. From that base we will expand the scope of our analysis to explain the current pattern of trade restrictions across countries, how they evolved over time, and how trade regulations are likely to change in the future.

The next section briefly reviews the history of U.S. trade policy before and after World War II and summarizes both current economic conditions and the political climate for protectionist legislation in the United States. The section that follows provides a simple analytical framework within which we can explain the evolution of both the pattern and the level of protectionism in the United States and other countries. That framework is used in Chapter 2 to explain the historical events touched upon in this chapter and to forecast the direction in which trade relations among nations are likely to move in the years to come.

THE PATTERN OF PROTECTION IN THE UNITED STATES

The value of a historical perspective to understanding current trade policy is apparent in the common caution that history does repeat itself but never in exactly the same way. Simple-minded extrapolations across time and circumstances can be as foolhardy as ignoring history altogether, but history provides useful information to us in some important respects. As explained below, the shift in political support toward protectionist legislation in the United States in the last decade is not a new phenomenon. There was also precedent for the political support for trade liberalization within the United States during the 1950s and 1960s. A brief review of the historical pattern of protectionism in the United States provides some insight into the means by which economic interest groups can serve and have served to reinforce or undermine federal government policies with respect to international economic cooperation.

In a study of trade policy in the United States during the last half of the nineteenth century, Baack and Ray (1983) identified a number of relationships worth noting here. First, contrary to the general thrust of U.S. trade policy throughout most of the post-World War II period, the United States pursued a policy of high tariffs throughout its period of rapid industrialization between 1870 and 1914. Referring to a sample of ninety-seven manufacturing industries including every industry that emerged as significant by 1914, the average tariff rate was 45.8 percent in 1870, 40.6 percent in 1910 and 26.3 percent in 1914 following the substantial tariff cuts of the Underwood-Simmons Tariff Act of October 1913.

Furthermore, they found that contrary to the characterization offered in Taussig's (1931) classic study, U.S. tariff policy appears to have been systematically geared to accommodate rapid industrialization. Specifically, Baack and Ray found that tariff protection was concentrated on finished manufactured goods rather than intermediate goods. That same general strategy has been used by developing countries in this century to promote import substitution in manufacturing. While the results for contemporary cases are mixed at best, the historical evidence suggests that manufacturing sectors that were highly protected by the tariff structure in 1870 in the United States emerged as the most rapidly expanding industries throughout the period from 1870 to 1914.[2] Finally, they found that tariffs were systematically higher on liquor, tobacco products and other price-inelastic commodities (price-inelastic goods are those for which price increases induce little or no decrease in the quantity demanded) that one would expect to be reliable sources of federal government revenue at a time when tariffs funded well over half of the federal budget.

The simple point here is that during its industrialization period the United States was highly protectionist, used tariff policy to promote the growth of its manufacturing sector and relied heavily on tariffs to fund central government programs. Those policies are characteristic of many developing countries today and are in sharp contrast to the trade liberalization stance that the United States has professed for the last fifty years. (Readers interested in protectionist policies in developing countries are referred to Balassa [1971], Bhagwati [1982], Krueger [1978] and Ray [1974]). One test that our analysis will have to pass is to explain why U.S. policy on trade restrictions shifted so dramatically over time.

There is another apparent paradox in American trade policy that a coherent analysis ought to be able to explain. Throughout the late nineteenth century, Democrats *opposed* the high tariffs adopted by Congress and fought to reduce them. Republicans were equally staunch in their support *for* high tariffs. In contrast, Democrats have systematically championed protectionist legislation in the post-World War II period over the objections of the Republicans, who have pushed for further trade liberalization. Are there underlying economic factors that we can identify as consistent in their impact on national policy positions to explain the apparent flip-flop of the major parties with respect to trade restrictions?

Except for the brief period under the Smoot-Hawley Tariff of 1930, which resulted in U.S. tariffs reaching an all-time high average of 59 percent in 1932, tariffs have declined steadily in the United States throughout the period from 1914 to 1986, when the Tokyo Round tariff cuts were scheduled to be fully implemented. The United States played the major role in establishing GATT in 1947 and in promoting its expansion from the original twenty-two member countries to more than ninety today. (The interested reader can find a good discussion of the background and operation of the GATT in Curzon [1964].) Moreover, the United States played a key role in setting the trade liberalizing agenda through each of the seven rounds of trade negotiations in 1947, 1949, 1950-1951, 1955-1956, 1961-1962, 1964-1967 and 1974-1979. The last three rounds have come to be known more commonly as the Dillon, Kennedy and Tokyo Rounds, respectively. The latest round of multilateral trade negotiations, the Uruguay Round, moved quickly through the planning stage and convened in Geneva in late 1987. However suspect U.S. motives may seem, President Reagan was among those calling for these negotiations since the completion of the Tokyo Round negotiations.

The rapid decline in U.S. tariffs from 59 percent in 1932 to a little over 7 percent after the implementation of the Kennedy Round tariff cuts by the early 1970s paralleled changes in other industrialized nations and contributed to a genuine sense of progress toward free international trade. A number of studies focused on the consequences of multilateral trade concessions within countries and found that benefits far outweighed any adverse effects associated with short-term adjustment costs (see for example Baldwin [1976a] and Baldwin and Lage [1971]).

However, even before the Kennedy Round had been concluded, a number of authors noted either that the multilateral agreements were not providing substantial access to industrial country markets for the manufactured exports of developing countries (Balassa [1967, 1971], or that remaining nontariff barriers to trade might affect trade differently than would tariffs (Bhagwati [1969], Fishelson and Flatters [1975], Kreinen [1970]). The negotiators at the Kennedy Round meetings abandoned their efforts to deal with NTBs when it became clear that their work on tariff cuts would be substantial enough to warrant their full attention. The negotiators at the Tokyo Round did succeed in hammering out codes of conduct for the use of NTBs, but actual agreements to reduce them in line with tariff cuts remained for the Uruguay Round and perhaps later rounds of multilateral negotiations.

The fact that international negotiations have dealt less effectively with NTBs is a crucial element in our story to explain the shifting pattern of protectionism in the last twenty-five years. As explained below, trade policy is determined by the impact of economic special interests within a country on the national political and economic agenda through the political process. The outcome at any point in time surely will be influenced by underlying political and economic circumstances. Which positions prevail in any given struggle for control of trade policy also will depend upon the means available for controlling trade flows. NTBs have become more effective and therefore more prevalent than tariffs as instruments for restricting trade. We will argue below that NTBs have increased the likelihood that protectionist interests will be successful in shaping the pattern of protection to suit their tastes in any given set of political and economic circumstances.

One did not have to look too hard in the early post-World War II period to find evidence that while protection in general was diminishing among the industrial countries, there were specific areas in which quantitative restrictions were expanding. For example, in 1956 the United States persuaded Japan to adopt a voluntary export restriction (VER), on exports of cotton textiles to the United States (specific studies of VERs include Fahnline [1987], Tarr and Morkre [1984], Tosini and Tower [1987] and Turner [1983]), and the United Kingdom concluded a similar agreement with Hong Kong. Needless to say, U.S. imports continued to grow when Hong Kong exports that were deliberately excluded from the United Kingdom were diverted to the United States. The GATT specifically restricts the use of quantitative restrictions unless they are applied on a most-favored-nation basis and compensation is provided to affected countries. Otherwise, the affected countries would have a right to retaliate against the offending nation. The diabolical genius behind the use of VERs stems from the fact that they are technically self-imposed limits on trade by the exporting country rather than discriminatory quantitative restrictions by an importing country.

Congressional approval of the Trade Expansion Act of 1962, giving the president authority to proceed with what came to be known as the Kennedy Round, was gained only after the administration concluded the Short Term Arrangement on Cotton Textiles in 1961 and the Long Term Agreement (LTA) on Tariffs and Trade in 1962. Passage of the Trade Act of 1974, authorizing the president to proceed with what came to be known as the Tokyo Round of trade liberalization, was threatened until the Multifiber Arrangement (MFA), was signed in December 1973, expanding the LTA to include manmade fibers and wool. By the end of 1986, the United States had agreements on almost 650 quotas with forty-one different countries. MFA IV, which was concluded in December 1986, added silk, linen, ramie and jute to the list of controlled fibers (see Fahnline [1987]).

Throughout the 1960s the rapidly changing nature of world commodity markets, of which the textile trade was only one example, raised questions about the determinants of a country's competitive position in world markets and changes in that position over time. Baldwin (1971) and Hufbauer (1970) provided some of the earliest and best analyses of the changing nature of comparative advantage in the United States. Among their principal findings were that the United States was relatively strong in exporting technologically sophisticated products that required skilled labor and relatively weak in competing for international sales of goods that could be mass produced using cheap, low-skilled labor.

Those findings quite naturally led to attempts to estimate whether or not the recently completed Kennedy Round had yielded a pattern of protection across industries that was consistent with the protection of less competitive, domestically produced, low-skill, labor-intensive goods. Cheh (1974, 1976) and Stone (1978) were among the first investigators to demonstrate a systematic bias in post-Kennedy Round protection in the United States in favor of low-skill, labor-intensive products. At the same time Pincus (1975), building on earlier work by Olson (1968) and Stigler (1971), provided empirical evidence that U.S. tariff protection in the early 1830s was structured to protect the special interests of producers in industries that could not compete effectively against imported goods for domestic sales of their products. Caves (1976) and Helleiner (1977) provided empirical evidence to support the contention that in Canada, too, the structure of tariff rates across industries seemed to be related to the needs of special interests rather than the economic benefit of society as a whole.

By the mid-1970s it was clear that while the trend in tariffs across industries within the United States and other industrial countries was toward freer trade, there remained considerable systematic differences in protection across industries that were worth explaining. However, there was no consensus that NTBs were a serious threat to continued trade liberalization. Neither was there particular concern that NTBs could be used to disguise the extent to which trade is restricted and thereby foster a false sense of satisfaction among policymakers about gains in international economic cooperation. National and international economic crises during the last half of the 1970s served to highlight the power of special interest groups in setting trade policies and the effectiveness of NTBs as protectionist instruments.

Special Interests and Trade Stratgegies

The public dialogue about trade policy in the United States changed quickly in the early 1970s when a foreign special interest group, the Organization of Petroleum Exporting Countries (OPEC), demonstrated its power to manipulate international trade relations to its own advantage. With one stroke OPEC dealt a serious blow to our national sense of security in international economic matters and undercut our collective political commitment to international economic cooperation. In addition, the fact that the rise in oil prices that followed affected a few key industries severely meant that the economic base on which our national commitment to trade liberalization rested was changing. In short, the shift in momentum away from trade liberalization was directly related to changed economic and political realities.

The first oil crisis in 1974 quickly led to public speculation about either retaliation against OPEC through trade restrictions such as oil import quotas or some agreement to negotiate long-term prices on OPEC oil. For a more detailed discussion of OPEC, see Pindyck (1978), MacBean and

Snowden (1981, Chapter 6) and Vernon (1983, Chapter 2). One popular but mindless retaliatory scheme was the withholding of bushels (of wheat) for barrels (of oil). Alternatively, Henry Kissinger advocated a buyers' cartel to negotiate guaranteed long-term prices for OPEC oil in the industrial countries. Fortunately, neither of those alternative paths for trade policy was adopted. However, public discussions in the United States regarding trade had shifted to a consideration of alternative strategies that we might employ. Without much fanfare, public discussions of the oil crisis expanded the menu of admissible trade policies for the United States to include various strategic alternatives and in the bargain signaled a shift in national consensus from a strong commitment to trade liberalization to the view that freer trade was only one of many options to be pursued and not necessarily the best one.

As a result of many factors, including accelerating inflation in the United States, high energy prices, government regulations on domestic oil prices and auto emissions, and the emergence of West Germany and Japan as genuine competitors for steel and auto sales in the United States, all pretense of a continuing commitment to unqualified free trade by the United States was abandoned by the time the Tokyo Round Agreements were concluded in 1979. Trigger prices for steel imports, Japanese voluntary quotas on auto exports to the United States, government loan guarantees to Chrysler, multifiber agreements, semiconductor agreements between the United States and Japan not to compete against each other for sales, arguments between the United States and the European Community over wheat sales to Egypt and compensation payments to the United States for lost export sales in Spain resulting from her membership in the European Community, arguments with Canada over lumber product sales by Canadians in the United States and numerous other conflicts and special agreements on a bilateral basis with our trading partners have made it clear that the United States has lost some of its credibility if not its resolve to promote trade liberalization.

Walter Mondale campaigned for the presidency in 1984 arguing that the United States should insist on an overall trade policy based upon *fair* trade rather than *free* trade. Although he lost the election, it is clear that as a nation we are still wrestling with the question of whether we advocate freer trade without conditions or a shift away from multilateral agreements to bilateral reciprocal trade agreements with individual trading partners. The ambivalence of our position as a nation is evident from the fact that the Reagan administration led the call for the current round of multilateral negotiations while also negotiating free trade agreements on a bilateral basis with Israel and with Canada.

Congress for its part produced a comprehensive trade bill that (before being changed in the conference committee) threatened trade restrictions on a bilateral basis against countries that have large trade surpluses with the United States. That idea was taken seriously enough to project its author, Congressman Richard Gephardt, into position as a legitimate candidate for the Democratic presidential nomination in 1988. The provision was removed from the trade bill after representative Gephardt dropped out of the primaries. Although a presidential veto of the trade bill was sustained in the Senate in early June 1988, the vote was close and required some assurance from the president that he actually supported much of the tough language in the bill regarding fair trade and retaliation against trade partners found in violation of U.S. understandings of acceptable trade practices. Once the plant closing requirement was separated from the rest of the trade legislation during the summer of 1988, both bills passed Congress and the trade legislation became law.[3]

Further evidence of the increasingly bilateral nature of U.S. trade policy is seen in the recently renewed generalized system of preferences (GSP), intended to provide developing countries with preferential treatment in trade by granting them duty-free access to U.S. markets for many of their exports. Similarly, the Caribbean Basin Initiative adopted in 1983 and implemented in 1984, is intended to provide countries in the Caribbean region with duty-free access to U.S. markets for key exports. Regardless of how well intentioned such programs may be or how effective they are in achieving their stated objectives, they clearly imply that the United States is no longer committed to most-favored-nation trade policies.

It is surely not surprising that, in the context of such times, trade research would increasingly focus on the determinants of the structure of protection within countries and the forces that shift the pattern of protection over time. We have already mentioned early attempts to estimate the influence of special interests on the pattern of tariffs and tariff changes within a country. Becker (1976, 1983) and Peltzman (1976) among others extended the work by Stigler (1971) on the political economy of industrial regulation. Peltzman (1976) provided insight into the trade-offs that governments face in voter support by acceding to the wishes of special interest groups at the expense of the general voting public. Becker (1983) expanded his earlier argument that government regulations establish a pattern for the distribution of economic rents (economic rents are pure profits or monopoly profits that can be redistributed without changing resource allocation decisions) and that changes in that pattern are likely only if political and/or economic conditions change enough to disturb the initial equilibrium distribution of rents. (An equilibruim distribution of rents is simply an allocation of monopoly profits that will persist through time unless it is disturbed by changing economic and/or political conditions.) While it may be useful to think of trade policy as an attempt to distribute rents generated by trade restrictions and to explain policy changes as the product of changed political and/or economic fortunes, such an approach can only have predictive content if we can explain precisely how changing economic-political conditions change policy. The next section provides an explanation of how changes in the regulation of trade are brought about.

THE MICRO- VERSUS THE MACROVIEW OF POLICY DECISIONMAKING

As elaborated below, there have been two general approaches to explain how trade policy is determined over time. On the one hand trade policy is viewed as the aggregate outcome of industry-level battles over protection. In that view government policy simply mirrors the preferences of industrial constituents. The view that aggregate national policy on trade issues is simply the sum of the demands of special interest groups might be called the *microview* of national policy determination. Alternatively, national governments are treated as individual players in international affairs who take positions on issues that are difficult to trace back to the underlying individual and/or industry interests or concerns. For obvious reasons we will refer to the notion that trade policy is the product of some collective interest called the nation or the government with no notion of how such aggregate interests can be traced back to the underlying constituent interests as the *macroview* of national policy determination.

A number of studies including those by Baldwin (1976b, 1984, 1986a, 1986b), Goldstein and Krasner (1984), Snape (1987) and Wihlborg (1987) have focused attention on how the mechanisms for making trade policies within countries or for adjudicating trade disputes between countries might be changed to move the United States and the rest of the world back toward a more consistent protrade liberalization stance. Implicit in many of these and related papers is the notion that trade policies are set by governments constrained by domestic concerns such as full employment, price stability and economic growth. Trade policy is viewed as an integral part of both domestic national economic and political policy and international political relationships. International economic tensions are the product of national conflicts in the economic arena that might be substantially reduced with appropriate changes in domestic and international mechanisms for determining how nations as individual participants reconcile their differing trade policies.

Alternatively, a number of papers have concentrated on the ability of special interest groups to influence the pattern of protection within a given country. Examples of such papers would include Cheh (1974, 1976), Clark (1987), Deardorff and Stern (1985), Pincus (1975), Pugel and Walter (1985), Ray (1974, 1981a, 1981b, 1987a), Riedel (1977),

Stone (1978), Taussig (1931) and Tosini and Tower (1987). Whether intended or not, such studies have often left the impression that government policy is either a weighted sum of the preferences of special interest groups adopted in a passive fashion or the end product of a sinister calculation by a group of frightened politicians who count votes before taking a position on any issue and are committed to nothing so much as they are to keeping their jobs.

While there are times when governments appear to behave in a way that is consistent with either the view that policy decisions are made at the macro- or aggregate level or the earlier view that collective decisions are built up from individual preferences, there is little evidence to suggest that either is superior to the other as a general model for predicting government behavior. There is a useful analogy here that can be made with the controversy surrounding the properties of light. Just as the properties of light are sometimes best understood by thinking of light as energy waves and at other times as particles, the properties of trade relations are sometimes best understood by thinking of nations as individual actors and at other times as simple aggregates of underlying special interests. The apparent need for such a dichotomous view of national policy determination is indicative of the need for a unifying theory of the properties of nations just as the dichotomous view of the nature of light is indicative of the need for a unifying theory of energy and matter.

Within the context of the Stigler-Peltzman-Becker framework, it is possible to argue that in conjunction with the equilibrium distribution of rents established in a regulated market, there is a political equilibrium as well that may be the product of both self-interest and shared values or concerns. In fact, we will argue below that contemporary trade policy is best understood by thinking of it as the product of a dynamic interaction between economic interest groups with immediate self-interest objectives and national economic and political agendas that represent shared or consensus positions of the populace. Shared values are slow to change and durable. In the sections that follow we will explain what the common values are and how effectively they have held protectionist demands in check within the United States in the last decade. The characterization of the alternative views of how trade policies are shaped as the microview and the macroview reflects our presumption that there are microfoundations to macropolicy positions with respect to international trade policy. The microview and the macroview must be integrated if we are to make substantial progress in understanding trade relations among nations. The first order of business, however, is to provide some evidence that shared values of consensus positions exist. Fortunately, we do not have to search long for that evidence.

For example, Marvel and Ray (1983) and Ray and Marvel (1984) assume that governments in industrialized countries are committed to providing a kind of safety net in the form of trade restrictions for industries that are vulnerable to foreign competition, but not to assisting rapidly expanding and profitable industries in exploiting monopoly profit positions in the home market. They provided empirical support for that view by demonstrating that Kennedy Round tariff cuts were minimized for declining industries and that NTBs were used to augment the tariff protection that less competitive industries already enjoyed. Note that we use the term safety net here in the same sense that the Reagan administration spoke of social security as part of the national "safety net" of welfare programs in the United States. Trade restrictions appear to have been used to protect vulnerable and declining industries rather than to create super profit opportunities for expanding and competitive industries in the United States.

In the foreign policy realm, Ray (1987a) argues that shifts in trade policy in the United States, including the adoption of the GSP and the CBI, were the result of national foreign policy commitments to developing nations trying to compete effectively in world markets for exports of manufactured goods. In effect, the paper implies a blending of the two extreme views of government behavior that characterize the literature on protectionism. Foreign policy objectives led the United States to adopt a trade program such as the GSP that is inconsistent with the country's long-standing policy of adhering to the most-favored-nation principle. Such an action suggests the presence of an activist government that is not simply responding to special interests or to alignments of voters. At the same time, that paper provides evidence that special interest groups influenced the content of the original version of the GSP that was implemented in 1975 and effectively sabotaged any hope that the legislation would achieve its advertised objective of opening U.S. markets for key exports from developing countries.

One could perhaps develop the thesis that U.S. policy is merely the servant of economic interest groups and that policies like the GSP and CBI are part of a cruel charade. However, the debate over trade policy in Congress over the last decade has reflected the kind of drift that is more consistent with a genuine clash between long-held principles and current special interest group tastes than the charade interpretation would lead one to expect.

The next section contains a simple and hopefully painless attempt to define an analytical framework within which to analyze the postwar phenomena of falling tariffs and rising NTBs that we have described generally in this section. That model will be useful in analyzing postwar trends and future prospects for world trade in Chapter 2.

AN ANALYTICAL FRAMEWORK

The discussion in the previous section cannot be extended unless we can be quite specific about who the various special interest groups are that try to influence trade policy, who the winners and losers are and how shared values or consensus positions are formed and changed. The purpose of this section is to begin the process of providing the necessary details of the analysis.

The set of major players in the struggle over whether trade policy is biased toward liberalization or protection at any point in time includes consumers, who always have an interest in freer trade in order to have access to a variety of products at the least possible cost. In fact, it is reasonable to assume that as incomes rise, consumer preferences for diversity intensify (see Krugman [1983]).

Producers and workers in import-sensitive sectors of the economy will always favor protection, while producers and workers in industries that have the potential to capture export market sales favor freer trade. The simple logic involved is that less competitive sectors will find that trade restrictions can preserve jobs and protect profits that would otherwise be lost to foreign competitors. Highly competitive export-oriented firms hoping to expand foreign sales will be concerned about the possibility that domestic trade restrictions will lead to retaliation abroad and reduce their access to foreign markets.

If we add four modest extensions to this simple list of the economic winners and losers from changes in trade policies, we can complete a summary of the key elements of all of the special interest models that correspond to the microview described earlier. Let us assume that consumers of final goods are a diverse group that cannot form an effective coalition to promote free trade. That assumption by itself suggests that final consumer goods are more likely candidates for protection than are producer goods or intermediate goods like capital equipment that would be imported by more homogeneous, better organized and smaller producer interest groups.

To the extent that the costs of producing an effective lobby for protection of a given industry from foreign competition increase with the size of the group, there is a presumption that concentrated industries in which a handful of firms are dominant would be more effective in organizing an effective lobbying effort and therefore in obtaining protection than industries with many small firms. Since we have already argued that firms that purchase capital equipment and/or other intermediate goods abroad will surely favor freer trade for those goods and are likely to be more concentrated as a group than consumers of final goods are as a group, there is a presumption that protection will be biased in favor of producers of final consumer goods whose production is dominated by a few large firms and away from intermediate inputs and capital goods that are produced under highly competitive conditions.

The final element of the story is that the government serves simply as the agent for all these diverse special interests and pursues a policy with respect to trade that is consistent with its own survival or electability. Empirical evidence supporting that simple, stylized view of the determination of trade policy is extensive and includes Caves (1976), Cheh (1974, 1976), Clark (1987), Deardorff and Stern (1985), Marvel (1980), Marvel and Ray (1987), Pincus (1975), Pugel and Walter (1985), Ray (1974, 1981a, 1981b), Stone (1978) and Tosini and Tower (1987).

One clue that we have that this model is incomplete is that it ignores foreign policy. Actions that we have already described such as the U.S. agreement to trade freely with Israel and with Canada, and the attempts to provide preferential access to U.S. markets for manufactured imports from developing countries through the implementation of the GSP and the CBI, suggest that as a nation we have staked out international political positions that do not follow easily from the microview model that we have at hand.

Furthermore, the battle in the United States between the executive branch and the legislature over trade policy throughout the 1980s highlights the fact that at a time when special interest groups are quite outspoken in their demands for protection, the executive branch of the government is working hard to maintain the nation's long-standing commitment to continued trade liberalization. That kind of conflict is not explicable in the context of a model in which the government proceeds to make policy decisions based solely on its appraisal of the summed wishes of special interest groups.

Domestic policy is also difficult to explain as the simple sum of special interest group preferences within the United States. The civil rights movement of the 1960s, the development, expansion and finally the indexing of social security payments in the early 1970s, which the Reagan administration promised to maintain, and the developing consensus on some form of catastrophic health insurance at the national level are examples of national policies that have evolved over many years and appear to respond slowly if at all to interest group pressures.

In general, then, we might characterize the federal government as the key player in the decision-making process regarding the regulation of trade. Particular government actions are guided by established national policies subject to feedback from special interest groups. When both national and net special interest group preferences favor trade liberalization, as we will argue they did in the early postwar period, national policy will be unambiguously in favor of freer trade. When national preferences are for freer trade and competition, but special interest preferences are on balance protectionist, as we will argue they have been in recent years, U.S. policy on international trade will reflect the kind of ambiguity we are now observing. The presumption here then is that national policy can be turned away from the current protrade stance if the special interest group bias continues to remain strong for a number of years.

The primary distinction between the model that we have proposed here and the special interest group models is that the government is explicitly included here as an active player with a long-term agenda. The government is sensitive to special interest group pressures, but it is not their captive. At the same time government policy is related to the overriding concerns of special interest groups. If special interest group preferences persist in favoring a particular stance on trade issues, the national agenda will shift to adopt that position. This model's contribution to the discussion of the formation and change in trade regulations is that it highlights the dynamic interaction between individual and collective interests that is so important to an understanding of current U.S. policy.[4]

There are a few key elements of this model that bear repeating. First, special interest groups, including groups of consumers and producers of imports and exports, do influence trade policy. The relative influence that such groups have on trade legislation is directly related to the effectiveness of their lobbying efforts, which in turn depend upon the size and cohesiveness of the coalitions they form. Small cohesive coalitions on trade issues are likely to be most effective in shaping policy. When national policy objectives are synchronized with the preponderant weight of special interest preferences with respect to trade, trade policies will be unambiguous. When national policies with respect to international economic relations lag behind changes in the sum of special interest objectives with respect to trade, policy positions will become blurred and inconsistent. The extent to which the government will respond quickly to shift national policies from an established course in response to special interest pressures will depend directly on the degree to which current policy and special interest preferences are in conflict with each other and on the relative importance of international trade to domestic economic progress. Finally, a nation's response to special interest pressures in reformulating trade policies will depend upon the international rules of the game in terms of admissible behavior as well as on the existing set of international millitary, political, cultural and economic relations.

While the model we are proposing here has not been tested explicitly, there are a number of studies of the regulation of trade that do provide support for the view that national as well as special interest considerations have influenced the structure and the pattern of change of trade restrictions in the United States. Baack and Ray (1983) provide evidence that in the late nineteenth century U.S. tariffs were structured to promote industrialization of the country. Specifically, they found that tariff protection was greatest for fast growth industries in late nineteenth-century America and that tariffs were reduced or removed as industries, including steel, became competitive in world markets. Marvel and Ray (1983) provide evidence consistent with the view that the Kennedy Round tariff cuts and the simultaneous expansion in the use of NTBs in the United States were intended to minimize the impact of trade liberalization on weak industries without augmenting the profitability of fast-growth industries. In particular, they found that Kennedy Round tariff cuts were greatest in fast growth, R&D-intensive industries and least in slow growth or declining industries and in consumer manufactures in which the United States was losing its competitive edge in international trade. Furthermore, they provide statistical evidence that nontariff trade restrictions were added to tariff protection for weak industries including manufactured consumer goods.

Ray (1987a) argues that the timing and nature of the original GSP and the CBI legislation adopted in the United States can be understood best when viewed as a compromise between a national commitment to help developing countries industrialize and the desire of affected special interest groups to blunt the threat of cheap imports in their domestic product markets. He provides direct evidence that both the GSP and CBI provided developing countries with duty-free access to U.S. markets for manufactured exports. However, that access was biased away from declining, noncompetitive industries such as textiles and processed foods. Unfortunately, those are the areas in which developing countries could benefit most from access to the U.S. market.

The point here is that the simple model we have in mind is robust enough to explain very different periods in U.S. history within a consistent framework. As suggested earlier and developed more fully in the next chapter, there have been historical periods when U.S. trade policy has been solidly committed to freer trade, including the early twentieth century and the early post-World War II years; there have been periods of commitment to protectionism, including the late nineteenth century and the early years of the depression; and there have been periods like the present when U.S. trade policy can best be described as unclear. We will review a number of those periods in Chapter 2 to illustrate how useful the framework outlined in this section is for understanding the many different policy stances that we have taken as a nation with respect to international trade and to explain why policy changed when it did.

Tariffs versus NTBs

There is one final point to be made before we turn to a more systematic discussion of U.S. trade policy with the model at hand. That issue is whether or not the government has any preferences regarding the form that protection of import-sensitive industries should take. Historically, as nation-states emerged, it was evident that central governments required funding and that tariff revenues were fairly easy to collect. Not until the early twentieth century, for example, did tariffs cease to provide the majority of federal government finances in the United States. In many developing countries, tariffs continue to play a major role in financing national government expenditures. Other things being equal, it should not be surprising that developing countries still rely more heavily on tariffs to restrict imports than do the industrialized nations (see Balassa and Associates [1971], Ray [1974]). Free of the revenue constraint associated with a heavy dependence on tariffs to finance government activities, the industrialized nations have led the way in developing NTB innovations for regulating international trade.

That preference for tariffs in developing countries is a direct outgrowth of the fact that fiscal or revenue-raising mechanisms are less well developed in such countries than in industrialized countries in North America and Europe. In developing countries tariffs serve the double duty of protecting domestic producers and providing a major share of the taxes collected by the national government. Quotas and other NTBs are more difficult and expensive to administer than tariffs and therefore less attractive as a primary source of revenue for government programs. Industrial countries that can use income taxes, value added taxes and other instruments to raise revenue are more likely to consider NTBs to restrict trade than are developing countries. As explained in more detail in the following section, special interest groups that are too large to demand tariff protection successfully may be able to secure NTBs. Their demands for protection along with the greater flexibility that governments of industrial countries have in entertaining alternative forms of trade restrictions combine to make the industrialized nations likely candidates for the adoption of innovations in NTBs.

Furthermore, there is always some political advantage to a government that can assist special interests without advertising the extent to which it is taking such action. NTBs have the advantage over tariffs of being more difficult to assess in terms of winners and losers and their general welfare effects. Governments of industrial countries that are not constrained to the use of tariffs for revenue purposes and can appreciate the value of NTBs in masking government support for special interest groups are likely to prefer NTBs to tariffs. Useful discussions of this issue can be found in Finger et al. (1982) and Ray (1981a, 1981b).

The Regulation of International Trade

Before reviewing the rise in the level of protectionist pressures in the United States in the last twenty years based upon the model discussed in this section, we can give some examples that help to explain why the shift in the pattern of protection on manufactured goods from tariffs to NTBs began when it did in the industrialized nations. The examples reinforce the observations that we have just made about why NTBs are preferred over tariffs and indicate the pervasiveness of NTBs in international trade.

The first observation is that effective income tax systems in industrialized countries make those countries less dependent on tariffs to finance central government operations than is the case for most developing nations. In that sense the industrialized nations have greater flexibility in choosing whether or not they want to restrict trade and what kinds of trade restrictions they want to implement.

The revenue issue was clearly important in explaining the timing of trade liberalization in England in the 1840s. Tariff rates were reduced sharply in England only after the central government instituted an income tax as a substitute for tariff revenue to finance the government. One of the most hotly contested issues in the United States during the 1890s was whether the expanding role of the central government in the economy would continue to be financed primarily with tariff revenues or through the adoption of an income tax. The adoption of the income tax amendment to the Constitution in 1913 appears to be critical in explaining the first dramatic cuts in tariffs in the United States in over fifty years (see Baack and Ray [1985a]).

The second observation is that, while the GATT is equally outspoken in its condemnation of tariff and NTB restrictions on trade, it has been much easier to agree on the quantitative effects of tariffs on trade flows than it has been to agree on the consequences of differences across countries of such NTBs as product standardization requirements, government biases toward awarding contracts to domestic producers and so on. Therefore, as successive GATT rounds achieved further reductions in tariff rates, new protectionist measures either to shore up already weak industries or to compensate industries that were adversely affected by tariff cuts took the form of NTBs. That shift is evident in the multifiber agreements beginning in the early 1960s (Fahnline, 1987) and in the creation of NTB protection in the footwear, steel and auto industries discussed in Tarr and Morkre (1984).

Recall that the Kennedy Round failed to deal with the problem of NTBs and that the Tokyo Round developed codes for use of NTBs but left the issue of how to proceed to dismantle NTBs for later GATT rounds. In a way, the successful elimination of much of the tariff protection that existed in the industrial countries following World War II may have played a role in promoting NTB innovations in the same way that arms agreements may at times promote the development of new weapons systems. In the arms race example, unless there is an honest intent to disarm, there is a strong incentive to agree to limit the use of weapons in order to gain strategic concessions from one's adversary while simultaneously developing new systems that will make the original agreement inconsequential. So too, if the commitment to trade liberalization is less than sincere, there is an incentive to surrender ineffective tariff protection while adopting new trade regulations that are even more effective.

Ray (1981a, 1981b) found clear evidence that NTBs had been used in the United States and abroad to substitute for lost tariff protection by industries that experienced tariff cuts in the Kennedy Round and that NTBs were systematically used to complement tariff protection in industries that already had relatively high tariff protection. Those studies indicated that industries that had the highest tariff rates before the Kennedy Round tariff cuts were implemented still had the highest tariff rates after the Kennedy Round. Furthermore, NTBs that were introduced during the late 1960s and 1970s did not go to industries with low tariff rates after the Kennedy Round but rather to those industries that benefitted most from tariff protection both before and after the Kennedy Round. Marvel and Ray (1983) provided a more precise test of the substitution and complementary protective effects of NTBs that were implemented in the United States in response to the Kennedy Round tariff cuts. They demonstrated that those industries like steel, textiles, processed foods and consumer durables that experienced small if any tariff cuts during the Kennedy Round were precisely the industries that gained NTB protection. In short, NTBs were not used to substitute for the general loss of tariff protection but rather to increase protection for industries least affected by Kennedy Round tariff cuts.

Along somewhat different lines, Ray and Marvel (1984) argued that part of the explanation for the popularity of NTBs has to do with their effective use by special interest groups that would be unable to get government support for tariff protection. Consider an industry composed of fifty firms, each losing domestic sales to foreign firms and therefore having a collective interest in getting the government to restrict imports with a tariff on foreign goods. One problem that the group faces is that if one firm opts not to help in the lobbying effort and the effort succeeds anyway, then that firm will benefit from the reduction in foreign competition along with the other forty-nine that worked for that outcome. In effect, the one firm is a free rider (a firm that can benefit from a policy change that other firms in the industry paid for without having to pay anything itself). The noncooperative producer of the product benefits from the collective effort of the other producers without bearing any costs. Clearly, the more firms there are in an industry, the more likely it is that the free-rider problem will prevent an effective coalition from being formed. In effect, each of the fifty firms has an incentive to try to get others to do the work and to be a free rider.

Alternatively, if the same group of fifty firms could get the government to restrict imports of competitive goods and distribute import licenses among existing producers who participated in the coalition to limit imports, the group would have a means by which it could reward participants in the coalition and exclude nonparticipants. In this case, each participant in the coalition gains the benefits of reduced foreign competition as well as part of the rent associated with the domestic sale of foreign goods that would have gone to the government with a tariff. Firms that try to free-ride will still benefit from the increased price of foreign goods, but they can be prevented from importing and selling those foreign goods at the higher domestic price. They will not capture any of the tariff-equivalent rents generated by the quota. Clearly, the free-rider problem is reduced substantially and the prospects for a successful coalition are enhanced. In fact, Ray and Marvel (1984) give empirical support for the notion that, other things being equal, NTBs are found predominantly among less concentrated industries. That finding is consistent with the argument that larger coalitions are sustainable when NTBs are at issue than when tariffs are at issue. One disturbing aspect of this finding is that the relatively greater effectiveness of NTBs as instruments to reward participants and exclude free riders in protectionist lobbying efforts is likely to increase the overall level of protection granted to domestic industries.

There is one particular NTB innovation in the protection of producers of manufactured goods worth mentioning in the current context. The voluntary export restraint (VER) poses a particular problem for international trade negotiations. The GATT is quite explicit in condemning the use of quantitative trade restrictions and in allowing for retaliatory sanctions by injured parties. However, it is difficult to imagine how to police self-imposed export restrictions to which trading partners agree on a bilateral basis. In effect, VERs provide a bribe (in the sense that the foreign government and producers gain control over the distribution of rents that would go to the importing country's government if a tariff were imposed) to foreign governments and producers in the form of tariff-equivalent revenue (the value of the rent captured by foreign governments and producers should be equal to the rent that would be generated by an equally restrictive tariff) if they agree to limit exports. Such a system avoids open confrontations that ordinary quotas would invite and, as in the case of Japanese restrictions on automobile exports to the United States, can be worth billions of dollars to existing exporters and to the government of the exporting country. The fact that VERs represent bilateral agreements between governments that include transfers of wealth to the exporting country means that nations involved in such agreements are not likely to complain to the GATT and therefore that VERs are likely to become increasingly recognized as the trade restriction of choice by all but the poorest nations.

NOTES

1. The adoption of the income tax in the United States accompanied the first major reduction in protectionism in the United States in 1913. That same combination of trade liberalization and adoption of an income tax occurred in England during the 1840s. Papers by Baack and Ray (1985a, 1985b, 1985c) explain the role that special interests played in moving the U.S. government to consider tariff cuts only after the income tax was adopted rather than cutting federal expenditures to allow for reduced tariff revenue.

2. It is curious that economists tend to view the value of protectionist policies in promoting industrialization as either always wrong or always right. The primary argument against the use of protection as a strategic device to promote industrialization is that protection insulates domestic markets from external market discipline and therefore increases the likelihood that bad bets are going to be propped up by government support. Perhaps U.S. policymakers were smart or perhaps just lucky. Whatever the case may have been, strategic intervention need not always fall. Recent experience among developing countries does suggest that government trade controls to promote domestic industrialization have generally failed in that regard and have fostered corruption and incompetence.

3. The plant closing bill requires firms to provide workers with at least sixty days' notice before closing down a plant. The debate surrounding the legislation never seriously considered the economic consequences of the legislation but was based on whether or not it seemed fair to provide notice of termination to workers. The political realities of a presidential election year resulted in strong support for the legislation in both houses of Congress.

4. A congenial alternative statement of the model would be to substitute median voter preferences for what we have referred to as shared national values. In effect, the government attempts to satisfy the median voter subject to the constraining influences of organized special interest groups. While this may appear to be a simpler statement of the model that we have in mind, it is important to realize that the model is useful only if we can explain what the shared values of society or the preferences of the median voter are and how they change over time.

REFERENCES

Arendt, Sven W. "Aspects of Trade and Protection." University of California at Santa Cruz and the Commons Institute for International Studies (June 1987).

Baack, Bennett D., and Ray, Edward John. "The Political Economy of Tariff Policy: A Case Study of the United States." *Explorations in Economic History* 20 (1983): 73-93.

_____. "The Political Economy of the Origins of the U.S. Military Industrial Complex." *Journal of Economic History* 65, no. 2 (June 1985a): 369-75.

_____. "Special interests and the Adoption of the Income Tax in the United States." *Journal of Economic History* 66, no. 3 (September 1985b): 607-25.

_____. "The Political Economy of the Origin and Development of the Federal

Income Tax System." *The Emergence of the Modern Political Economy, Research in Economic History* Supp. 4 (1985c): 121-38.

Balassa, Bela. "The Impact of the Industrial Countries' Tariff Structure on Their Imports of Manufactures from Less Developed Areas." *Economica* 34 (November 1967): 372-83.

_____. "The Changing Pattern of Comparative Advantage in Manufactured Goods." *Review of Economics and Statistics* 41, no. 2 (May 1979): 260-66.

Balassa, Bela, and Associates. *The Structure of Protection in Developing Countries.* Baltimore: Johns Hopkins University Press, 1971.

Baldwin, Robert E. "Determinants of the Commodity Structure of U.S. Trade." *American Economic Review* 61 (March 1971): 126-46.

_____. "Trade and Employment Effects in the United States of Multilateral Tariff Reductions." *American Economic Review Papers and Proceedings* 66 (May 1976a): 142-48.

_____. "The Political Economy of Postwar U.S. Trade Policy." *Bulletin.* New York University Graduate School of Business, no. 4 (1976b).

_____. "The Changing Nature of U.S. Trade Policy since World War II." In Robert E. Baldwin and Anne Krueger, eds., *The Structure and Evolution of Recent U.S. Trade Policy.* Chicago: National Bureau of Economic Research, 1984: 5-27.

_____. "The New Protectionism: A Response to Shifts in National Economic Power." *National Bureau of Economic Research Working Paper* no. 1823 (January 1986a).

_____. "Alternative Liberalization Strategies." *National Bureau of Economic Research Working Paper* no. 2045 (October 1986b).

Baldwin, Robert E., and Lage, Gerald M. "A Multilateral Model of Trade Balancing Tariff Concessions." *Review of Economics and Statistics* 53 (August 1971): 237-44.

Becker, Gary. "Comment." *Journal of Law and Economics* 19 (August 1976): 245-48.

_____. "A Theory of Competition Among Pressure Groups for Political Influence." *Quarterly Journal of Economics* 98 (August 1983): 317-400.

Bhagwati, Jagdish. "Shifting Comparative Advantage, Protectionist Demands, and Policy Response." In Jagdish Bhagwati, ed., *Import Competition and Response.* Chicago: National Bureau of Economic Research, 1982: 153-84.

Caves, Richard E. "Economic Models of Political Choice: Canada's Tariff Structure." *Canadian Journal of Economics* 9 (May 1976): 278-300.

Caves, Richard E., and Jones, Ronald W. "Tariff Policy and Trade Liberalization." *World Trade and Payments; An Introduction,* 2d ed. Boston: Little, Brown, 1977.

Cheh, John H. "United States Concessions in the Kennedy Round and Short-Run Labor Adjustment Costs." *Journal of International Economics* 4 (November 1974): 323-40.

_____. "A Note on Tariffs, Nontariff Barriers, and Labor Protection in United States Manufacturing Industries." *Journal of Political Economy* 84, no. 2 (April 1976): 389-94.

Clark, Don P. "Regulation of International Trade: The United States' Caribbean Basin Economic Recovery Act." University of Tennessee (July 1987).

Curzon, Gerard. *Multilateral Commercial Diplomacy*. London: Michael Joseph, 1964.

Deardorff, Alan V., and Stern, Robert M. "American Labor's Stake in International Trade." In *Tariffs, Quotas and Trade: The Politics of Protectionism*. San Francisco: Institute for Contemporary Studies, 1979: 125-48.

_____. "The Structure of Tariff Protection: Effects of Foreign Tariffs and Existing NTBs." *Review of Economics and Statistics* 67 (November 1985): 539-48.

Fahnline, Kathryn, "An Economic Analysis of Protection in the Textile Industry." Ohio State University (August 1987).

Fieleke, Norman S. "The Incidence of the U.S. Tariff Structure on Consumption." *Public Policy* 19 (Fall 1971): 639-52.

Finger, J. M., et al. "The Political Economy of Administered Protection." *American Economic Review* 72 (June 1982): 452-66.

Fishelson, Gideon, and Flatters, Frank. "The (Non)Equivalence of Optimal Tariffs and Quotas Under Uncertainty." *Journal of International Economics* 5 (November 1975): 385-93.

Goldstein, Judith L., and Krasner, Stephen D. "Unfair Trade Practices: The Case for a Differential Response." *American Economic Review Papers and Proceedings* 74, no. 2 (May 1984): 282-87.

Grossman, Gene. "Import Competition for Developed and Developing Countries." *Review of Economics and Statistics* 64 (May 1982): 271-81.

Helleiner, G. K. "The Political Economy of Canada's Tariff Structure: An Alternative Model." *Canadian Journal of Economics* 10 (May 1977): 318-26.

Hufbauer, Gary C. "The Impact of National Characteristics and Technology on the Commodity Composition of Trade in Manufactured Goods." In Raymond Vernon, ed., *The Technology Factor in International Trade*. New York: Columbia University Press (for the National Bureau of Economic Research), 1970.

Kaempfer, William H. "Explaining the Mode of Protection: A Public Choice Perspective." University of Colorado (March 1987).

Kreinen, Mordechai E. "More on the Equivalence of Tariffs and Quotas." *Kyklos* 23, fasc. 1 (1970): 75-79.

Krueger, Anne. "Alternative Trade Strategies and Employment in LDCs." *American Economic Review* 68, no. 2 (May 1978): 270-74.

Krugman, Paul. "New Theories of Trade Among Industrialized Countries." *American Economic Review Papers and Proceedings* 73 (May 1983): 343-47.

MacBean, A. I., and Snowden, P. N. *International Institutions in Trade and Finance*. London: Allen and Unwin, 1981.

Marks, Stephen V. "Empirical Analysis of the Determinants of Protection: A Survey and Some New Results." Pomona College and the Claremont Graduate School (February 1987).

Marvel, Howard P. "Foreign Trade and Domestic Competition." *Economic Inquiry* 18, no. 1 (January 1980): 103-22.

Marvel, Howard P., and Ray, Edward John. "The Kennedy Round: Evidence on the Regulation of International Trade in the United States." *American Economic Review* 73, no. 1 (March 1983): 190-97.

_____. "Intraindustry Trade: Sources and Effects on Protection."*Journal of Political Economy* 95, no. 6 (December 1987): 1278-91.

Olson, Mancur, Jr. *The Logic of Collective Actions: Public Goods and the Theory of Groups.* New York: Schocken, 1968.

Peltzman, Sam. "Toward a More General Theory of Regulation." *Journal of Law and Economics* 19 (August 1976): 211-40.

Pincus, J. J. "Pressure Groups and the Pattern of Tariffs." *Journal of Political Economy* 83, no. 4 (August 1975): 757-78.

Pindyck, Robert S. "Gains to Producers from the Cartelization of Exhaustible Resources." *Review of Economics and Statistics* 60 (May 1978): 238-51.

Pugel, Thomas A., and Walter, Ingo. "U.S. Corporate interests and the Political Economy of Trade Policy." *Review of Economics and Statistics* 67 (August 1985): 465-73.

Ray, Edward John. "The Optimum Commodity Tariff and Tariff Rates in Developed and Less Developed Countries." *Review of Economics and Statistics* 56 (August 1974): 369-77.

_____. "The Determinants of Tariff and Nontariff Trade Restrictions in the United States." *Journal of Political Economy* 89, no. 1 (February 1981a): 105-21.

_____. "Tariff and Nontariff Barriers to Trade in the United States and Abroad." *Review of Economics and Statistics* 63 (May 1981b): 161-68.

_____. "The Impact of Special Interests on Preferential Tariff Concessions by the United States." *Review of Economics and Statistics* 69, no. 2 (May 1987a): 187-93.

_____. "U.S. Protection and Intraindustry Trade: Evidence and Implications." Ohio State University (May 1987b).

Ray, Edward John, and Marvel, Howard P. "The Pattern of Protection in the Industrialized World." *Review of Economics and Statistics* 66, no. 3 (August 1984): 452-58.

Riedel, James. "Tariff Concessions in the Kennedy Round and the Structure of Protection in West Germany." *Journal of International Economics* 7 (May 1977): 133-43.

Snape, Richard H. "Bilateral-Multilateral Tension in Trade Policy." Monash University and the World Bank (July 1987).

Stern, Robert M. "The U.S. Tariff and the Efficiency of the U.S. Economy." *American Economic Review Papers and Proceedings* 54 (May 1964): 459-70.

Stigler, George J. "The Economic Theory of Regulation." *Bell Journal of Economics and Management Science* 2 (Spring 1971): 3-21.

Stone, Joe A. "A Comment on Tariffs, Nontariff Barriers, and Labor Protection in United States Manufacturing Industries." *Journal of Political Economy* 86, no. 5 (October 1978): 959-62.

Tarr, David G., and Morkre, M. E. *Aggregate Costs to the United States of Tariffs and Quotas on Imports: General Tariff Cuts and Removal of Quotas on Automobiles, Steel, Sugar and Textiles.* Federal Trade Commission Staff Report. Washington, D.C.: U.S. Government Printing Office, 1984.

Taussig, Frank. *The Tariff History of the United States.* New York: Putnam, 1931.

Tosini, Suzanne, and Tower, Edward. "The Textile Bill of 1985: The Determinants of Congressional Voting Patterns." *Public Choice* 54 (1987): 19-25.

Turner, Charlie G. "Voluntary Export Restraints on Trade Going to the United States." *Southern Economic Journal* 49 (January 1983): 793-803.

Vernon, Raymond. *Two Hungry Giants: The United States and Japan in the Quest for Oil and Ores.* Cambridge, Mass.: Harvard University Press, 1983.

Verreydt, Eric, and Waelbroeck, Jean. "European Community Protection Against Manufactured Imports from Developing Countries: A Case Study in the Political Economy of Protection." In Jagdish Bhagwati, ed., *Import Competition and Response.* Chicago: National Bureau of Economic Research, 1982: 362-93.

Wihlborg, Clas. "Proposals for Reforming National Structures for Policy Making in International Trade." University of Southern California and the Claremont Graduate School (March 1987).

2

GATT and the Developing Countries

THE HISTORY OF PROTECTIONISM IN THE UNITED STATES

As indicated in the background discussion in Chapter 1, the historical position of the United States with respect to trade restrictions has changed in response to shifts in the underlying economic and political conditions at home and abroad. The simple model that we discussed in Chapter 1 is sufficient to help us to sort out why changes in policy have occurred and what the driving forces for change are within the United States. Recall that the major elements of the model were individual producers and consumers and the government. We argued that the relatively greater concentration of producers' interests in the consumer goods area relative to consumers' interests gave those producers an advantage in influencing trade policy. We also indicated that producer interests would be more likely to succeed in gaining protectionist support from the government if they are not opposed by other producer interests as they would be if they specialized in the production of capital equipment or other kinds of inter-mediate goods. Producers seeking protection are also more likely to suc-ceed if they are not opposed by producers of similar products with strong export markets, who have reason to fear retaliatory trade restrictions by offended trading partners.

When those pieces are put together, a fairly clear picture emerges of the underlying forces that try to move government policy in one direction or another. Protectionist pressures that ultimately succeed are most likely to come from producers of consumer goods who cannot compete effectively in international markets. Their lack of competitiveness is important because it assures that there are few if any exporters of closely related goods who could serve to offset their coalition to foster protectionist policies. In the aggregate then, policy is more likely to be protectionist if import interests are stronger than export interests. When export growth is vigorous, underlying special interests are likely to tip the balance in favor of freer trade. The weaker the balance-of-trade position of the country is at any point in time, the more likely it is that protectionist interests will have the stronger voice among special interest groups.

How the government responds to the special interest pressures placed on it, we argued, will depend upon the shared values that we indicated in vague terms serve to guide overall international policy. This is not the place to attempt a generalized theory of collective choice. However, there are a few general observations that can be made about government policy with respect to international trade. The most obvious point is that the more open a country is to trade, the more likely it is that domestic economic conditions will be perceived as influenced by what is happening in foreign markets. Therefore, in the event that domestic economic problems are severe and seem to call for government intervention, that intervention is more likely to include changes in trade policies if the economy is highly open rather than autonomous.

Two other characteristics of U.S. national policy that influence international economic relations are worth mentioning here because they have been fairly consistently reflected in American foreign policy positions for much of the last century. First, the market orientation of the U.S. economy has tended to promote a desire to compete internationally rather than protect domestic markets. The emergence of the United States as a major industrial power after the Civil War gave impetus to a desire to compete that was only briefly interrupted in the depths of the depression of the 1930s. The country toyed with economic isolationism in the guise of the Smoot-Hawley Tariff of 1930.

The wavering that did occur in the U.S. determination to compete internationally was in response to another overriding element of national policy that began to emerge with the antitrust movement in the United States a hundred years ago. In effect, the federal government in the United States has been perceived as having ultimate responsibility for making the market system work fairly. During the 1880s the preference for fairness was best reflected in antitrust policies to promote competition among firms. During the 1930s that preference for fairness became identified with the need for the government to get people back to work and to provide a legal framework within which workers could organize and take collective action. In effect, the brief experiment with isolationist trade policies during the 1930s arose in response to the apparent failure of the market economy to sustain full employment of those who wanted to work. In a sense it was not fair that people who were willing to work could not find jobs. The possibility of using trade restrictions to fix the domestic employment problem undercut the general preference to compete internationally.

We do not want to make extravagant claims here to having identified inherent values in the American psyche. We only wish to suggest that two very strong and persistent values with respect to economic issues that help to explain collective policy positions of the central government in the United States are preference for competition over collusion and fairness in economic outcomes. There are others. Our purpose here is to provide some sense of what we mean by shared values and how they can constrain the central government from simply adding up special interest votes and deciding policy questions on the basis of which special interest groups have the most support at the moment.

The changing pattern of protectionism in the United States over the course of the last century is less difficult to explain if we keep the discussion of Chapter 1 and the beginning of this chapter in mind. Recall that we argued that trade policies are ultimately defined by governments, which act in accordance with shared social values subject to special interest groups pressures. Changes in national and international economic and political conditions as well as innovations in methods of protection all contribute to changes in the protectionist regime within any given country.

Political Parties and Trade Policies

With the defeat of the South in the Civil War, Congress was dominated by Eastern economic interests, which included government support for rapid industrialization. Therefore, apart from individual firm or industry interests, there was a consensus to try to promote industrialization in the United States. The key to understanding what happened next is not whether such a strategy succeeded, but rather that rapid industrialization did take place and did undercut the argument for continued protection for industrialization purposes. Consequently, export interests became more important over time, and on balance special interest groups favored freer trade. Democrats with traditional strength in the South and West favored freer trade throughout the late nineteenth century in support of western agricultural interests and consumers who wanted cheap imports. As industrialization proceeded, probusiness Republicans shifted from favoring protection to favoring foreign sales and foreign direct investments.

The shift from protectionism to substantial trade liberalization rested on the perception by the beginning of the 1890s that a long-term change had been realized in the international competitiveness of U.S. manufacturers. The actual shift toward trade liberalization took nearly twenty years and did not materialize until the income tax amendment was ratified in 1913. That act resolved the conflict between a general consensus to liberalize trade while continuing to provide financing for rapidly expanding federal programs, including the first major peacetime military buildup in the country's history, which began in the early 1880s.[1] The shift away from protectionism in the United States in the late nineteenth century was the direct result of its earlier success in industrialization (Baack and Ray [1985b]). On balance, special interest groups in industry contributed to the national preference for freer trade.

Republicans supported protectionism during the period of rapid industrialization in the United States because that policy supported the general preferences of manufacturers. Democrats supported trade liberalization because it conformed to the interests of their predominantly agriculture-based constituents in the West and South. Both parties endorsed reductions in tariffs once the government finance bottleneck had been removed and it was clear that manufacturers wanted to go after foreign market sales.

Even before the depression of the 1930s solidified labor support for the Democrats, the basic division between Democrats and Republicans put farmers and industrial workers in the Democrat camp and business in the Republican camp. What has changed since World War II was not the constituencies that supported the two parties but rather the economic interests of those constituencies. During the 1950s and early 1960s Democrats and Republicans supported trade liberalization, and U.S. agricultural and manufactured products dominated competition in world markets.

Democrats became divided on the trade issue during the late 1960s and early 1970s when it became clear that the U.S. maintained strong export capabilities in agricultural products and capital equipment but specific industries like textiles, footwear, steel and automobiles were beginning to lose sales in the United States and abroad to foreign competitors. Programs to provide unemployment assistance to steel and auto workers, trigger prices and quotas in steel, textiles and others were pushed by Democrats in Congress. By the late 1970s Republicans from states like Michigan, Ohio, Indiana and Illinois that were particularly affected by the decline in U.S. steel and auto sales also supported relief from import competition.

The push for protectionist legislation in Congress that culminated in the Omnibus Trade and Competitiveness Act of 1988 was largely attributable to Democrats but did have some Republican support. In effect, some of the traditional constituents of the Democrats and of the Republicans pushed for trade restrictions. The current and previous positions of the two major political parties on trade issues have changed in response to the changing preferences of their constituent special interest groups that have in turn been shaped by changing economic conditions.[2]

Figure 1
Protection and Income Growth, 1913-1980

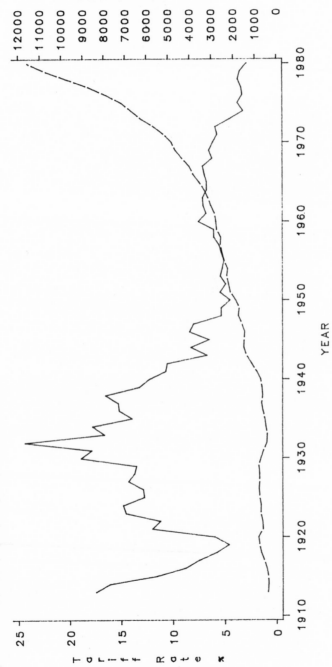

YEAR

Tariff Rate — Solid Line
GNP/Capita — Broken Line

SOURCE: See Appendix A

Table 1
U.S. Tariffs and Economic Conditions

YEAR	Tariff Rate (%)	GNP/Capita ($)	Recessions (1.0)	Relative Net Exports (%)
1913	17.4353	407	0	17.4080
1914	16.1058	389	1	10.2596
1915	11.5713	398	1	34.0607
1916	8.7984	473	0	39.2960
1917	7.5170	585	0	36.0698
1918	5.8008	740	0	34.9135
1919	4.6172	804	0	37.9947
1920	5.9975	860	0	22.3368
1921	11.9970	641	1	28.1364
1922	11.1948	673	1	10.4738
1923	14.5352	760	0	4.9188
1924	14.8110	742	0	12.5460
1925	12.7607	804	0	7.7403
1926	12.8762	826	0	4.4789
1927	14.2807	797	0	8.0460
1928	13.6808	805	0	11.5859
1929	13.4946	848	0	9.0112
1930	18.9111	738	1	11.7304
1931	17.8469	615	1	8.1058
1932	24.4047	467	1	10.7641
1933	16.6060	444	1	6.9624
1934	17.7784	516	1	11.8720
1935	13.9461	570	1	-1.1919
1936	15.1929	647	1	0.8567
1937	15.2894	706	1	4.0712
1938	16.5295	656	1	19.7563
1939	13.2352	698	1	16.2960
1940	12.2683	757	1	20.9030
1941	10.6850	937	1	22.0002
1942	10.5459	1175	0	44.8368
1943	6.6971	1405	0	53.3428
1944	8.2689	1522	0	54.1795
1945	6.5014	1518	0	40.7947
1946	8.3679	1484	0	39.7897
1947	7.9859	1617	0	45.8722
1948	5.3328	1770	0	27.4133
1949	5.3390	1731	1	27.9719
1950	4.4819	1889	1	5.8183
1951	5.4492	2144	0	12.0658
1952	4.9179	2217	0	10.7506
1953	5.4305	2299	0	6.1444
1954	5.2352	2259	0	11.0643
1955	5.0750	2420	0	11.1633
1956	5.3269	2507	0	15.6560
1957	5.5301	2592	0	19.0881
1958	6.0377	2582	1	11.7891
1959	6.0418	2755	0	3.6137
1960	7.4946	2802	0	14.2641

Source: See Appendix A.

Table 1 (continued)

1961	6.7636	2855	1	16.1382
1962	7.0416	3028	0	12.3280
1963	7.0837	3152	0	13.3484
1964	6.7142	3323	0	15.4810
1965	6.7082	3556	0	10.3100
1966	6.9395	3845	0	6.9845
1967	7.08773	4023	0	6.643
1968	6.18250	4351	0	0.920
1969	6.47838	4656	0	1.378
1970	6.10568	4841	1	2.647
1971	5.68464	5189	0	-2.542
1972	5.89100	5649	0	-6.100
1973	4.52205	6258	0	0.642
1974	3.21663	6705	1	-2.646
1975	3.74945	7173	1	4.410
1976	3.28413	7878	0	-4.015
1977	3.39510	8708	0	-11.329
1978	3.73863	9720	0	-10.620
1979	3.51196	10741	0	-6.900
1980	2.87247	11566	1	-5.376

U.S. TRADE POLICY IN THE TWENTIETH CENTURY

Historical data are often useful in highlighting long-term relationships that are blurred by the idiosyncrasies of each particular period of time. For the purpose at hand, a paper by Baack and Ray (1985c) provides evidence on the relationship between tariffs in the United States and key economic variables related to our model for the period from 1913 to 1980 (see Figures 1 through 4 and the underlying data that are presented in Table 1). Reference to that material will help illustrate that there is a direct and predictable link between changes in domestic and international economic conditions and the course of U.S. trade policy over the course of the last century. Specifically, we will provide evidence that when special interests and national policies coincided to support or oppose trade restrictions, U.S. trade policies were unambiguous. When the net impact of special interest groups is poised in opposition to declared national policy on trade issues, as seems to be the case today, expressed U.S. trade policy appears contradictory and/or ingenuine.

Referring to Figure 1, it is clear that tariffs have declined substantially over the period while income per capita has increased. A more careful look at the actual data in Table 1 makes it clear that rising incomes between 1913 and 1920 were accompanied by tariff cuts from 17.4 percent to 6 percent (the measure of tariffs referred to in this section is the average tariff rate for all imports rather than the tariff rate on dutiable imports that is used in much of the empirical literature). As income declined during the 1920s and particularly during the early 1930s, tariffs rose quickly to almost 12 percent in 1920 and a high of 24 percent in 1932.

Average income hit bottom in the United States in 1933, and as incomes recovered, tariff rates began to come down again. Tariffs declined generally throughout the post-World War II period as incomes increased steadily. That relationship between tariffs and incomes is consistent with our assumption that rising incomes are associated with increasing consumer preferences for product variety and therefore a liberalization of international trade.

Figure 2 shows the relationship between tariff protection and business cycles (most simply defined as periods of national economic activity that include an expansion, peak, slowdown and negative economic growth). In the post-World War II period, expansions have averaged two to four years and slowdown periods or recessions have averaged one to two years) as indicated by the occurrence of recessions in the U.S. economy between 1913 and 1980. Based on the discussion in Chapter 1, we would expect special interest groups to be most united against free trade when economic conditions are depressed and most solidly in favor of free trade during relatively prosperous economic periods. Therefore, protectionism should be strongest during depressed economic periods and least during periods of economic prosperity. Tariffs increased with the recession of 1921 and 1922 and with the beginning of the depression in 1930. In fact, the average tariff rate on imports did not fall below the predepression (1929) level of 13.5 percent until 1939. The steady decline in tariffs ended during the recession of 1950, and tariffs rose slightly in 1951. Tariffs increased slightly during the recessions of 1958 and 1974-1975 and following the recession in 1961.

It is clear that at least since the adoption of the Smoot-Hawley Tariff in 1930, there has been a national commitment to protect jobs and declining industries in the United States. Economic downturns and the job losses and business failures that they inevitably bring have served to rally support for restrictions on international trade. Therefore, it is not surprising that pressures to restrict trade were less during the 1950s and 1960s when recessions were less frequent and severe than during the 1970s and early 1980s, when the United States experienced its most severe recessions since World War II. Marvel and Ray (1983) identified that "safety-net" aspect of U.S. trade policy when they observed that tariff cuts under the Kennedy Round were least for slow-growth and declining industries.

Figure 3 illustrates the relationship between tariff protection and the relative commodity export strength of the United States in international trade. This relationship highlights the association discussed earlier that we would expect between special interest group demands for protection from import competition and the ability of U.S. firms to compete. We would expect support for trade liberalization to rise and fall in concert with our success and failure to sell more of our goods and services abroad

Figure 2
Tariff Rates and Business Cycles, 1913-1980

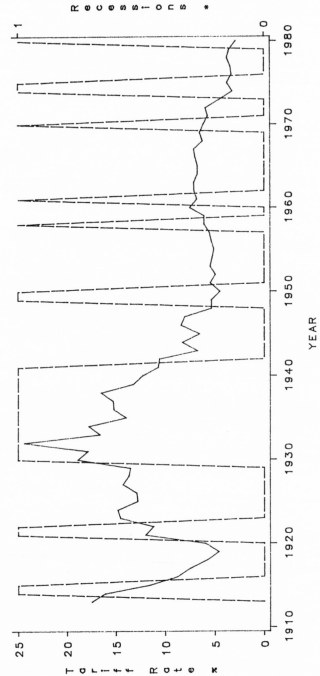

YEAR

Tariff Rate — Solid Line
Recessions — Broken Line

SOURCE: See Appendix A

* Value is 1 during a recession and 0 otherwise

Figure 3
Tariff Rates and Relative Export Strength, 1913-1980

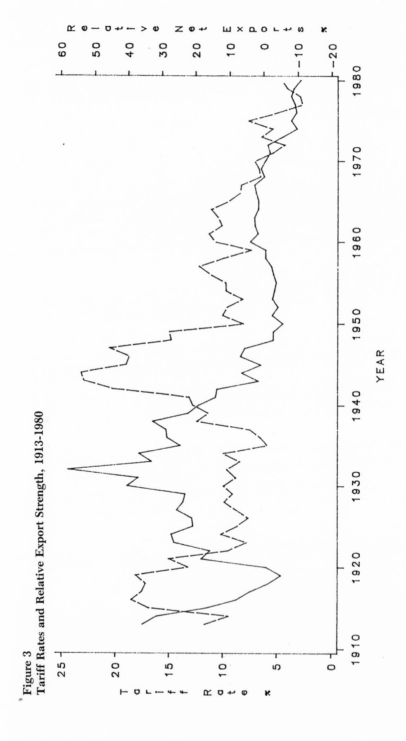

Tariff Rate — Solid Line
Relative Export Strength — Broken Line

SOURCE: See Appendix A

than foreigners sell in the United States. For every year from 1936 to 1970, net merchandise exports from the United States were positive, often quite high, relative to the sum of imports and exports. The relative net export figure avreaged 37.7 percent during the 1940s, 10.7 percent during the 1950s, 9.8 percent during the 1960s, − 4.2 percent during the 1970s and − 16.0 percent during the 1981-1986 period. In effect, during the early postwar period, the United States took the lead in promoting trade liberalization, in part for foreign policy reasons including the desired reindustrialization of wartorn Europe and Japan and the inclusion of developing nations among our non-Communist trading partners. Throughout the 1950s and the 1960s, those policies also corresponded to general trading interests of American businesses as reflected by their net positive export position relative to the rest of the world.

It is no accident that the U.S. commitment to further trade liberalization has seemed less certain in the last ten years and that the net merchandise export position for the United States has been negative in every one of those years. In fact, based on the discussion of our model in Chapter 1 and earlier in this chapter, we should expect the recent deterioration of the net merchandise export position of the United States to generate special interest group efforts to undermine the historical commitment to trade liberalization. The coincident preference for liberalized international trade embodied in U.S. foreign policy and among industry special interest groups that experienced great success in selling their products abroad throughout much of the period from World War II until the early 1970s resulted in an unambiguous commitment to freer trade by the United States. The rapid deteriorization of the merchandise export position of the United States since the mid-1970s has created a conflict of interests between trade-sensitive industries and government with respect to trade. That conflict continues and is reflected in the late 1980s in the ongoing disagreement between the Congress and the executive branch of government regarding trade policy.

Figure 4 illustrates tariff movements and changes in the relative size of the trade sector (measured by the value of commodity imports and exports as a percentage of Gross National Product) in the United States since 1913. The more important the trade sector is compared to the overall economy, the more significant will be the concern of special interest groups with respect to international trade relations. In simplest terms, the more important the trade sector is to the overall well-being of the economy the more likely domestic economic conditions will be identified as the result of trade policies. Those observations follow directly from the argument in Chapter 1 that trade policy is the result of government enforcement of consensus policies subject to the influence of special interest groups.

Figure 4
Tariff Rates and the Size of the Trade Sector, 1913-1980

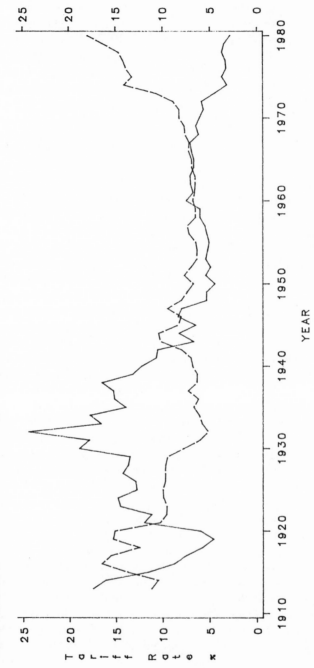

Tariff Rate — Solid Line
Relative Trade Sector — Broken Line

SOURCE: See Appendix A

First, it is worth noting that the recent rapid expansion in the relative size of the trade sector represents a return to pre-World War II proportions. That was the last period that tariffs averaged well over 10 percent and that domestic economic problems in the United States were closely identified with international economic conditions. In effect, the rapid relative growth of the trade sector in the United States in the last twenty years, accompanied by a deterioration in the net merchandise export position and the two worst post-World War II recessions, has helped to fuel the protectionist argument that our domestic economic problems are somehow the fault of our trading partners. Because tariff increases are prohibited by the GATT agreements, protectionist measures have had to take the form of NTBs since the early 1970s when the protectionist threat became serious.

In effect, we have argued that U.S. trade policy has become muddled because of the conflict between industry special interest groups that on balance have been tilting more toward favoring protection in recent years and the federal government, which still tries to maintain the thrust toward trade liberalization. The severity of the protectionist threat is easily underestimated. Recall our earlier observation that the shift toward NTBs rather than tariffs as the predominant form of protection against imports reduces the free-rider problem and increases the likelihood that special interest groups seeking protectionist legislation will be successful.

These points are important and bear repeating. Imposition of a tariff is a hostile economic action that is multilateral in its effect and easily observed. Given the common interest of Western nations to liberalize trade after World War II, the GATT had no trouble rejecting the unilateral imposition of tariffs without just cause. So effective was that commitment that tariffs declined dramatically throughout the period. Special interest groups seeking added tariff protection for their industries generally failed in their efforts because of the obvious international economic and political harm that tariffs might cause. Multilateral quotas have many of the same effects and are not a likely vehicle for the successful creation of protection.

Unfortunately, voluntary export restraints are extremely well suited to the needs of special interest groups seeking protection. First, they are bilateral as opposed to multilateral agreements that are worked out by consenting as opposed to competing nations. They can be structured to provide protection to import-sensitive industries and to provide rents to governments and/or producers in the exporting countries. In effect, domestic producers in both the importing and exporting countries can collude with their own governments in restraining competition and capturing monopoly rents at the expense of the consuming public. The GATT has no effective means for preventing such collusive agreements. Multilateral tariffs and quotas are likely to generate international retaliation, and that retaliatory threat reduces the likelihood that special interest groups within a country could get them adopted. Voluntary export restraints are bilateral collusive agreements that carry no such retaliatory threat and therefore retaliatory restraint.

Special Interest and National Trade Policy Conflicts

The ongoing conflict over trade policy between industry special interest groups and the national government has resulted in some surprising and disturbing changes in U.S. trade policy that have been evident in recent empirical work. Ray and Marvel (1984) examined the structure of tariff and NTB protection in the United States, Canada, Japan, and the European Community (EC) following the Kennedy Round tariff cuts. As indicated below, the statistical evidence gathered in their study and others that followed indicated that by the mid-1970s protectionist interests had become strong enough to impose conditions that crippled legislation that was intended to assist developing countries in their efforts to expand exports of manufactured goods to the United States and other industrial nations. During the early 1980s protectionist interest groups continued to gain strength. The issue at hand now is not whether protectionist special interest groups are sufficiently powerful to undermine the effectiveness of trade liberalizing legislation but whether there is any life left in the free trade movement. The following review of some of that empirical work will help to illustrate how special interest groups effectively undermined trade liberalizing legislation.

A general finding of the Ray and Marvel (1984) study was that the post-Kennedy Round structure of tariffs and NTBs among the industrialized nations was systematically biased against imports of consumer durables, processed agricultural products and textiles. Since those are manufacturing product areas in which developing countries are expected to have the best chance of competing for sales in world markets, the message is clear. Trade liberalization through various GATT rounds has not been effective in increasing access to industrial country markets for competitive exports of manufactured goods from developing countries. (Papers dealing with the impact of U.S. trade policies on imports from developing countries include: Bhagwati [1982], Clark [1987], Grossman [1982], Ray [1987a, 1987b], Ray and Marvel [1984]. Papers on comparative advantage among developing countries include: Balassa [1979, 1986], and Grossman [1982]).

In fact, many developing countries complained that the Kennedy Round had not provided them with much in the way of potential export gains. Most industrial countries including the United States adopted their own generalized system of preferences (GSP) to provide developing countries with duty-free access to markets for their exports. Unfortunately, the same industry-level special interest groups that attempted to minimize the trade liberalizing effects of the Kennedy Round in the United States worked to prevent the GSP, first adopted in 1975 and renewed in 1985, from undercutting the protection that had been preserved through the Kennedy Round. Ray (1987a) found that the GSP and the Caribbean Basin Initiative (CBI), adopted in 1983 to provide expanded preferential access to U.S. markets for exports from the Caribbean, were both sabotaged. Based on an analysis of U.S. imports in 1984, it is apparent that the GSP and CBI did not provide preferential access to U.S. markets for exports from developing countries in consumer goods, textiles or manufactured foods or, for that matter, for goods that were particularly heavily protected by tariffs before the preferences were granted. If one presumes that both the GSP and the CBI began as genuine efforts to provide developing countries with access to U.S. markets for key manufactured exports, the fact that special interest groups could influence the final legislation to the point of making it irrelevant in both cases is a bit chilling. In terms of our model it suggests that the long-standing commitment to trade liberalization by the United States is close to being canceled by the power of special interest groups to thwart government efforts at international economic cooperation.

Krugman (1983) argued that intraindustry trade or trade in closely related products, which has been expanding rapidly in recent years, may serve as an engine for trade liberalization over time. In the context of our model, the argument would be that as intraindustry trade expands, the clash between import and export interests diminishes, and therefore the relevance of special interest groups in shaping trade policy declines. Intraindustry trade would reduce protectionist pressures.

Marvel and Ray (1987) found that intraindustry trade does reduce protection in the form of tariffs, since export interests undercut the effectiveness of importers in obtaining tariff protection on closely related goods. Unfortunately, they also found that intraindustry trade occurs primarily in made-to-order, labor-intensive, intermediate goods that are produced in small firms. Those are not the kinds of goods commonly exported from developing countries. Marvel and Ray conjectured that the impact of expanding intraindustry trade may be to promote further trade liberalization among the industrialized countries to the exclusion of developing nations.

Following up on that point, Ray (1987b) analyzed the characteristics of U.S. intraindustry trade on a bilateral basis with Canada, Japan, the EC, Mexico, Brazil, South America and the Caribbean Basin using 1984 trade data for manufacturing. The evidence obtained indicated that U.S. intraindustry trade with developing countries and regions is also biased toward made-to-order intermediate goods. In fact, U.S. intraindustry trade with developing countries is systematically biased away from industries that enjoy substantial tariff and/or NTB protection in the United States such as textiles, consumer manufactures and processed food products.

A second result that Ray and Marvel (1984) obtained is worth noting here, since it does provide some sense of what protectionist trends may be in the future. They found that among the industrialized areas the EC exhibited the most pervasive use of trade restrictions when tariffs and NTBs are viewed together. They suggested that one effect of the expansion of the EC to include less homogeneous members such as Spain and Portugal may be to increase the group's common external trade restrictions. If so, that would imply that as the EC has expanded over time, the trade-diverting effects of that expansion may have begun to outweigh the trade-expansion effects of those additions.

To understand this point, it is important to understand how the European Community decides on common external trade barriers. When a country like Spain joins the EC, it must adopt the external trade restrictions that special interest groups within the smaller EC have already secured. Since Spain's production mix and competitive industries are somewhat different from those of other members, Spain will bring its own special interest groups to the bargaining process. Those groups seek supporters in other EC countries and in some cases succeed in generating trade restrictions for the expanded European Community that it did not have before the new member joined. The increase in trade diversion arises from the adoption by the original members of the EC of new trade restrictions on imports from nonmember nations. As indicated earlier, the magnitude of the trade-diversion effects of continuing expansion of the EC is reflected in the finding by Ray and Marvel (1984) that the EC has uniformly higher levels of protection across manufacturing than any of the other major industrial areas. Expansion of the EC to include countries like Spain and Portugal, whose economies are quite different from those of other members that joined earlier, does expand the scope for competition within the community, but it also increases the likelihood that special interest groups may gain the additional political clout they need to generate new trade restrictions.

THE CURRENT TRANSITION IN U.S. TRADE POLICY

Figures 5 to 7 and the data they reflect (Table 2) show why U.S. trade policy is in transition in the late 1980s. Figure 5 illustrates how rapidly the trade sector (exports plus imports of commodities relative to Gross National Product) has increased in importance relative to overall economic activity in the U.S. since the early 1970s. The rise in trade figures relative to GNP and the deterioration in the merchandise trade statistics were obviously related to the rapid rise in oil prices in 1974 and

Table 2
U.S. Trade and Economic Conditions: 1947-1986

(1) YEAR	(2) Trade Relative to GNP (%)	(3) U.S. Dollar Exchange Rate	Civilian Unemployment Rate (%)
1947	9.4699	--	5.40
1948	8.0238	--	4.49
1949	7.3890	--	7.28
1950	6.7319	--	6.35
1951	7.6849	--	3.86
1952	6.9797	--	3.50
1953	6.3761	--	3.34
1954	6.3465	--	6.55
1955	6.4871	--	5.12
1956	7.1992	--	4.78
1957	7.4000	--	4.92
1958	6.5306	--	8.01
1959	6.5111	--	6.33
1960	6.7904	--	6.39
1961	6.6010	--	7.79
1962	6.5477	--	6.33
1963	6.5799	--	6.45
1964	6.9192	--	5.84
1965	6.9364	--	5.04
1966	7.2422	--	4.17
1967	7.1861	120.0	4.22
1968	7.6186	122.1	3.91
1969	7.6899	122.4	3.81
1970	8.2360	121.1	5.44
1971	8.2495	117.8	6.60
1972	8.8689	109.1	6.21
1973	10.6988	99.1	5.35
1974	14.0812	101.4	6.19
1975	13.2409	98.5	9.62
1976	13.8838	105.6	8.67
1977	14.2055	103.3	7.88
1978	14.6895	92.4	6.69
1979	16.3906	88.1	6.43
1980	18.0023	87.4	7.96
1981	16.4498	102.9	8.53
1982	14.4927	116.6	11.11
1983	13.8215	125.3	10.10
1984	14.6699	138.3	8.40
1985	13.8387	143.2	8.00
1986	13.8783	112.0	7.74

Source: See Appendix A.

Figure 5
Commodity Trade Relative to GNP, 1947-1986

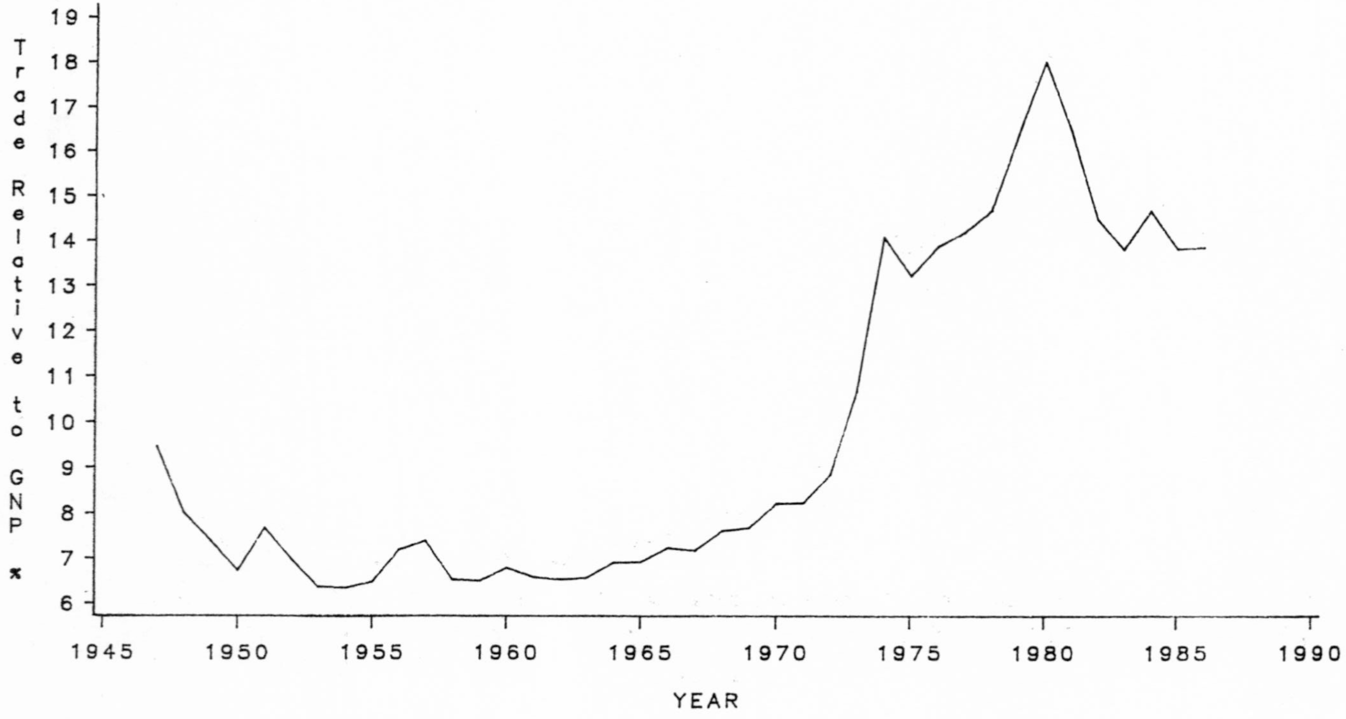

SOURCE: See Appendix A

again in 1980. The oil shocks played a significant role in generating the recessions in 1974-1975 and in 1980. That juxtaposition of increased trade relative to GNP, a deterioration of the merchandise trade statistics, and economic recessions surely contributed to public sympathy with the idea that domestic economic problems in the United States were induced by foreign economic conditions and policies. We have already made the point, and it is not surprising that both the Carter and Reagan administrations were under substantial political pressure to do something about the international trade problems of the United States in the late 1970s and 1980s.

What is not clear based on the information we have been discussing so far is why protectionist pressures have continued to increase. Since 1983, there has been a continuous economic recovery and expansion in the United States. The dramatic decline in OPEC oil prices in 1986 that has not been fully reversed in 1987 or 1988 could hardly have contributed to a continuing decline in relative net exports. We used our simple analysis to suggest that a deterioration in the relative net exports of commodities played a significant role in explaining the shift in U.S. policy away from wholehearted support for continuing trade liberalization.

The first point is that, despite the leveling off and eventual decline in imported oil prices in the United States during the 1980s, the relative net merchandise export position (the value of commodity exports less the value of commodity imports divided by imports plus exports) of the United States continued to deteriorate from an average of -9.3 percent for 1981-1983 to -20.4 percent in 1984, -22.5 percent in 1985 and -25.1 percent in 1986. In the context of our model there is a direct relationship between the net export position of the United States and the extent to which special interest groups favor trade liberalization. The negative and worsening trade balance for the United States in recent years would lead us to expect special interest groups, on balance, to lobby against trade liberalization with increasing intensity. If we could understand why the merchandise trade position of the United States continued to deteriorate throughout the 1980s, we would have a clearer perspective on the cause of continuing protectionist pressures on Congress.

The proximate cause for the continuing deterioration in the commodity trade position (the net merchandise export position) of the United States throughout the 1980s has been the dramatic increase in the trade-weighted value of the U.S. dollar between 1980 and 1985 that began to reverse itself in 1986 (see Figure 6). Based on an index of exchange rates with 1973 equal to approximately 100, the value of the dollar increased almost 60 percent between 1980 and 1985. By itself, that change in the value of the dollar would lower the price of imports 60 percent and raise the foreign price of our exports by 60 percent. Not surprisingly, that kind

Figure 6
The Value of the Trade Weighted U.S. Dollar, 1967-1986

Index values with 1973=100
SOURCE: See Appendix A

of change in import and export prices would and did generate a serious deterioration in our commodity trade position. With some lag, we can expect the rapid fall in the value of the U.S. dollar in trade that began in 1986 and has continued throughout 1987 and 1988 to reduce the merchandise trade deficit and in the process the pressure from industry special interest groups on Congress for protection. How much improvement can be expected will depend upon the extent to which the original rise in the value of the dollar was the result of high interest rates in the United States, presumably associated with large federal government deficits, and upon the continuing rapidity of expansion among our major trading partners relative to economic growth in the United States. We will return to a consideration of those factors shortly.

For the present, it is noteworthy that much of the impetus in Congress for tough trade legislation was gone by the spring of 1988 as it became apparent that the merchandise trade deficit was beginning to drop quickly. The most controversial element of the original trade bill was the amendment by Representative Richard Gephardt that would have required bilateral trade sanctions against individual countries that did not take concerted action to reduce their trade surpluses with the United States. That amendment was discretely dropped from the bill by the conference committee almost as soon as Gephardt announced his withdrawal from the presidential race.

The final trade bill was passed by Congress and vetoed by the president with the veto sustained by the Senate in June 1988. Apart from some tough language concerning the need to make sure that trade competition is fair and shifting responsibility to act in response to unfair foreign trade practices to the special trade representative, the trade bill lacked much bite. The most highly publicized element of the bill was a call for mandatory prior notice of sixty days for plant closings by businesses. While the issue has political value because it does have the appeal of seeming to require fair treatment of workers, it is not strictly a trade issue. Indeed by the end of June 1988 the amendment's sponsor, Senator Howard Metzenbaum of Ohio, indicated that the plant-closing notice requirement would be removed from the next draft of the trade bill and submitted as separate legislation. In effect, as the economy continued to expand and the merchandise trade deficit continued to decline, trade policy lost much of its political appeal.

The Democrats recognized the decline in interest in trade issues and shifted their focus to the question of whether or not U.S. workers are treated fairly within the United States when businesses move from one location to another. The removal of the prior notice amendment from the trade bill indicated that the trade issue itself had lost much of its appeal and hindered rather than bolstered support for the plant-closing part of the bill.

With respect to the use of the fairness issue, Figure 7 and the related data on civilian unemployment rates in the United States since World War II help us to understand the increase in protectionist pressures in the last decade or so. We argued earlier that there is a national commitment to provide a safety net for failing industries and protection for jobs that might be lost to foreign competition dating back at least to the Smoot-Hawley Tariff of 1930. The fairness issue here has two components. First, there is the question of whether foreign producers receive unfair government assistance in exporting goods to the United States. Americans have great faith in the value of competition and are not likely to support protectionist efforts to avoid competition unless they can be persuaded that the rules of the game are not fair. The second element of the fairness issue involves whether people who are willing to work are unable to do so through no fault of their own. Obviously, if one could piece together an argument that foreigners do not compete fairly in international trade and that as a result people who are willing to work and to compete are unable to do so through no fault of their own, one has a potent political issue.

To the extent that we can show that the unemployment problem became more severe in the United States in recent years, our model would lead us to expect our national commitment to freer international competition to slacken. Figure 7 illustrates that the overall unemployment picture has been significantly worse since 1974 than it had been before. The civilian unemployment rate in the United States averaged 5.49 perceent throughout the period 1947-1974 and 8.43 percent between 1975 and 1986. The average unemployment rate during the latter period exceeded the unemployment rate in any year between 1947 and 1974. It is perhaps not surprising, then, that politicians were especially sensitive about the possible impact that trade policies might have on domestic employment during the recent period. It also is not surprising that as the unemployment rate declined to 6 percent at the end of 1987 and to 5.4 percent by the middle of 1988, public interest in the trade issue declined substantially.

Before proceeding to an assessment of possible trends in international trade and economic conditions, we should note one positive aspect of the story that emerges from our discussion to this point. The general increase in the relative importance of the trade sector relative to GNP in the United States in conjunction with continued high unemployment rates and the prolonged adverse movement in the U.S. commodity trade statistics combined to intensify pressure on the federal government to restrict trade. Nevertheless, although protectionist interests have enjoyed some successes in the proliferation of NTBs and in undermining the effectiveness of trade liberalizing programs like the GSP and the CBI, basic U.S. policy continues to tilt toward trade liberalization.

The pure special interest group explanation of trade policy would not

Figure 7
U.S. Unemployment in the Postwar Period, 1947-1986

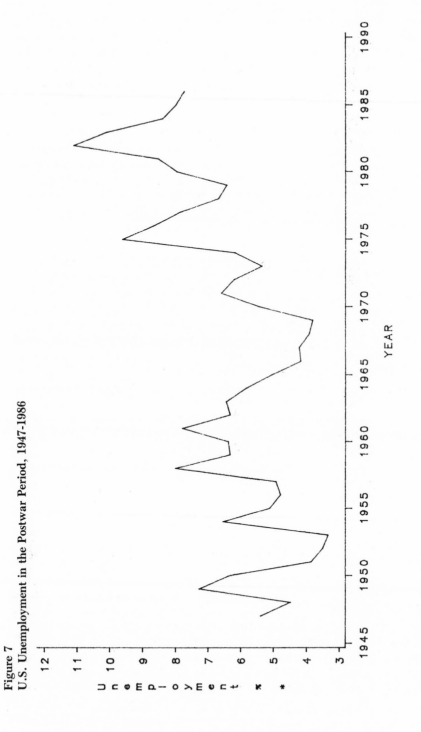

Source: See Appendix A
* Nonfarm Civilian Unemployment

lead us to expect such a persistent commitment to freer international trade as part of the national agenda, given economic conditions in the United States between 1974 and 1986. The positive message that follows is that current ongoing changes in economic conditions in the United States and abroad are shifting away from patterns that contributed to the original intensification of protectionist pressures. If those trends continue, the traditional commitment to trade liberalization in the United States will continue and become even more apparent to our trading partners than it has been in recent years. In the following section, we will discuss the likely course that economic conditions will follow in the United States and other industrial countries and thereby provide some indication of the seriousness of the generalized protectionist threat in the foreseeable future.

THE EMERGING PATTERN OF PROTECTIONISM

The direction that trade policies will take in the United States and abroad over the next few years will obviously be affected by economic conditions particularly among the major industrial countries. Our discussion of the basic model in Chapter 1 and the introduction to this chapter made it clear that the prospects for renewed international economic cooperation depend directly on the relative size of the trade sector in the economy, the net export position of the United States, the severity of the unemployment problem in the United States, the extent to which international economic competition is perceived to be fair, and growth in real income over time. The purpose of this section is to discuss the likelihood that world economic conditions with regard to these and other key variables will change in ways that will promote or impede trade liberalization. Table 3 summarizes the World Bank's estimates of exports and imports for industrial countries from 1969 through 1988. The average growth rates for imports and exports for all of the industrial countries for the ten years ending in 1988 (4.5 percent and 4.1 percent compared to the ten-year averages of 6.9 percent and 7.3 percent for 1969-1978) suggest that the slowdown in growth of world trade that began in the decade after 1969 has continued since. The special interests approach to the determination of trade policy would lead one to conclude that the absence of dramatic growth possibilities in world trade among the industrialized nations of the sort realized in the first two decades after World War II will continue to blunt enthusiasm for further trade liberalization. With specific reference to the United States, the combined effects of the rise in the relative share of trade in aggregate income in the last fifteen years and the slowdown in growth in world trade will be to slow growth in real income per capita in the United States compared to earlier decades.

Table 3
Industrial Countries: Export Volumes and Terms of Trade, 1969-1988 (Annual changes, in percent)

| | | | | | | | | Export volumes[1] | |
	Canada	United States	Japan	France	Germany, W.	Italy	United Kingdom	Other Industrial Countries	All Industrial Countries
Average									
1969-78[2]	6.8	6.8	11.4	10.1	5.9	8.1	5.6	7.1	7.3
1979	4.0	14.1	0.2	8.7	5.1	7.7	4.8	8.2	7.2
1980	2.6	9.8	17.1	3.3	1.4	-7.8	0.9	1.9	3.9
1981	4.9	-1.6	10.6	4.1	6.5	5.5	-0.8	2.2	3.7
1982	-0.8	-10.9	-2.3	-3.8	2.9	-0.5	2.6	1.0	-2.0
1983	7.4	-3.8	8.7	3.4	-0.2	3.5	1.8	5.6	2.8
1984	18.5	7.5	16.0	5.7	9.6	6.6	8.4	8.8	9.7
1985	5.9	1.6	4.4	1.7	6.4	7.5	5.5	4.9	4.4
1986	2.6	7.8	-1.4	0.2	1.2	2.2	3.7	4.0	2.9
1987	3.3	12.7	-4.0	3.0	0.5	2.5	2.4	3.4	2.4
1988	4.0	13.4	2.5	4.1	2.4	3.5	2.4	3.5	4.6

Notes: Trade in goods only.
[1] Composites for country groups are averages of percentage changes for individual countries weighted by the average U.S. dollar value of their respective merchandise exports over the preceding three years.
[2] Compound annual rates of change.

Table 3 (continued)

Import volumes[1]

	Canada	United States	Japan	France	Germany, W.	Italy	United Kingdom	Other Industrial Countries	All Industrial Countries
Average									
1969-78[2]	7.5	7.5	7.8	8.8	10.1	6.2	3.6	6.2	6.3
1979	14.6	1.6	11.3	11.6	7.8	13.2	13.6	9.4	8.9
1980	5.1	-7.9	-5.0	5.8	-0.2	2.6	-5.4	1.0	-1.6
1981	10.1	0.6	-2.2	-3.9	-5.0	-11.1	-3.7	-3.4	-2.3
1982	-16.2	-3.7	-0.5	3.3	1.0	3.3	5.4	1.3	-0.3
1983	9.5	13.0	1.2	-1.3	4.1	2.0	8.1	1.0	4.8
1984	19.3	24.3	10.8	2.7	5.5	9.1	11.1	7.1	12.4
1985	9.3	5.1	0.4	4.9	4.6	8.9	3.4	5.6	5.0
1986	6.0	14.6	13.5	7.9	6.1	6.0	6.2	7.0	8.9
1987	4.9	1.8	8.5	4.8	3.6	7.5	6.0	4.0	4.3
1988	3.3	4.0	7.0	5.4	3.5	6.0	4.6	4.4	4.6

Notes: Trade in goods only.

[1] Composites for country groups are averages of percentage changes for individual countries weighted by the average U.S. dollar value of their respective merchandise exports over the preceding three years.

[2] Compound annual rates of change.

Table 3 (continued)

Terms of Trade[1]

	Canada	United States	Japan	France	Germany, W.	Italy	United Kingdom	Other Industrial Countries	All Industrial Countries
Average									
1969-78[2]	0.3	1.7	-1.1	-0.2	0.7	-1.8	-1.3	-0.4	-0.6
1979	8.6	-3.9	-15.9	-0.5	-5.4	-1.8	4.3	-1.0	-2.9
1980	7.8	-13.5	-19.5	-6.3	-6.4	-6.2	4.7	-4.0	-7.1
1981	1.7	1.9	1.5	-4.8	-6.7	-10.5	0.9	-2.1	-2.1
1982	-2.3	3.0	0.9	1.9	3.8	6.8	0.1	1.5	2.1
1983	-0.1	3.3	2.9	2.6	1.7	4.6	0.3	-0.8	1.6
1984	-0.5	2.0	2.4	0.9	-2.3	-1.5	-2.2	1.0	0.3
1985	-1.5	-1.0	4.6	2.6	1.4	0.6	1.3	0.4	0.9
1986	-3.7	0.9	40.3	10.9	15.1	16.9	-5.4	3.3	9.4
1987	0.4	-5.4	5.2	0.7	3.3	3.1	0.9	0.1	0.6
1988	-0.6	0.3	0.5	-0.3	-0.9	--	0.6	0.3	-0.1

Notes: Trade in goods only.

[1] Composites for country groups are averages of percentage changes for individual countries weighted by the average U.S. dollar value of their respective merchandise imports over the preceding three years.

[2] Compound annual rates of change.

Source: I.M.F., *World Economic Outlook*, Washington, D.C., April 1987, Table A-22, p. 140.

On the other hand, the expected improvement in the export performance of the United States relative to growth in imports for 1988 and beyond, which is largely associated with the fall in the international value of the U.S. dollar, should help to swing the net impact of industry special interest groups on the trade issue within the United States back toward favoring freer trade. There is another element of the dynamic story involving the effectiveness of special interest lobbying that we have not yet discussed. If the linkage between domestic unemployment and trade deficits is critical for selling protectionist arguments, the ongoing restructuring of employment in the economy has been working against protectionist interests. The more resilient the economy proves to be in relocating workers laid off by steel firms, automakers and textile and shoe manufacturers, the smaller the base of support for protection in those industries becomes and the more difficult it becomes for the associated special interest groups to convince the general populace that those industries and workers require special help in the form of trade restrictions.

The presumption that the decline in the value of the U.S. dollar will substantially improve the balance-of-trade position of the United States (commodity exports less commodity imports) may prove incorrect for at least three reasons. First, the value of the U.S. dollar has declined relative to the Japanese yen and the German mark, but it has changed very little relative to the currencies of many other countries with which we trade, particularly developing nations. Therefore, the impact of the falling value of the U.S. dollar on world markets is likely to be to encourage exports to and discourage imports from only a few of our major trading partners and not with respect to others. Second, U.S. exports to developing countries grew rapidly during the years before the world debt crisis. The debt problems of developing countries have persisted, and efforts to deal with the debt problem within those countries have resulted in slower real growth and dampened demand for imports from the United States. Finally, the rate of inflation in the United States has begun to accelerate and rates of interest are beginning to rise. To the extent that the Federal Reserve System in the United States responds to rising inflationary pressure by cutting back substantially on the rate of monetary expansion, real as well as nominal interest rates will rise further and the dollar will rise in value on world markets. If movement in the value of the dollar is reversed, net exports will decline.

Whether or not the recent decline in the value of the U.S. dollar persists is particularly important at this time. Any success that might come from the Uruguay Round of multilateral trade negotiations in Geneva will depend heavily on the leadership provided by the United States, and the extent of such leadership will surely depend upon these issues.

The slowdown in the rate of growth of imports and exports among the industrial nations is mirrored in data pertaining to developing countries presented in Table 4. The decline in the rate of growth of exports from developing countries was particularly severe after 1980. One clue to the slowdown in export growth for developing countries is the fact that GNP growth among their trading partners declined from an average of 4.9 percent between 1969 and 1978 to 2.8 percent per year from 1979 to 1988. It is critical to developing nations to have rapid growth in exports to hard-currency, industrialized nations to provide the capital they need to sustain the industrialization process. Unless economic conditions turn much more favorable for growth among the industrial countries including the United States, the capital scarcity problem facing the developing countries is likely to become increasingly severe.

Limits on the possible hard-currency earnings attainable by developing countries through exports to industrialized countries would be bad enough if many of them were not already faced with staggering inter-national debts. Current actions by major banks such as Citicorp, Chase and Morgan to write off bad loans to developing countries have created a false impression about the international debt problem. The fact is that while the banks themselves have been successfully working their way out from under the burden of their bad loans to developing countries, the burden of those debts on the countries themselves has actually grown worse. Table 5 shows the international debt positions of developing countries between 1979 and 1988. Generally, bankers consider an external debt-to-export ratio in excess of 300 percent to be unsustainable. Only those developing countries that have been successful in exporting manufactured goods have been able to avoid external debt problems of close to crisis proportions. The magnitude of the debt problem facing the most heavily indebted and the poorest developing countries has actually increased in the late 1980s.

Table 6 provides some perspective on the magnitude of the external debt problem facing developing countries by indicating the ratio of ex-ternal debt to domestic productive capacity. Except for exporters of manufactured goods, the external debt burden is generally as much as half as large as domestic output and is continuing to increase in size relative to the ability of developing countries to create goods and services.

On balance, the continued growth within the United States and the accompanying decline in the unemployment rate to 5.4 percent by the middle of 1988 has reduced the pressure on the federal government to use protectionist measures to provide a safety net to weak industries and protection to domestic workers. The decline in the international price of the U.S. dollar has already begun to reduce the commodity trade deficit and moderate the effectiveness of industry interest groups to rally support for further trade restrictions. The United States has not abandoned its commitment to further trade liberalization although the commitment has been somewhat shaky in recent years.

Table 4
Developing Countries: Merchandise Trade, 1969-1988 (Annual changes, in percent)

| | Developing Countries [1] | | | | | | | |
| | Total Value (in U.S. $) | | Volume | | Unit value (in U.S. $) | | Terms of Trade | Purchasing Power of Exports [2] |
	Exports	Imports	Exports	Imports	Exports	Imports		
Average								
1969-78 [3]	19.8	18.4	4.6	7.2	14.6	10.5	3.7	8.5
1979	34.6	21.3	4.4	3.5	28.9	17.2	10.0	14.9
1980	31.7	26.8	-4.2	7.3	37.4	18.2	16.3	11.4
1981	-1.7	8.9	-6.0	7.8	4.6	1.0	3.6	-2.7
1982	-11.8	-7.5	-7.6	-4.0	-4.5	-3.6	-1.0	-8.5
1983	-4.6	-6.4	3.2	-2.4	-7.6	-4.2	-3.5	-0.5
1984	6.6	0.2	7.1	1.8	-0.4	-1.5	1.1	8.2
1985	-3.8	-3.6	1.0	-0.2	-4.7	-3.4	-1.4	-0.4
1986	-6.2	0.9	8.2	-3.1	-13.3	4.2	-16.8	-10.0
1987	8.4	8.3	2.8	-0.2	5.5	8.4	-2.7	--
1988	9.2	7.4	5.8	2.9	3.2	4.3	-1.0	4.7

Table 4 (continued)

Developing Countries[1]

	Memorandum Real GNP Growth of trading Partners	Non-fuel Exporters (Value in U.S. $)		Volume (in U.S. $)		Unit Value (in U.S. $)		Terms of Trade	Purchasing Power of Exports[2]
		Exports	Imports	Exports	Imports	Exports	Imports		
Average									
1969-78[3]	4.9	16.4	15.9	6.1	4.8	9.7	10.5	-0.8	5.3
1979	4.1	24.7	27.3	6.9	7.4	16.6	18.6	-1.7	5.1
1980	2.6	22.7	26.1	8.5	4.9	13.1	20.2	-5.9	2.1
1981	2.2	2.2	4.6	5.2	3.2	-2.8	1.4	-4.2	0.8
1982	0.7	-4.6	-8.7	1.1	-5.2	-5.7	-3.7	-2.1	-0.9
1983	2.6	3.7	-3.1	8.2	1.7	-4.1	-4.6	0.6	8.0
1984	4.3	11.8	4.0	11.6	5.3	0.2	-1.2	1.4	13.1
1985	2.7	-0.3	0.2	5.2	4.5	-5.2	-4.1	-1.1	4.0
1986	2.9	9.3	5.6	7.7	3.9	1.5	1.7	-0.2	7.5
1987	2.8	9.2	11.5	3.9	3.3	5.1	7.9	-2.6	1.2
1988	3.1	9.6	8.3	6.2	4.0	3.2	4.2	-1.0	5.1

[1]Excluding China prior to 1978.
[2]Export earnings deflated by import prices.
[3]Compound annual rates of change.

Source: I.M.F., *World Economic Outlook*, Washington, D.C., April 1987, Table A-23, p. 141.

Table 5
Developing Countries: External Debt Relative to Exports, 1979-1988 (In percent)

Ratio of external debt to exports of goods and services [1]

	By region						By predominant export		
	Developing Countries	Africa	Asia	Europe	Middle East	Western Hemisphere	Primary product exports	Agricultural exporters	Mineral exporters
Average									
1979	90.8	107.1	75.7	130.1	32.6	197.7	165.5	181.3	132.2
1980	81.6	90.2	71.9	127.4	26.6	183.5	159.1	182.3	114.4
1981	94.6	116.3	74.5	136.7	33.2	210.3	193.2	210.5	153.0
1982	120.1	153.8	88.4	147.0	45.7	273.8	240.8	259.9	194.2
1983	133.3	170.4	93.6	150.0	59.8	290.3	251.3	274.9	204.8
1984	133.7	170.1	88.1	146.4	69.7	277.1	254.8	261.9	220.6
1985	147.8	181.0	100.0	161.9	82.2	295.5	268.3	280.8	230.7
1986	167.5	219.6	101.6	160.7	120.4	354.7	287.3	304.9	237.4
1987	168.6	227.7	100.0	156.8	129.0	367.6	297.8	321.0	234.7
1988	160.7	220.0	95.8	148.6	127.3	342.2	284.3	305.3	225.9

Table 5 (continued)

Ratio of external debt to exports of goods and services [1]

	Exporters of manu- factures	By financial criteria		By miscellaneous criteria		
		Countries with debt- servicing problems	Countries without debt- servicing problems	Fifteen indebted countries	Small low- income countries	Sub- Saharan Africa [2]
Average						
1979	79.1	164.3	85.9	182.3	229.9	149.2
1980	75.1	151.2	79.1	167.1	227.2	146.3
1981	74.3	185.8	81.1	201.4	272.3	181.3
1982	80.2	241.5	92.8	269.8	325.0	213.9
1983	81.5	254.3	100.0	289.7	341.9	226.9
1984	75.8	247.2	96.3	272.1	352.1	222.8
1985	84.0	263.9	109.2	284.2	398.8	256.6
1986	80.8	302.4	114.0	337.9	432.7	282.3
1987	77.8	312.7	112.4	349.6	451.1	294.3
1988	73.7	295.8	107.0	324.7	449.1	301.1

[1]Ratio of year-end debt to exports of goods and services or GDP for year indicated, excluding debt owed to International Monetary Fund.
[2]Excluding Nigeria and South Africa.

Source: I.M.F., World Economic Outlook, Washington, D.C., April 1987, Table A-50, p. 187

Table 6
Developing Countries: External Debt Relative to GDP, 1979-1988

Ratio of external debt to exports of goods and services[1]

| | Developing Countries | By region | | | | | By predominant export | | |
		Africa	Asia	Europe	Middle East	Western Hemi- sphere	Primary product exports	Agricul- tural exporters	Mineral exporters
Average									
1979	24.7	30.6	16.7	30.9	18.6	32.2	29.4	26.6	42.4
1980	24.4	27.2	17.2	35.1	16.2	32.2	30.2	28.5	36.6
1981	27.6	31.4	19.1	40.8	18.8	35.7	34.9	33.4	40.5
1982	32.0	37.5	23.4	43.0	21.9	42.9	40.4	38.2	50.3
1983	34.3	39.8	22.1	49.2	24.1	47.3	42.9	40.3	54.7
1984	35.3	40.3	-24.0	54.7	25.6	47.6	45.5	42.4	60.7
1985	37.5	44.9	27.2	57.9	27.5	46.8	48.2	44.2	71.1
1986	39.8	49.2	29.6	52.6	31.4	48.5	47.9	44.2	68.7
1987	41.3	54.4	31.7	51.2	31.5	49.8	48.4	45.0	67.7
1988	39.7	52.6	30.6	49.4	31.7	47.0	46.6	43.4	65.3

Table 6 (continued)

Ratio of external debt to exports of goods and services[1]

	Exporters of manu-factures	By financial criteria			By miscellaneous criteria	
		Countries with debt-servicing problems	Countries without debt-servicing problems	Fifteen indebted countries	Small low-income countries	Sub-saharan Africa[2]
Average						
1979	19.1	34.0	20.1	30.2	34.1	38.8
1980	19.6	33.6	20.5	30.8	33.5	36.4
1981	21.4	38.5	22.1	34.6	40.6	44.9
1982	22.8	45.5	24.9	41.7	46.0	51.9
1983	23.1	50.0	26.3	47.0	47.5	55.7
1984	23.7	51.1	27.3	46.8	49.4	59.4
1985	26.1	52.2	30.7	46.3	58.4	65.6
1986	26.5	54.8	32.5	48.4	67.6	68.2
1987	27.2	57.5	33.7	50.8	77.6	73.8
1988	26.0	54.7	32.5	47.9	77.5	74.7

[1]Ratio of year-end debt to exports of goods and services or GDP for year indicated, excluding debt owed to International Monetary Fund.
[2]Excluding Nigeria and South Africa.

Source: I.M.F., *World Economic Outlook*, Washington, D.C., April 1987, Table A-50, p. 187

However, the international debt crisis is far from over. Prudence would suggest that the developing nations should not miss the opporutunity to make themselves heard in Geneva on their need for a relatively unrestricted opportunity to compete for sales of their manufactured exports in the industrialized countries. How effective the next round of negotiations will be in liberalizing international trade will depend upon the ability of the participants to agree on curbs on the use of NTBs. As we have already noted, the relative effectiveness of NTBs as a means of avoiding the free-rider problem of effective coalition formation virtually insures that the protectionist threat will never be safely put to rest.

In conclusion, it seems clear that the period of U.S. dominance in international economic competition is not going to return, and therefore the unanimity with which U.S. politicians pushed for trade liberalization in the early post-World War II period is also gone. It also seems clear that innovations in the use of NTBs to restrict trade have had the net effect of strengthening protectionist interests. The world seems poised for a long period of struggle over further efforts to promote international economic cooperation. Without an acceleration in growth rates in industrial and developing countries, the drive to liberalize world trade will be thwarted by special interest groups. Yet, without further genuine liberalization in world trade the prospects for accelerated real growth rates are not good. The product of the inquiry of the last two chapters was never intended to be a flat prediction on how the struggle will end between free trade and protectionist interests but rather an understanding of some of the key factors that have brought us to this moment and that will determine which path we follow in the years to come.

The purpose for our extended discussion of the history of protectionism in the United States has been to place the primary issue for this study—the potential impact of U.S. preferential trade concessions on the ability of the developing countries to deal with their international debt problems—in context. Chapter 3 will include an explicit analysis of the terms of the generalized system of preferences that was adopted by the United States in 1975 and revised in 1984. Our general discussion of the determinants of trade policy in the United States in the last two chapters will be useful in explaining the intent of specific sections of the original GSP and in evaluating the impact that the GSP had on the ability of developing countries to export manufactured goods to the United States.

Chapter 4 will focus on both the export capabilities and debt problems of seven key international debtor nations: Argentina, Brazil, Indonesia, Korea, Mexico, Philippines and Venezuela. Those seven countries were singled out by the World Bank in 1986 as the group of debtor nations that are primarily indebted to foreign private lenders and also had the largest outstanding debts. We are interested in studying them on the presumption that when they incurred the foreign debts, they were worthwhile candidates for foreign loans. Now they are faced with the immediate problem of settling existing debts and the long-term problem of attracting new foreign capital to help to finance their economic development. Surely, a long-term market solution to the debt problems of those nations will require vigorous export expansion. The potential for export expansion by the major foreign private debtors will also depend crucially on whether or not the United States and other industrial countries allow manufactured exports from the debtor countries to have free access to their domestic markets.

The expressed purpose of the GSP was to provide easier access to U.S. markets for exports of manufactured goods from developing countries. Therefore, we proceed with the intention of clarifying the likelihood that the original GSP and the amended version adopted in the autumn of 1984 contributed to a lessening of the debt problem and/or to the prospect of reducing the problem in the future.

NOTES

1. As indicated in Chapter 1, the adoption of the income tax in the United States was critical to the process of trade liberalization. The linkage between the two arose because cutting federal spending was never seriously entertained as an alternative method of accommodating the revenue losses that would accompany tariff cuts. The two major programs that dominated federal spending were the military buildup that began during the 1880s and represented the first major peacetime military expansion in the history of the United States and the rapid growth in the veterans' pension program. See Baack and Ray (1985a) for a more detailed discussion of the issues involved in the military buildup. The growth in the veterans' pension program and the legislative ties between that program and the adoption of the social security program in the United States are traced in Baack and Ray (1988).

2. It has become somewhat fashionable to discuss issues of political economy in terms of ideological commitments and changes in ideology. The meaning of ideology and how one would measure its influence on policy is a slippery matter. The point of the present discussion is not to suggest that there are no major philosophical differences between the two major political parties in the United States or that those differences have played no major role in shaping policy positions. The present discussion simply makes the point that political party positions on trade issues have changed over time in ways that are consistent with traditional constituent interests and responsive to changes in economic factors.

REFERENCES

Baack, Bennett D., and Ray, Edward John. "The Political Economy of the Origins of the U.S. Military Industrial Complex." *Journal of Economic History* 45, no. 2 (June 1985a): 369-75.

_____. "Special Interests and the Adoption of the Income Tax in the United States." *Journal of Economic History* 45, no. 3 (September 1985b): 607-25.

_____. "The Political Economy of the Origin and Development of the Federal Income Tax System." *The Emergence of the Modern Political Economy, Research in Economic History* Supp. 4 (1985c): 121-38.

_____. "Federal Transfer Payments in America: Veterans' Pensions and the Rise in Social Security." *Economic Inquiry* 26 (October 1988): 687-702.

Balassa, Bela. "The Changing Pattern of Comparative Advantage in Manufactured Goods." *Review of Economics and Statistics* 61, no. 2 (May 1979): 260-66.

_____. "Comparative Advantage in Manufactured Goods: A Reappraisal." *Review of Economics and Statistics* 68, no. 4 (November 1986): 315-19.

Bhagwati, Jagdish. "Shifting Comparative Advantage, Protectionist Demands, and Policy Response." In Jagdish Bhagwati, ed., *Import Competition and Response.* Chicago: National Bureau of Economic Research, 1982: 153-84.

Clark, Don P. "Regulation of International Trade: The United States' Caribbean Basin Economic Recovery Act." University of Tennessee (July 1987).

Grossman, Gene. "Import Competition for Developed and Developing Countries." *Review of Economics and Statistics* 64 (May 1982): 271-81.

Krugman, Paul. "New Theories of Trade Among Industrialized Countries." *American Economic Review Papers and Proceedings* 73 (May 1983): 343-47.

Marvel, Howard P., and Ray, Edward John. "The Kennedy Round: Evidence on the Regulation of International Trade in the United States." *American Economic Review* 73, no. 1 (March 1983): 190-97.

_____. "Intraindustry Trade: Sources and Effects on Protection." *Journal of Political Economy* 95, no. 6 (December 1987): 1278-91.

Ray, Edward. "The Impact of Special Interests on Preferential Tariff Concessions by the United States." *Review of Economics and Statistics* 69, no. 2 (May 1987a): 187-93.

_____. "U.S. Protection and Intraindustry Trade: Evidence and Implications." Ohio State University (May 1987b).

Ray, Edward John, and Marvel, Howard P. "The Pattern of Protection in the Industrialized World." *Review of Economics and Statistics* 66, no. 3 (August 1984): 452-58.

Appendix A: Variable Sources for Figures 1 Through 7

VARIABLE DEFINITIONS

Average Tariff Rate	(Customs Revenue/Merchandise Imports) × 100
GNP per Capita	Nominal GNP/population
Recessions	This is a dummy variable with a value of 1 for years with double-digit unemployment in the nonfarm sector between 1913-1941 and in years classified by the National Bureau of Economic Research (NBER) from 1942-1980, and zero otherwise. This variable equals 1.0 for the following years: 1914, 1915, 1921, 1922, 1930, 1931, 1932, 1933, 1934, 1935, 1936, 1937, 1938, 1939, 1940, 1941, 1945, 1949, 1954, 1958, 1961, 1970, 1974, 1980.
Relative Net Exports	$\dfrac{\text{Merchandise Exports } - \text{ Merchandise Imports}}{\text{Merchandise Exports } + \text{ Merchandise imports}} \times 100$
Trade Relative to GNP	(Merchandise Exports/Nominal GNP) × 100
Value of the Trade Weighted U.S. Dollar	A composite of the exchange rate between the U.S. dollar and a market basket of foreign currencies weighted by their value of trade with the United States.
U.S. Unemployment in the Postwar Period	The nonfarm civilian unemployment rate. From 1971-1986 constructed as: (civilian unemployment/nonfarm employment) × 100.

DATA SOURCES

Nominal GNP	1913-1928, *Historical Statistics of the United States*, F1, p. 224; 1929-1976, *National Income and Product Accounts 1929-1976*, pp. 1, 2; 1977-1986, *Economic Report of the President* 1983, 1987.

GNP per Capita	1913-1928, *Historical Statistics of the United States*, Series F-5, p. 224; 1929-1976, *National Income and Product Accounts 1929-1976*, pp. 318, 319; 1977-1980, *Economic Report of the President* 1983, 1987.
Customs Revenue	1913-1970, *Historical Statistics of the United States*, Series Y344, Y353, pp. 1105-1106; 1971-1980, *Economic Report of the President* 1974, 1981.
Merchandise Imports	1913-1970, *Historical Statistics of the United States*, Series U9, p. 864; 1971-1986, *Economic Report of the President* 1974, 1980, 1987.
Merchandise Exports	1913-1970, *Historical Statistics of the United States*, Series U2, p. 864; 1971-1986d, *Economic Report of the President*, 1974, 1982, 1987.
Recessions	1913-1941, see the nonfarm unemployment rate; 1942-1980, *Statistical Abstract of the United States*, 1984, No. 19, p. 545.
Trade Weighted Dollar	1967-1986, *Economic Report of the President*, 1987.
Nonfarm Unemployment Rate	1913-1970, *Historical Statistics of the United States*, Series D-10, p. 126; 1971-1986, *Economic Report of the President* 1983, 1987.

3

The GSP: 1975-1985

BACKGROUND TO THE ADOPTION OF THE GSP

The Generalized System of Preferences, or GSP, was adopted in the United States in 1974 and implemented beginning in 1975. The original document was intended to provide access to U.S. markets on a duty-free basis to key exports from developing countries. The original legislation was subject to review and was actually revised and renewed in October 1984. At the same time that the United States was adopting legislation to grant exports from developing countries preferential access to the U.S. market, the other industrialized nations adopted their own versions of the GSP. The Lomé Agreement adopted in 1975 by the EC constituted that area's version of the GSP. Given the multilateral nature of the GATT Rounds and the much-heralded work by the negotiators during the Kennedy Round, the motivation for the United States and other industrial nations to adopt preferential trade programs aimed at assisting developing countries within two years after the Kennedy Round tariff cuts were fully in place deserves some explanation.

The Kennedy Round negotiators agreed to the rather ingenious procedure of adopting a linear rule for tariff cuts. The basic idea was that all tariffs should be cut by 50 percent except in a limited number of cases for which countries could make effective arguments for exceptions. Unlike the procedures used in previous GATT Rounds in which there was debate over every item considered, the linear rule was intended to maximize agreement on cuts with a minimum of debate. The burden of defending one's position was shifted from proponents of tariff cuts to those who did not want to cooperate with tariff reductions. Measured in broad terms, the Kennedy Round seemed to be an extraordinary success. Tariff rates among the participating nations were cut an average of 50 percent (U.S. tariffs were cut from 14 percent to 7 percent).

Unfortunately, two elements of the negotiating procedure made it possible for countries to undercut much of the effectiveness of the tariff reductions. First, as already noted, the participants had the right to take exception to the 50 percent cut rule and therefore to protect domestic industries from serious losses in protection if those industries had substantial domestic political clout. Second, negotiators agreed that the task of keeping to the 50 percent cut rule would be difficult and that they would defer the problem of defining and controlling nontariff trade barriers (NTBs) for subsequent negotiating rounds. That decision assured participating nations that they could use NTBs to compensate industries for any protection that they might have lost due to tariff cuts. Furthermore, the decision to defer the problem of regulating the use of NTBs to protect industries that had traditionally been shielded from foreign competition as well as new claimants for protection meant that the practice could continue unabated.

Given the ground rules for the Kennedy Round negotiations that we have just outlined, our model would suggest that industries with particular characteristics would be those least likely to experience reductions in tariff rates as a consequence of the Kennedy Round agreements. For example, we would have expected producers of consumer goods to be more successful in maintaining tariff protection in the United States, and they were. Producers would be more likely to form effective coalitions to defend themselves from the threat of foreign competition if they constituted a relatively small group rather than a large group. Not surprisingly, industries in which production is relatively concentrated absorbed the smallest tariff cuts as a result of the Kennedy Round negotiations.

We also argued that the fairness issue could be used most effectively to sustain protection in industries that are having difficulty competing and in which workers are in danger of losing their jobs "through no fault of their own." That observation would lead us to expect protection to be used to shelter declining industries but not to protect domestic profits for firms that are experiencing a growing demand for their products and/or could compete effectively against foreign producers. It is not surprising then that the pattern of tariff protection in the United States after the Kennedy Round tariff cuts were phased in indicated that industries that had experienced relatively slow growth in the years preceding the tariff agreement experienced the smallest tariff cuts. Furthermore, industries that relied heavily on research and development inputs in production and therefore corresponded to industries in which the United States would be highly competitive internationally experienced the largest tariff reductions.

Tariff Cuts and NTBs

Perhaps the most troubling findings with respect to the Kennedy Round tariff cuts had to do with the use of NTBs in the United States. We have already suggested that the negotiators chose to defer the problem of defining and regulating the use of NTBs for later trade rounds and that countries had the opportunity to use NTBs to restore protection lost through tariff cuts as well as to create protection for newly distressed industries. The question that we have not discussed systematically within the context of the model is: Which special interest groups are likely to be most successful in obtaining unregulated NTB protection?

We already have a good deal of information about who will receive NTB protection based on our model. Consumer goods producers are more likely to obtain protection of any kind than are makers of producers' goods such as capital equipment. In fact, unless market and or political conditions in the country have changed dramatically in recent years, we would expect to find that industries that historically benefitted from high tariff rates would be good candidates for other forms of protection as well. Marvel and Ray (1983) found that producers of consumer goods and of goods that had received the greatest tariff protection before the Kennedy Round were more likely than other producers to receive NTB protection.

The interesting dynamic question is whether or not NTB protection went primarily to industries that had experienced the greatest tariff cuts during the Kennedy Round negotiations in order to compensate them for their losses. Such a finding would suggest that in general the Kennedy Round tariff cuts overstated the degree of trade liberalization because some of the protection that individual industries lost from tariff cuts were compensated for by the simultaneous imposition of NTBs. The actual picture that emerges is more disturbing than that. NTB protection was most strongly associated with industries that on average had experienced the least amount of lost protection through the tariff cuts. In effect, the most highly protected industries in the United States not only avoided the trade-liberalizing effects of the Kennedy Round tariff cuts but also managed to obtain NTB protection. It is not unlikely that highly protected industries in the United States faced less threat from foreign competitors after the Kennedy Round than they had before it.

At the end of Chapter 1 we discussed the proliferation in the use of NTBs in the United States at the same time that the United States was taking a leading role in the international effort to reduce trade restrictions. At one level such paradoxical behavior is explained by the general national commitment to market competition and the simultaneous effort by special interest groups that would not prosper in a more competitive world economy working at cross purposes. We suggested that an analogy exists between the pattern of liberalization and increased protectionism that emerged from the Kennedy Round and the results one obtains from bad-faith arms negotiations.

Arms Talks and Trade Negotiations

In the arms negotiations case, there are two key elements. First, there must exist actual or potential innovations in weaponry that substitute for or even exceed existing systems in military effectiveness. That creates the possibility that one can gain an advantage over a potential adversary in negotiations without taking any substantial risk. For example, the United States might agree to limit the deployment of land-based missiles while simultaneously increasing the deployment of missile-armed submarines. If a potential adversary agrees to the land-based missile limitations without simultaneously matching the U.S. deployment of missile-launching submarines, the United States will gain an advantage.

The international trade counterpart to the innovation in weaponry is the development of numerous forms of nontariff trade restrictions such as government domestic procurement rules, health and safety standards that discriminate against differentiated foreign products as well as marketing agreements and voluntary export restraint agreements. The easier it is to compensate for competitive advantages lost through tariff cuts by deploying NTBs, the easier it is to reach agreements on tariff cuts. It is no accident that the major participants in recent rounds to cut tariffs were the highly industrialized nations. Unlike many developing nations, industrialized countries have significant internal taxing capabilities and little need for tariff revenue to finance fiscal programs. The fact that they do not depend on tariff revenue to finance government programs means that the developed countries have more latitude than developing nations to choose among measures to restrict international competition that meet the needs of important domestic special interest groups.

The second key element in the strategic arms negotiation case is the existence of a certain amount of mistrust or bad faith. Clearly, nations that cooperate economically, socially and politically do not have arms races and arms negotiations. The less earnest either participant is in arms talks and/or the less genuine one believes one's adversary is about reducing military forces, the more likely it is that one will view arms talks as an opportunity to gain an advantage rather than make any real progress toward reducing the threat of military confrontation.

There are two aspects of the bad-faith component to the Kennedy Round negotiations that deserve mention. First, there is the issue of whether the Kennedy Round was unique in continuing protection for various special interest groups. Second, the timing for the use of NTBs both to sustain and to increase protection of some industries from international competition requires some explanation.

Recall that the pattern of tariff protection across industries in the United States after the Kennedy Round was quite similar to the pattern that existed before the tariff cuts were implemented. In a sense the simple linear rule of 50 percent tariff cuts across all industries would have produced that result. However, there is further evidence (Lavergne 1983) that the pattern of tariff protection across industries in the United States after the Kennedy Round was quite similar to the pattern that was observed during the 1930s long before the GATT was formed and long before anything like the linear rule was adopted for negotiating purposes. The durability of the pattern of protection across time suggests that specific industries remained vulnerable to foreign competition throughout the mid-twentieth century in the United States and that those industries were able to influence the pattern of concessions associated with a strong trend toward freer trade over the last fifty years that blunted the impact on their domestic profits and sales. In short, the Kennedy Round was not uniquely associated with successful efforts by special interest groups to undercut some of the trade liberalizing effects of the negotiations.

The Kennedy Round was unique with respect to the proliferation of NTBs that accompanied tariff cuts. We have already pointed out that the negotiators did not address the issue of regulating NTBs. But previous multilateral negotiations had not dealt with NTBs either, and the rapid spread in the use of NTBs does not appear to have been part of other tariff rounds. The simplest explanation for the proliferation in the use of NTBs accompanying the Kennedy Round tariff cuts is that market forces had shifted in a protectionist direction. The slowdown in growth at the end of the 1960s was accompanied by rising rates of unemployment in the United States that paralleled declining growth rates and increased unemployment problems throughout much of the world. Growth in world trade slowed dramatically beginning in the late 1960s, and the commodity trade surplus narrowed in the United States as we indicated in more detail in Chapter 2. Under those circumstances special interests seeking protection from imports became stronger relative to competitive industries. At the national level, increasing domestic unemployment and a shrinking commodity trade surplus pushed the federal government further in the direction of worrying about whether or not world trade was fair enough rather than free enough. In effect, many of the economic conditions that existed during the period 1948-1968 and were so conducive to a strong U.S. commitment to trade liberalization reversed themselves during the next twenty years.

There is a final element of the story of falling tariffs and rising NTBs that was discussed in some detail in Chapter 1 but bears repeating here.

NTBs represent a much more serious threat to efforts to liberalize international trade than one would expect if they are viewed simply as comparably effective alternatives to tariffs to protect markets from foreign competition. NTBs are not simple tariff substitutes that advocates of freer trade have not figured out how to control yet. NTBs are potentially more potent barriers to trade than tariffs.

One reason for the lack of control over the use of NTBs is that their effects are harder to quantify than the effects of tariffs. Tariffs directly increase the prices of imports by some measurable amount. The implications of the artificial price increase associated with a tariff can be determined if we have some idea what domestic demand and supply elasticities are for the product we are considering. The implicit price effects of nationally imposed safety standards, government domestic procurement requirements, marketing agreements and voluntary export restraints are difficult to determine and confound efforts to rally consumer support against such trade restrictions.

We discussed the free-rider problem in Chapter 1 to explain why industries in which production is relatively more concentrated are likely to be more successful in obtaining tariff protection. Tariffs protect all current and potential domestic producers of a product from the threat of foreign competition whether they have contributed to the effort that gained tariff protection or not. Consequently, every firm has an incentive to free-ride on the efforts of others to restrict trade. NTBs not only restrict competition but also generate revenues from the sale of import licenses and other measures that can be distributed among protected domestic firms or foreign countries and/or foreign producers according to the role they played in a successful attempt to limit competition in a market. That added element of control that allows a successful coalition to restrict trade to reward supporters and exclude free riders makes concentration in production less critical as a prerequisite for gaining trade restrictions.

As a result, Marvel and Ray (1983) found that NTBs were systematically associated with less concentrated industries. In effect, industries that were less concentrated and therefore unable to form successful coalitions to restrict imports through the imposition of tariffs were successful in obtaining NTB protection. NTBs expand the feasible set of industries that may successfully restrict trade and thereby extend the range of products over which advocates of trade liberalization must be prepared to do battle.

Furthermore, as discussed in Chapter 1, voluntary export restraints (VERs) and orderly marketing agreements (OMAs) are particularly diabolical means for restricting trade because they can be used to co-opt much of the opposition to protection that exists when tariffs are imposed. When tariffs are used to restrict trade, foreign producers and therefore foreign governments are among those who protest and threaten retaliation. OMAs and VERs provide means of restricting competition internationally in response to domestic political pressures and simultaneously sharing the spoils with cooperating foreign governments and producers.

Trade Regulation versus Trade Liberalization

If one thinks of trade negotiations as efforts to reregulate international competition, one is in a better position to differentiate between the advertised intent of the negotiations and the results that may emerge.[1] Each of the major tariff rounds, including the Uruguay Round, began with the advertised objective of liberalizing international trade. The extent to which any given set of negotiations has succeeded or failed in that endeavor has depended in large part on whether or not the underlying economic conditions within the major participating nations were compatible with expanded international competition. Despite the ingenious use of the linear negotiating rule, the Kennedy Round was less successful in liberalizing international trade than would have been the case if national growth rates and employment conditions had been more like they were during the 1950s. The Tokyo Round of trade negotiations between 1974 and 1979 generated trade liberalization measures that were phased in within the United States during the period 1979-1985. It seems clear that the trade-liberalizing effects of the Tokyo Round were much less dramatic than those of the Kennedy Round as one would have expected, given the relative deterioration in the strength of underlying economic conditions that are conducive to trade liberalization between the late 1960s and the late 1970s.

The reregulation description for international trade negotiations is useful to keep in mind because it suggests that regulatory control can increase or decrease in general and/or within specific industries regardless of the advertised intentions of those who come together to negotiate. Special interest groups that attempted to influence U.S. positions during the Kennedy Round did not simply include groups that traditionally sought protection from foreign competition or access to foreign markets but new protectionist and export-oriented interests as well. Unfortunately, changing domestic and international market conditions weighed in more heavily among the new interest groups on the side of increased protection for the United States and many of the other industrialized nations.

Recall that Marvel and Ray (1983) found that industries that had surrendered the least amount of protection in the form of tariff cuts as a result of the Kennedy Round were the most likely to obtain nontariff trade barriers to supplement their remaining tariff protection. That raises the real possibility that a number of key sectors of the economy emerged from the most successful tariff-cutting round in history with more real protection from international competitors than they enjoyed before the negotiations began. In short, while the general impact and certainly the intent of the Kennedy Round was to deregulate competition in international trade dramatically, specific industries may well have managed to increase regulatory restraints on international competition.

THE KENNEDY ROUND AND THE DEVELOPING COUNTRIES

While it is interesting to sort out the paradox of declining tariffs and the simultaneous increasing use of NTBs, the more germain issue at hand is whether Kennedy Round-period tariff cuts and NTB increases systematically affected the ability of developing countries to export commodities to the United States and to other industrial nations. To answer that question, we need to know whether the experience described above with respect to the United States is unique or characteristic of developed countries in general. That is, did the Kennedy Round lead to the systematic use of NTBs to substitute for lost tariff protection in industrial countries other than the United States? And did other industrial countries use NTBs to supplement protection in already highly protected sectors of their economies? Assuming that a similar pattern existed in other industrialized countries, is there any evidence that those industries that gained NTB protection and gave up the least amount of tariff protection within the industrial country markets were industries in which developing countries have competitive export capabilities?

To be more precise, we note that a number of studies have suggested that developing countries have a comparative advantage in exporting such manufactured goods as textiles, processed foods and light consumer goods (for example see Balassa [1967], Balassa and Associates [1971], Bhagwati [1982], Keesing [1983], and Verrydt and Waelbroeck [1982]). Thus, the issue to be addressed is whether or not the United States and other industrialized countries have used NTBs to compensate for lost tariff protection and/or to supplement already relatively high tariff protection for textiles, processed foods and consumer goods in the post-Kennedy Round period. Ray and Marvel (1984) addressed those points in a study that investigated the patterns of post-Kennedy Round tariff and NTB protection across manufacturing sectors for the United States, Japan, Canada and the European Community.

Post-Kennedy Round tariff rates in the United States were found to be positively related to the production of consumer goods and textiles but not to the production of processed foods. The finding with respect to processed foods is less surprising when we recall that the infrastructure of tariff protection in the United States remained fairly stable for the last fifty years. The GATT has been effective in preventing member countries from introducing substantial increases in protection for distressed industries in the form of tariffs. To the extent that the loss of comparative advantage for the United States in the production of manufactured foodstuffs is a post-World War II phenomenon, we would expect to find little evidence of the effective use of tariffs to protect processed food manufacturers in the United States. On the other hand, we argued earlier that the lack of international control over the use of NTBs to protect domestic producers who were losing their ability to compete internationally should lead to the systematic use of NTBs to create new protection possibilities. In fact, the evidence clearly indicates that post-Kennedy Round NTBs are positively associated with consumer goods, textiles and processed food manufacturing in the United States.

The fact that NTB protection was provided to consumer goods and textile manufacturing industries exemplifies the phenomenon of using NTBs to supplement protection through tariffs that were already in place. As a result, tariffs for consumer goods and textiles understate the actual levels of protection that those sectors of the U.S. economy enjoy. The positive association between NTB protection and production of processed foods reflects the fact that, as expected, NTBs were used to provide new protection to domestic manufacturers in response to changing inter-national market conditions. Therefore, the combined effects of tariffs and NTBs in the United States in the post-Kennedy Round period was to discriminate against imports of precisely the kinds of goods that developing countries hoped to export to the United States and other industrial nations: consumer goods, textiles and processed foods.

The post-Kennedy Round tariff structure in Japan systematically discriminated against consumer goods and processed foods but not textiles in which the Japanese have traditionally been more competitive. In more recent years, the Japanese have become major world competitors in the production of manufactured consumer goods. Not surprisingly, Japanese NTBs are not significant in the consumer goods area, but they are significant in the processed foods area. In effect, tariffs in Japan in the post-Kennedy Round period continued to protect manufacturers of con-sumer goods and manufactured foodstuffs but not textiles. And NTBs sup-plemented tariff protection in the processed foods category, which is consistent with Japan's continued lack of competitiveness in that area. Consistent with the view that NTBs have played the critical role of restructuring the pattern of protection within a country in response to changing world market conditions because tariff agreements have been effectively enforced is the observation that Japan used NTBs to add additional protection in the processed foods area but not in the production of consumer goods in which the Japanese have become competitive in world markets.

One of the more intriguing findings with respect to protectionism in Japan is that NTBs have been used to protect high-tech or R&D-intensive manufacturing industries. Given the rapid pace with which the Japanese have emerged as world-class competitors in the sale of technologically sophisticated products, it appears that Japan used its freedom of action with respect to the imposition of NTBs to promote domestic production of skill-intensive products. If so, Japan's success in fostering such industries is analogous to the use of tariffs by the United States in the last third of the nineteenth century to promote the development of steel and other heavy manufacturing industries in the United States. In between lie countless examples of developing countries that protected domestic producers from foreign competition in the failed hope that domestic firms could develop the capacity to compete for international market sales.

An analysis of post-Kennedy Round tariff protection in the European Community (EC) indicates a bias in protection in favor of domestic producers of consumer goods and textiles as well as strong support for producers of processed foods. NTB protection in the EC is biased in favor of consumer goods and processed foods. As a consequence of the combined use of tariffs and NTBs the European Community protects producers in member countries in the consumer goods, textiles and processed foods sectors from foreign competition. Tariff protection alone understates the extent to which the European Community protects internal suppliers of consumer goods and processed foods.

Post-Kennedy Round Canadian tariff protection systematically protected producers of all three categories of goods: consumer goods, textiles and processed foods. Canada also used NTBs to protect domestic producers of textiles and processed foods. Again, in Canada as in the other cases we have discussed, tariff protection alone understates the extent to which domestic producers of products such as textiles and processed foods are protected from foreign competition that would come primarily from developing countries.

On a comparative basis, the United States is relatively less protectionist in its use of tariffs than the other industrial areas. The simple average tariff rates across manufacturing industries in the United States following the Kennedy Round were 7.26 percent in terms of nominal tariffs and 11.55 percent in terms of effective protection rates. Comparable measures for the other areas were 9.60 percent and 15.91 percent for Japan, 7.85 percent and 15.20 percent for the EC and 11.35 percent and 20.63 percent for Canada. With respect to the use of NTBs, the pattern of protection across manufacturing sectors is quite similar for Canada, Japan and the United States. All three areas have concentrated the use of NTBs primarily in the three commodity categories we have focused on in this section with little use of NTBs in other sectors. The outlier in terms of the use of NTBs has been the European Community, which not only has relatively high concentrations of NTBs in the three areas we are interested in here but in almost all other areas of manufacturing as well.

The picture that emerges from a systematic analysis of the pattern of protection across the major industrialized nations of the world following the Kennedy Round of trade liberalization shows continued and perhaps even increased barriers against imports of consumer goods, textiles and manufactured foodstuffs from the rest of the world. Within that context developing nations complained that the Kennedy Round had provided them with little in the way of meaningful access to the domestic markets of the industrialized economies for sales of key manufactured exports.

That the developing countries could compete for sales of manufactured products in international markets was evident from their success during the 1970s despite the continued presence and expansion of trade barriers against their exports. Between 1970 and 1975 the ratio of manufactured exports from developing countries to industrialized countries divided by manufactured exports from developed economies to developed economies rose from 0.13 to 0.18. That same ratio equaled 0.22 by 1979. Measured in comparable terms the ratio of textile export sales in the developed economies from the developing countries increased from 0.32 to 0.44. It is difficult to believe that developing countries would not have experienced even more dramatic gains in exports of manufactured goods to the industrialized nations if tariffs and NTBs had not been targeted against key export categories for the developing countries by the industrialized nations.

THE GENERALIZED SYSTEM OF PREFERENCES IN THE UNITED STATES

The surprising element in the adoption of the U.S. Generalized System of Preferences is not that the developing countries demanded some compensatory action to remedy the bias in U.S. trade restrictions against manufactured exports from developing countries. The surprising element in the story is that the United States as well as other industrial countries responded positively to the demand for preferential trade arrangements with developing nations. In our discussion in Chapter 1 regarding factors that make U.S. national trade policy more than the simple sum of special interest pressures at each point in time we suggested that national values in the United States include a strong preference for market competition wherever possible as well as a concern for fairness. On those grounds alone it is easy to imagine how U.S. policymakers could have accepted preferential trade agreements with developing countries as an appealing way to deal with any inequities that remained in U.S. treatment of trade partners in the post-Kennedy Round period.

On a more practical level the United States and other industrial nations valued political, economic and military ties with many developing countries that were of strategic importance in terms of broad global economic and political alliances and differences. If for no other reason than to discourage a drift of developing country support from the West to the Soviet bloc, the United States and other industrial nations had significant interests in trying to accommodate their need to expand their export markets in manufactured goods. The interesting question is whether those general interests in helping developing countries to expand their exports of manufactured goods to the industrialized countries' markets was any match for the host of special interests that had succeeded during the Kennedy Round period in sheltering some sectors of the economy from substantial tariff cuts while actually increasing protection in the form of NTBs in those and other areas.

There are two kinds of evidence worth reviewing. First, it is instructive to review the GSP document itself for telltale signs of backsliding on the effort to give duty-free access to U.S. markets for manufactured exports from developing countries in the three key areas we have been discussing: consumer goods, textiles and processed foods. The second kind of evidence worth reviewing is data on the composition of exports to the United States that evolved under the influence of the GSP. Did the GSP tilt toward those exports? More generally, did GSP exports occur primarily in industries that were associated with high tariffs and/or the presence of NTBs in the United States?

Public Law 93-618

Public Law 93-618, passed on January 3, 1975, authorized the president of the United States to extend duty-free treatment to beneficiary developing countries for any eligible article. The first two qualifications quite reasonably required the president to take into account the extent to which the legislation would further the development of the affected countries and the extent to which other developed countries undertook comparable efforts to assist developing countries. Statements contained in the GSP and in the European Community's Lomé Convention, which was the EC counterpart of the U.S. GSP, appear in Appendix B. The third qualification on the president's authority to extend preferential treatment to developing countries was that he should consider the impact on domestic producers of the same or competitive products. That is the opening through which special interests would have the opportunity to deflect imports from the developing countries that threatened their domestic markets.

With respect to who gets on the list and who does not, Congress required the president to notify both the House and Senate of any intention to designate a country as a beneficiary and to provide an explanation for doing so. Furthermore, the president could not remove a country from the list of designated beneficiaries without providing both the House and the Senate and the country involved with notification of the intended action at least sixty days before reclassification. Finally, to make certain that the president did not become confused about what constituted a developing country, Congress specifically excluded Canada, Japan, the EC, the USSR, Eastern Europe, most of the rest of Europe, Australia and New Zealand.

The exclusion of Eastern Europe for political reasons is quite straightforward. One might expect that it would be fairly easy to define eligible articles. In fact, the matter is quite complicated. First, there is the requirement that the article is produced primarily in the developing country and not simply passed through the developing country with little or no value added there. That restriction would prevent producers from ineligible countries from shipping goods in a round-about fashion to the United States by way of a developing country simply to take advantage of duty-free access to the United States. That condition is sensible and not surprising.

However, the bill goes on to list articles that are not eligible regardless of where they originate. The excluded "import-sensitive" areas enumerated by the GSP include: textile and apparel articles that are subject to textile agreements, watches, import-sensitive electronic articles, import-sensitive steel articles, footwear articles specified in items 700.05 through 700.27, 700.29 through 700.53, 700.55.23 through 700.55.75, and 700.60 through 700.80 of the Tariff Schedules of the United States, import-sensitive semimanufactured and manufactured glass products, and any other article that the president deems to be import-sensitive in the context of the Generalized System of Preferences. In short, textiles, shoes, glass products, electronic products, steel-industry products and just about any other semimanufactured or manufactured product that the president chooses to classify as import-sensitive can be excluded from the list of eligible articles. It is not difficult to imagine that under the right circumstances any given article that was initially designated as eligible could be removed from the list of duty-free imports from developing countries.

In addition, Congress limited the eligibility of any beneficiary country based on the success of that country in exporting a product to the United States. For example, eligibility could be lost if a country exported more than 50 percent of total imports to the United States of a particular product in a calendar year. Eligibility could also be lost if a country's exports of the product to the United States exceeded an assessed value bearing the same relationship to $25 million that the previous year's value of the gross national product of the United States had in relationship to the gross national product of the United States in 1974, which was $1.4728 trillion. Therefore, a country could become ineligible if direct or indirect exports to the United States exceeded $25 million in 1975. By 1985 the upper limit on imported value for any single article from an eligible country was $63.1 milion, since 1984 GNP in the United States was $3.7175 trillion.

As a final limitation on the effects that the GSP could have on domestic import-competitive industry interests, Congress required the president to report on the effects of the legislation within five years of its adoption and mandated that the legislation would be in force for ten years. Renewal legislation was adopted in October 1984 and will be discussed in detail in Chapter 5.

The European Community adopted legislation granting preferential access to EC markets for exports from developing countries in February 1975. Like the GSP legislation adopted in the United States, the Lomé Convention included language that permitted member states to withdraw preferential status from countries and articles that created difficulties for domestic industries. Specifically, Article 3 stated: "If the offers made by firms of the ACP (African, Caribbean, Pacific Countries) states are likely to be detrimental to the functioning of the Common Market and if any such detriment is attributable to a difference in the conditions of competition as regards prices, Member States may take appropriate measures, such as withdrawing concessions." Even if imports under the convention had no significant impact on the EC as a whole, actions could be taken to limit imports if a sector or region within a member state was seriously affected. Article 10 stated in part: "If as a result of applying the provisions of this Chapter, serious disturbances occur in a sector of the economy of the Community or of one or more of its Member States, or jeopardizes their external financial stability, or if difficulties arise which may result in a deterioration in a sector of the economy of a region of the Community, the later may take, or may authorize the Member State concerned to take, the necessary safeguard measures."

While the language of both the GSP legislation adopted in the United States and the Lomé Convention indicated that protectionist interests had some success in limiting the extent to which developing countries would have duty-free access to developed country markets for their exports, there remains the possibility that substantial benefits were realized. Even in the case of the U.S. legislation that specifically excluded textiles, shoes and other items, there was no explicit exclusion of consumer goods or processed foods. The question remains whether or not the GSP provided to developing countries preferential export opportunities in commodity categories in which they would have been expected to compete for sales in the United States.

Developing Country GSP Exports to the United States

Regardless of how the legislative record reads, the issue of interest is whether the GSP served the advertised role of providing developing countries with compensatory access to the U.S. market for exports of key manufactured goods. We have already noted that post-Kennedy Round tariffs and NTBs in the United States and other developed countries systematically discriminated against imports of manufactured textiles, processed foods and consumer goods. Yet, those are the manufactured commodity groups in which the developing countries would be expected to have a competitive advantage in world markets. Thus, compensatory access to U.S. markets for key manufactured exports from developing countries would be reflected either in evidence of a bias in GSP exports to the United States in the direction of textiles, consumer goods and/or processed foods or more generally in evidence that GSP imports into the United States were biased toward products that received substantial tariff and/or NTB protection.

Whether or not the United States succeeded in providing compensatory access to U.S. markets for key manufactured goods from developing countries, it is clear that the United States remained the most important overseas market for manufactured exports from developing countries throughout the period 1975-1984, when the original GSP legislation was in effect. Non-OPEC developing country exports to the United States grew from $71.5 billion in 1982 to $98.8 billion in 1984. The United States accounts for 60 percent of industrialized country imports of manufactures from developing countries. GSP imports into the United States were equal to $10.8 billion in 1983 and $13.0 billion in 1984. In overall terms, the GSP did contribute significantly to the value of manufactured exports to the United States from developing countries.

In one study focusing on the commodity composition of imports of manufactured goods into the United States in 1984, Ray (1987) found that the U.S. share of imports of consumer goods from the Caribbean was significant and that the import shares of processed foods and textiles from Brazil, South America as a whole and the Caribbean Basin were significant, too. That evidence by itself is consistent with the conjecture that the developing countries have a competitive advantage in exporting consumer goods, processed foods and textiles to developed countries like the United States. The question is how much of a contribution the GSP made to developing country export performance in those commodity areas.

The view that international trade agreements represent attempts to reregulate markets in response to changing economic and/or political conditions is useful in anticipating the impact of the GSP. Political concerns about the drift of developing country loyalties away from Western industrialized countries helped to generate an effort to include them in the gains from trade liberalization. Unfortunately, changing economic conditions in the United States and other industrialized nations pushed in the opposite direction. Increased concern over rising unemployment rates, plant closings and slow economic growth in the United States undercut the strength of the national commitment to trade liberalization.

The fact that overall economic conditions in the United States did not support vigorous trade liberalization efforts meant that special interest groups would have a significant role to play in shaping the structure of tariff concessions granted by the GSP. It is difficult to imagine that the same mix of special interest groups that was successful in undercutting the liberalizing effects of the Kennedy Round cuts would have failed to blunt much of the intended effects of the GSP since it was targeted at the most highly protected and most vulnerable industries in the United States. In short, we would expect to find that there were few if any strong incentives for developing countries to expand exports of processed foods, textiles and/or consumer goods to the United States under the terms of the GSP. More generally, we would expect to find little evidence that GSP imports into the United States were biased toward commodities that maintained high tariff and/or NTB protection following the Kennedy Round.

Ray (1987) provided evidence about the characteristics of GSP imports into the United States in 1984, the last year that the original GSP law was in effect. The likelihood that a product was imported under the conditions of the GSP was negatively related to whether the good was in the textile or processed food category and somewhat positively related to whether or not it was a consumer good. More generally, the likelihood that goods entered the United States under the terms of the GSP in 1984 was negatively related to post-Kennedy Round tariffs and to the presence of NTB protection for those goods.

This second finding is particularly striking. If the GSP had worked as advertised, one would have expected GSP imports to be concentrated in what would otherwise have been highly protected industries in the United States. Successful efforts by lobbyists to blunt the compensatory nature of the GSP would be reflected in a lack of evidence that GSP imports were related to protection in the United States. The actual negative association found between protectionist measures during the post-Kennedy Round period and GSP imports suggests that the GSP actually biased exports from developing countries to the United States away from vulnerable industries in the United States.

The fact that the results apply to 1984 data is also significant. It is quite likely that the observed results reflect equilibrium conditions and not some transitional phase because they represent market responses to the GSP program nine years after its implementation.

Obviously, aggregate relationships may not be representative of the impact of the GSP program on exports to the United States by specific developing countries and regions that are of particular interest. For example, Brazil and Mexico are two of the countries that we will be discussing in subsequent chapters that have serious external debt problems. To the extent that export earnings have the potential to relieve the burden of their external debt problems, it is worth asking whether or not they have benefitted from the GSP program. In fact, it is of general interest to know whether access to the U.S. market under the terms of the GSP has helped countries in South America and the Caribbean Basin to expand their export earnings in key commodity categories.

In 1984 the share of U.S. imports of manufactured goods from Mexico was not significant in processed foods, textiles or consumer goods. The share of imports from Mexico that entered the United States in 1984 under the terms of the GSP was systematically biased away from textiles. More generally, GSP imports into the United States from Mexico in 1984 were systematically biased away from industries with substantial tariff and/or NTB protection. So, at the margin the GSP discouraged exports of textiles to the United States from Mexico and promoted a shift in Mexican exports of manufactured goods away from vulnerable industries in which Mexico might be most effective as a competitor.

The share of U.S. imports from Brazil in 1984 was strongly related to whether a product was in the processed food or textile category. In contrast, Brazilian exports to the United States under the terms of the GSP as a share of Brazilian exports to the United States were systematically biased away from textiles and unrelated to processed foods. As a general matter then, the GSP promoted a shift in Brazilian exports away from two of the three areas we have been discussing and in which Brazil has already proven to be competitive with respect to U.S. sales. Moreover, as in the case of Mexico, the impact of the GSP has been to shift Brazilian exports to the United States away from industries that are highly protected by tariffs and/or NTBs.

Argentina and Venezuela are two other Latin American countries that are plagued with severe external debt problems that we will be discussing in subsequent chapters. In the current context, then, it is worth inquiring whether exports from South America to the United States in general are biased toward more or toward less competitive areas by the GSP program. The share of U.S. imports from South America in 1984 was positively related to processed foods and textiles. However, the share of South American exports to the United States associated with the GSP program in 1984 was biased away from both processed foods and textiles. As in the earlier cases, the general impact of the GSP on exports of manufactured goods from South America to the United States was to shift them away from sectors in the United States that are highly protected from foreign competition in the absence of GSP concessions.

The share of U.S. imports from the Caribbean Basin in 1984 was positively related to each of the three categories of commodities that we suggested should be good export prospects for developing countries: consumer goods, textiles and processed foods. The marginal impact of the GSP on manufactured exports from the Caribbean Basin to the United States was not strong in any of the three categories, but it was negative in each of them. As in the earlier cases described here, the impact of the GSP on the share of U.S. imports from the Caribbean Basin was to shift imports away from highly protected manufacturing sectors in the United States.

Whether we refer to aggregate GSP imports into the United States or imports from specific regions like South America and the Caribbean Basin or individual countries like Brazil and Mexico, there is a consistently disturbing message. The Generalized System of Preferences in the United States failed to provide developing countries with preferential access to the U.S. market in product areas in which the developing countries would be competitive. Even more striking is that the GSP actually induced shifts in developing countries' exports to the United States that run contrary to long-term competitive market forces. In a sense, the GSP as originally crafted may have decreased rather than increased the long-term possibility that an expansion in export sales of manufactured goods to the United States could play a major role in helping countries like Brazil and Mexico handle their external debt problems.

One can always conjure up images of dark forces and sinister elements at work to create the counterproductive structure of trade incentives and disincentives embodied in the GSP. In fact, there is a simple explanation for why the GSP assumed the characteristics we have been describing in this section. Protectionist interests in the United States succeeded in minimizing tariff cuts and in extending NTBs in product lines such as textiles, consumer goods and processed foods for reasons that we have already discussed. Therefore, it is not surprising to find that when the GSP was adopted two years after the full implementation of the Kennedy Round tariff cuts, those same special interests succeeded in maintaining protectionist measures against key imports from developing countries. Like the Kennedy Round before it, the GSP gained reductions in protection in commodity areas in which protection was least important to domestic manufacturing interests in the United States. Gains in cutting protection were greatest in areas of manufacturing in which they were worth the least. Consequently, the trade-creating impact of the GSP was greatest in commodity groups of least long-term importance to developing countries.

The part of the story that is most interesting and significant for policy purposes is what happened next. At the time when the original GSP legislation was adopted, the debt crisis did not exist. International debt problems for developing countries did not become general until after the first oil shock in 1973. The enormity of the debt problem facing industrializing nations did not gain general recognition until after the second oil shock of 1979 and the subsequent deceleration of inflation in the United States in 1981. When the GSP was renewed in late 1984, the magnitude of the debt problems of countries like Argentina, Brazil,

Mexico and Venezuela were well advertised. The fact that export earnings would have to play a substantial role in helping debtor nations meet their external financial obligations was also well understood. The question to be answered in the chapters ahead is whether the severity of the world debt problem had any significant influence on the characteristics of the revised GSP legislation in the United States.

To the extent that the international debt problem had no impact on the GSP program, we would expect to find the same pattern of irrelevant to counterproductive incentives to exports from developing countries to the United States that we observed in the original GSP legislation. In that case, we would have to draw a rather pessimistic conclusion regarding the role that expanded manufactured goods exports to the United States can play in assisting developing countries to meet their external debt obligations.

Our concern with the ability of debtor nations to meet their external financial obligations as opposed to simply repudiating their debts is straightforward. Developing countries need external capital inflows for industrialization purposes. Debt repudiation may seem like a solution to current financial problems, but it is a myopic solution at best. New capital inflows will be directly related to the extent to which developing countries meet their current financial obligations.

In Chapter 4 we will discuss the external debt positions of the seven major borrowers from international markets: Argentina, Brazil, Indonesia, Korea, Mexico, the Philippines and Venezuela. As explained in more detail in Chapter 4, the success that private banks have had in writing off a substantial part of the bad debts they were holding has contributed to a false sense that the international debt problem is behind us. At the same time that bad debts have been written off, there has been very little new money going into debtor nations.

An acceleration in the growth of manufactured exports from debtor nations to the United States could contribute substantially to an improvement in the creditworthiness of those countries. Chapter 5 will provide evidence regarding the impact of the revised GSP on manufactured exports to the United States from developing countries.

NOTE

1. The basic idea that international trade negotiations could be constructively analyzed as systematic attempts to reregulate international markets in response to changes in economic and political factors associated with the equilibrium distribution of rents was highlighted in Marvel and Ray (1983). That approach is a clear application of the ideas of Stigler (1971), Peltzman (1976) and Becker (1976, 1983) on industry regulation and the distribution of rents.

REFERENCES

Balassa, Bela. "The Impact of the Industrial Countries' Tariff Structure on Their Imports of Manufactures from Less Developed Areas." *Economica* 34 (November 1967): 372-83.

Balassa, Bela, and Associates. *The Structure of Protection in Developing Countries.* Baltimore: Johns Hopkins University Press, 1971.

Becker, Gary. "Comment." *Journal of Law and Economics* 19 (August 1976): 245-48.

_____. "A Theory of Competition among Pressure Groups for Political Influence." *Quarterly Journal of Economics* 98 (August 1983): 317-400.

Bhagwati, Jagdish. "Shifting Comparative Advantage, Protectionist Demands, and Policy Response." In Jagdish Bhagwati, ed., *Import Competition and Response.* Chicago: National Bureau of Economic Research, 1982: 153-84.

Keesing, Donald B. "Linking up to Distant Markets: South to North Exports of Manufactured Consumer Goods." *American Economic Review Papers and Proceedings* 73 (May 1983): 338-42.

Lavergne, Real P. *The Political Economy of U.S. Tariffs.* Toronto: Academic Press, 1983.

Marvel, Howard P., and Ray, Edward John. "The Kennedy Round: Evidence on the Regulation of International Trade in the United States." *American Economic Review* 73, no. 1 (March 1983): 190-97.

Peltzman, Sam. "Toward a More General Theory of Regulation." *Journal of Law and Economics* 19 (August 1976): 211-40.

"Public Laws," 93rd Congress, Second Session, 1974. *United States Statutes at Large* 88, part 2: 1363-2545.

Ray, Edward John. "The Impact of Special Interests on Preferential Tariff Concessions by the United States." *Review of Economics and Statistics* 69, no. 2 (May 1987): 187-93.

Ray, Edward John, and Marvel, Howard P. "The Pattern of Protection in the Industrialized World." *Review of Economics and Statistics* 66, no. 3 (August 1984): 452-58.

Stigler, George J. "The Economic Theory of Regulation." *Bell Journal of Economics and Management Science* 2 (Spring 1971): 3-21.

Verreydt, Eric, and Waelbroeck, Jean. "European Community Protection Against Manufactured Imports from Developing Countries: A Case Study in the Political Economy of Protection." In Jagdish Bhagwati, ed., *Import Competition and Response.* Chicago: National Bureau of Economic Research, 1982: 362-93.

Appendix B: Public Law 93-618—
January 3, 1975

TITLE V – GENERALIZED SYSTEM OF PREFERENCES

19 USC 2461.

SEC. 501. AUTHORITY TO EXTEND PREFERENCES.

The President may provide duty-free treatment for any eligible article from any beneficiary developing country in accordance with the provisions of this title. In taking any such action, the President shall have due regard for—

(1) the effect such action will have on furthering the economic development of developing countries;

(2) the extent to which other major developed countries are undertaking a comparable effort to assist developing countries by granting generalized preferences with respect to imports of products of such countries; and

(3) the anticipated impact of such action on United States producers of like or directly competitive products.

19 USC 2462.
"Beneficiary developing country"

SEC. 502. BENEFICIARY DEVELOPING COUNTRY.

(a)(1) For purposes of this title, the term "beneficiary developing country" means any country with respect to which there is in effect an Executive order by the President of the United States designating such country as a beneficiary developing country for purposes of this title. Before the President designates any country as a beneficiary developing country for purposes of this title, he shall notify the House of Representatives and the Senate of his intention to make such designation, together with the considerations entering into such decision.

(2) If the President has designated any country as a beneficiary developing country for purposes of this title, he shall not terminate such designation (either by issuing

an Executive order for that purpose or by issuing an Executive order which has the effect of terminating such designation) unless, at least 60 days before such termination, he has notified the House of Representatives and the Senate and has notified such country of his intention to terminate such designation, together with the considerations entering into such decision.

"Country."

(3) For purposes of this title, the term "country" means any foreign country, any overseas dependent territory or possession of a foreign country, or the Trust Territory of the Pacific Islands. In the case of an association of countries which is a free trade area or customs union, the President may by Executive order provide that all members of such association other than members which are barred from designation under subsection (b) shall be treated as one country for purposes of this title.

(b) No designation shall be made under this section with respect to any of the following:

Designation restriction

Australia	Japan
Austria	Monaco
Canada	New Zealand
Czechoslovakia	Norway
European Economic Community member states	Poland
	Republic of South Africa
Finland	Sweden
Germany (East)	Switzerland
Hungary	Union of Soviet
Iceland	Socialist Republics

19 USC 2463.

SEC. 503. ELIGIBLE ARTICLES.

(a) The President shall, from time to time, publish and furnish the International Trade Commission with lists of articles which may be considered for designation as eligible articles for purposes of this title. Before any such list is furnished to the Commission, there shall be in effect an Executive order under section 502 designating beneficiary developing countries. The provisions of sections 131, 132, 133, and 134 of this Act shall be complied with as though action under section 501 were action under section 101 of this Act to carry out a trade agreement entered into under section 101.

Ante, pp. 1994, 1995
Ante, p. 1982.

After receiving the advice of the Commission with respect to the listed articles, the President shall designate those articles he considers appropriate to be eligible articles for purposes of this title by Executive order.

(b) The duty-free treatment provided under section 501 with respect to any eligible article shall apply only—

(1) to an article which is imported directly from a beneficiary developing country into the customs territory of the United States; and

(2)(A) if the sum of (i) the cost of value of the materials produced in the beneficiary developing country plus (ii) the direct costs of processing operations performed in such beneficiary developing country is not less than 35 percent of the appraised value of such article at the time of its entry into the customs territory of the United States.

(B) if the sum of (i) the cost of value of the materials produced in two or more countries which are members of the same association of countries which is treated as one country under section 502(a)(3), plus (ii) the direct costs of processing operations performed in such countries is not less than 50 percent of the appraised value of such article at the time of its entry into the customs territory of the United States.

(C)(1) The President may not designate any article as an eligible article under subsection (a) if such article is within one of the following categories of import-sensitive articles— *import-sensitive articles.*

(A) textile and apparel articles which are subject to textile agreements,

(B) watches,

(C) import-sensitive electronic articles,

(D) import-sensitive steel articles,

(E) footwear articles specified in items 700.05 through 700.27, 700.29 through 700.53, 700.55.23 through 700.55.75, and 700.60 through 700.80 of the Tariff Schedules of the United States,

19 USC 1202.

(F) import-sensitive semimanufactured and manufactured glass products, and

(G) any other articles which the President determines to be import-sensitive in the context of the Generalized System of Preferences.

(2) No article shall be an eligible article for purposes of this title for any period during which such article is the subject of any section 19 action proclaimed pursuant to section 203 of this Act or section 232 or 351 of the Trade Expansion Act of 1962.

Ante, p.2015.
USC 1862,
1981

19 USC 2464.

SEC. 504. LIMITATIONS ON PREFERENTIAL TREATMENT.

(a) The President may withdraw, suspend, or limit the application of the duty-free treatment accorded under section

501 with respect to any article or with respect to any country; except that no rate of duty may be established in respect of any article pursuant to this section other than the rate which would apply but for this title. In taking any action under this subsection, the President shall consider the factors set forth in sections 501 and 502(c).

Beneficiary developing country, designation or withdrawal

(b) The President shall, after complying with the requirements of section 502(a)(2), withdraw or suspend designation of any country as a beneficiary developing country if, after such designation, he determines that as the result of changed suspension circumstances such country would be barred from designation as a beneficiary developing country under section 502(b). Such country shall cease to be a beneficiary developing country on the day on which the President issues an Executive order revoking his designation of such country under section 505.

(c)(1) Whenever the President determines that any country—

(A) has exported (directly or indirectly) to the United States during a calendar year a quantity of an eligible article having an appraised value in excess of an amount which bears the same ratio to $25,000,000 as the gross national product of the United States for the preceding calendar year, as determined by the Department of Commerce, bears to the gross national product of the United States for calendar year 1974, or

(B) except as provided in subsection (d), has exported (either directly or indirectly) to the United States a quantity of any eligible article equal to or exceeding 50 percent of the appraised value of the total imports of such article into the United States during any calendar year,

Publication Federal Register.

then, not later than 60 days after the close of such calendar year, such country shall not be treated as a beneficiary developing country with respect to such article, except that, if before such 60th day, the President determines and publishes in the Federal Register that, with respect to such country—

(i) there has been an historical preferential trade relationship between the United States and such country.

(ii) there is a treaty or trade agreement in force covering economic relations between such country and the United States, and

(iii) such country does not discriminate against, or impose unjustifiable or unreasonable barriers to, United States commerce,

then he may designate, or continue the designation of, such country as a beneficiary developing country with respect to such article.

(2) A country which is no longer treated as a beneficiary developing country with respect to an eligible article by reason of this subsection may be redesignated, subject to the provisions of section 502, a beneficiary developing country with respect to such article if imports of such article from such country did not exceed the limitations in paragraph (1) of this subsection during the preceding calendar year.

(d) Subsection (c)(1)(B) does not apply with respect to any eligible article if a like or directly competitive article is not produced on the date of enactment of this Act in the United States.

(e) No action pursuant to section 501 may affect any tariff duty imposed by the Legislature of Puerto Rico pursuant to section 319 of the Tariff Act of 1930 (19 U.S.C. sec. 1319) on coffee imported into Puerto Rico.

Puerto Rico, imported, coffee duty.

19 USC 2465.

SEC. 505. TIME LIMITED ON TITLE; COMPREHENSIVE REVIEW.

(a) No duty-free treatment under this title shall remain in effect after the date which is 10 years after the date of the enactment of this Act.

(b) On or before the date which is 5 years after the date of the enactment of this Act, the President shall submit to the Congress a full and complete report of the operation of this title.

Presidential report to Congress.

LOMÉ AGREEMENT

European Economic Community — African, Caribbean and Pacific (ACP) Countries: Documents Lomé home meetings [Doneut Lomé, Togo, February 28, 1975], *The Courier* #31 (Special Issue), March 1975, pp. 596-622.

Key provisions of the Lomé Convention that allowed the EEC to structure the pattern of trade concessions granted to developing countries in accordance with pressures from domestic special interest groups include the following:

"Article 3

If the offers made by firms of the ACP states are likely to be detrimental to the functioning of the Common Market and if any such detriment is attributable to a difference in the conditions of competition as regards prices, Member States may take appropriate measures, such as withdrawing concessions." (p. 603)

Title 1
"Article 10

1. If, as a result of applying the provision of this Chapter, serious disturbances

occur in a sector of the economy of the Community or of one or more of its Member States, or jeopardizes their external financial stability, or if difficulties arise which may result in a deterioration in a sector of the economy of a region of the Community, the latter may take, or may authorize the Member State concerned to take, the necessary safeguard measures. These measures and the methods of applying them shall be notified immediately to the Council of Ministers."

4

The World Debt Problem

UNITED STATES TRADE POLICY AND WORLD DEBT

This chapter, in conjunction with Chapters 5 and 6, assesses the role that the U.S. preferential trade agreement referred to as the Generalized System of Preferences (GSP) is likely to play in providing major debtor nations with expanded export opportunities. If developing countries are to succeed in meeting their external debt obligations, they will have to increase their export earnings substantially. This study focuses on the seven countries classified by the International Monetary Fund as the major market borrowers. They are countries that obtained at least two thirds of their external borrowings from 1978 to 1982 from commercial creditors and have the largest total external indebtedness. The countries are Argentina, Brazil, Indonesia, Korea, Mexico, the Philippines and Venezuela.

The reason for focusing on the major market borrowers is that their former ability to obtain commercial loans suggests that under favorable economic conditions they have the potential to attract private capital. One favorable change would be a substantial increase in export earnings from trade with the United States and other industrialized markets. If the GSP, which was first implemented in 1975 and revised in late 1984, cannot be shown to provide much opportunity for export expansion for the seven major market borrowers, it is unlikely that the GSP will make a substantial contribution to the efforts of developing countries generally in their efforts to avoid repudiating their debts. Obviously, the more dramatically debtor nations fall short of meeting their external debt obligations, the harder it will be for them to attract foreign capital in the future to reinvigorate their development efforts.

The countries included in the study are a diverse group. Indonesia, Mexico and Venezuela are considered fuel exporters, with fuel exports constituting at least 50 percent of their export earnings in 1980. Based on similar export percentages, Argentina, Brazil and the Philippines are classified as primary product exporters and Korea as an exporter of manufactures. Balassa (1967, 1979, 1986), Keesing (1983), Krueger (1978) and others have argued that developing countries should have a comparative advantage in exporting manufactured textiles, consumer goods and agricultural products. Obviously, that characterization would hold to varying degrees among the seven countries considered here.

Both Chapter 5 and Chapter 6 will assess the extent to which the GSP provides positive incentives to exports of each of those categories of manufactures from each of our sample countries. In addition, we will be interested in testing the more general proposition that the GSP provides our sample countries with access to the United States in product categories that would be heavily protected otherwise. In other words, we will explore the possibility that the GSP provides compensatory duty-free access to U.S. markets for exports from our sample countries in those product areas that are most highly protected.

As we indicated in our earlier discussion of the original GSP legislation (Chapter 3) previous studies by Clark (1987), Ray 1987a, 1987b, 1987c, 1987d), Ray and Marvel (1984), Verreydt and Waelbroeck (1982) and others have provided evidence that protection in the form of tariffs and nontariff trade barriers in the United States and other industrialized nations in the post-Kennedy Round period have been biased against imports of manufactured textiles, processed agricultural products and consumer goods. Furthermore, the original GSP legislation not only failed to redress the discriminatory aspects of U.S. trade policy but actually increased the disincentives for manufactured exports to the United States faced by the developing countries. The issue at hand is whether the severity of the international debt problem has had any impact on the incentives embodied in the revised GSP program with respect to manufactured exports from developing countries with severe debt problems.

We review the basic economic conditions and debt problems faced by the seven countries that are the major market debtors in this chapter in the sections that follow. Chapter 5 addresses the issue of the incentive effects of the revised GSP. That assessment includes a brief review of the changes in the 1984 legislation itself. Chapter 6 includes empirical evidence regarding the incentive effects of the GSP on exports from each of the debtor countries to the United States during the first two years of the revised program, 1985 and 1986.

ECONOMIC CONDITIONS AMONG MAJOR MARKET DEBTORS

The objective of the next few chapters is to review the external debt positions of the major market debtors as a group and to assess the potential contribution that exports to the United States under the conditons of the revised GSP can make to resolving their individual and collective debt problems. Addressing such a broad agenda in a reasonable amount of space requires trade-offs in terms of details with respect to individual country cases that must be sacrificed in order to develop some overall perspective. There are a great many studies that develop details concerning the international debt problem including causes and potential solutions such as Dornbusch (1986) and Watson et al. (1986).

Domestic Conditions in Developing Countries

Real growth in gross domestic product (GDP) averaged 6 percent in developing countries and 6.8 percent among our seven major borrowers during the period 1967-1976. In contrast, average real growth for official borrowers, countries that obtained external funds primarily from international institutions and foreign governments during the same period, was only 3.5 percent. In fact, through 1980, growth rates in major market borrowers continued to exceed those in developing countries in general. Real growth in GDP in 1980 averaged 4.7 percent for the major market borrowers compared to 3.4 percent for all developing countries and 3.0 percent for official borrowers.[1] In short, countries that were major borrowers from commercial lenders during the late 1970s and early 1980s were distinguishable from other developing countries by their rapid growth in absolute terms and relative to developing countries in general. As illustrated in Figure 8, the pattern of growth for developing countries in general and for debtor nations in particular changed dramatically after 1980.

From 1981 through 1985 our sample countries grew less rapidly than developing countries in general and much less rapidly than they had over the previous fifteen years. The fuel and primary product exporters, which included all our sample countries except Korea experienced the greatest slowdown in economic growth among developing countries. As Figure 8 indicates, real growth in major market borrower countries as a group was less than real growth in developing countries in general throughout the 1981-1986 period. In general indebted developing countries as a group also outperformed the major market borrowers with respect to real economic growth in the first half of the 1980s.

Developing countries in general have been plagued by rapidly rising consumer prices throughout the post-World War II period including the

Figure 8
Growth of Real GDP, 1967-1986

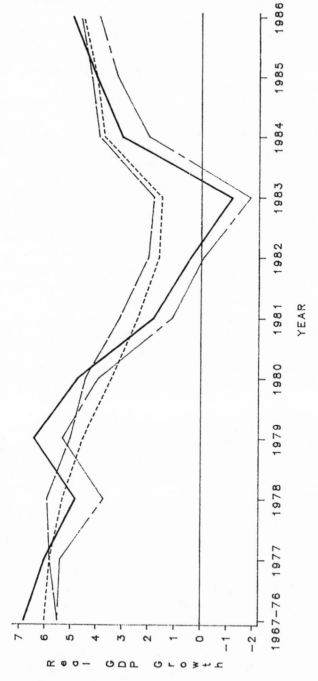

Major Market Borrowers — Wide Solid Line
Indebted Developing Countries — Long Dashed Line   Developing Countries — Short Dashed Line
Countries With Recent Debt Servicing Problems — Broken Line
SOURCE: Adapted from numerical data in IMF, World Economic Outlook,
April 1985, Washington, D.C., Table 5, p. 210.

past twenty years. The major market borrowers were even less successful in containing inflationary pressures than developing countries in general. As illustrated in Figure 9, the seven major market borrower nations as a group had higher annual rates of consumer price inflation during the 1967-1976 period (22.4 percent) than indebted developing countries (15.1 percent) or developing countries in general (13.8 percent).[2] Furthermore, the relative performance of major borrowers in dealing with consumer price inflation deteriorated during the 1977-1986 period. Consumer price inflation per year rose to 62.24 percent for the major borrowers compared to 30.06 percent for indebted developing countries and 27.13 percent for all developing countries. In effect, while inflationary pressure has been a nagging problem for the developing country subgroups we have been discussing in this section for many years, it is clear that inflation rates generally jumped 100 percent across developing countries and almost tripled in the major market borrower countries.

Inflationary pressure is often symptomatic of internal financial problems. Therefore, it is perhaps not surprising that the inflation rate in consumer prices in 1984 was 10.7 percent in developing countries without debt-servicing problems, 37.7 percent in developing countries as a group, 89 percent among countries with debt-servicing problems and 106 percent among the major market borrowers. By 1986 developing countries in general had reduced their price inflation rates to 22.6 percent, which compared favorably to the comparable measure of 24.8 percent in 1977. Even the seven major market borrowers reduced their average consumer price inflation rate down to 47.1 percent in 1986 compared to 45.4 percent in 1977. However, those rates of inflation were still double what they had been in the 1967-1976 period. Clearly, something must have induced such a generalized ratcheting up of inflation rates.

International Exchange Rate Regimes

There were significant changes in international financial markets during the 1970s that are often overlooked when discussing trends in inflationary pressures in developing countries that bear repeating here. Prior to 1967 global inflation rates were moderate and the overall expansion in liquidity in the world economy, associated primarily with U.S. monetary policy, did not appear to be greatly out of step with the demands of a growing world market. The major symptoms of impending problems in the way the international financial markets worked under the pegged exchange rate system that prevailed at the time were the ongoing arguments about how fast U.S. dollar balances held abroad should grow, the realization that absent some political crisis, exchange rate adjustments rarely occurred in timely fashion and that when exchange rate adjustments did take place, they were virtually always incurred by countries with balance-of-payments deficits like the United Kingdom

Figure 9
Changes in Consumer Prices, 1967-1986

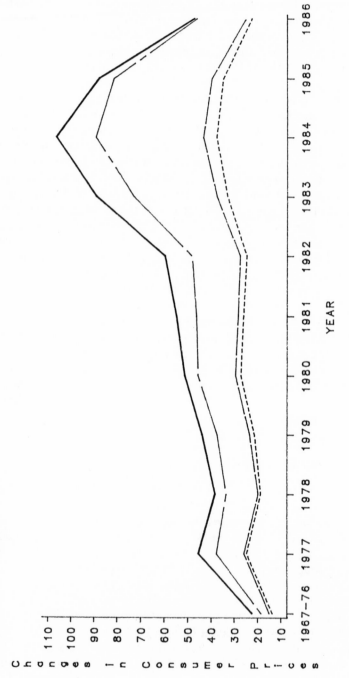

Major Market Borrowers — Wide Solid Line
Indebted Developing Countries — Long Dashed Line   Developing Countries — Short Dashed Line
Countries With Recent Debt Servicing Problems — Broken Line
SOURCE: Adapted from numerical data in IMF, World Economic Outlook,
April 1985, Washington, D.C., Table 10, p. 215.

rather than countries with balance-of-payments surpluses like West Germany and Japan.

While pursuing this discussion takes us somewhat off the main path of our inquiry, it is important to make certain that we have the history of international financial market problems associated with the pegged exchange rate system of the early post-World War II period correctly in mind. Part of the ongoing debate about the causes of the international debt problems and what to do to avoid such problems in the future has been to question the value of the current flexible exchange rate system. Proposals have ranged from calls for reestablishing the gold standard to pegging exchange rates to some bundle of commodities.

The twin problems associated with any pegged exchange rate system, regardless of what the standard is that currencies are pegged to, remain the same. Whether exchange rates are pegged once more on a gold standard (although economic historians are hard-pressed to define when that was), a pound sterling standard or a U.S. dollar standard, agreement will be difficult to reach on the rate of growth in international liquidity. In addition, there will be an inherent bias in the system for countries with balance-of-payments deficits to deflate their economies, that is, slow down the rate of inflation and perhaps the rate of economic growth, with no help from surplus countries.

With respect to the first problem, let us assume that the world adopts a Japanese yen standard. Expansion in world trade and international financial activity may suggest that yen balances around the world should grow faster or slower than the Japanese government wants to allow them to, based on economic conditions within Japan. How does the rest of the world convince Japan to accommodate the demands for increased liquidity around the world when those demands are incompatible with the economic self-interests of the Japanese?

If, alternatively, all currencies are pegged to a bundle of consumer goods with each country expanding its money supply to maintain stable prices for the bundle relative to prices in other currencies, how do we determine which goods are to be included in the bundle and the weights to be attached to them? How do we change the weights and composition of the bundle over time to match changes in patterns of consumption, relative commodity prices and product quality? How do we convince governments faced with strong political opposition domestically because of slow growth and high unemployment at home that they should resist the urge to accelerate monetary expansion in an effort to come up with a temporary or quick fix for their political problems?

With respect to the second problem, the early post-World War II experience taught us that countries that develop chronic balance-of-payments difficulties will ultimately have to adjust their exchange rates by devaluing or lowering the price of their currency in terms of other currencies. By itself, that action, perhaps with a considerable delay, would tend to stimulate exports and discourage imports and reduce trade deficits in the same way that the recent decline in the U.S. dollar internationally has finally begun to reduce this country's trade deficit. However, there is no guarantee that some major trading partners will not also change their exchange rates in order to avoid lost export sales to the devaluing country. Furthermore, unless the devaluing country is well below full employment, there will be accompanying pressure on the devaluing country to tighten monetary policy to keep inflationary pressure down. The risks of slower growth and increased unemployment for the devaluing country are obvious.

If the system worked symmetrically so that surplus countries (countries with balance-of-payments surpluses) were equally willing to raise the international value of their currencies, the risks of unemployment and slow growth in the devaluing country would be minimized. But such a revaluation of one's currency would tend to hurt domestic producers and workers in exporting industries that would become less competitive abroad, and it would tend to hurt producers and workers in industries in which imports are significant by reducing domestic prices of imported goods. The experience of the 1950s and 1960s made it clear that adjustment in a pegged system is not symmetrical. Surplus countries like Japan and West Germany strongly resisted pressures to revalue their currencies despite substantial and continuous balance-of-payments surpluses at the same time that chronic deficit countries like the United Kingdom faced recurring pressure to devalue. That lack of symmetry is sometimes referred to as the deflationary bias in the pegged exchange rate system. It is a real problem that would be present under any pegged system regardless of how the pegs are established.

After 1967, it became apparent that U.S. monetary policy was too expansionary to maintain fairly stable prices either in the United States or the world market. Ultimately, the rapid monetary expansion in the United States in the late 1960s and early 1970s brought about an end to the fixed exchange rate system created by the Bretton Woods agreement after World War II. On August 15, 1971, President Richard Nixon formally announced that the United States would no longer maintain an official price of gold in terms of U.S. dollars. In effect, the United States simply made it official that the pegged exchange rate system of the early post-World War II period that had begun to unravel by 1968 was no longer in effect. Despite several attempts to reestablish a pegged exchange rate system over the course of the next two years, the current flexible exchange rate system was recognized as the established international regime in December 1973.

Monetary Policy in Developing Countries. The end of the fixed exchange rate system meant that individual countries would have greater independence to set monetary growth targets within their own countries in conformity with internal economic conditions. Despite the fact that in a flexible exchange rate environment there are fewer external pressures to maintain moderate domestic monetary growth, countries like West Germany and Japan continued to keep inflation rates at home well below the rates in other industrialized countries including the United States. That is, there was no automatic reason for the adoption of the flexible exchange rate system that emerged during the 1971-1973 interval to be associated with accelerated inflation rates around the world. We have to look elsewhere for an explanation for the rapid acceleration of inflation in developing countries since 1973. At least two factors can be identified as having played an important role in accelerating inflation rates in developing countries after 1973.

The first factor was the emergence of OPEC as an effective price-setting cartel in the crude oil market. The quadrupling of crude oil prices in 1974 and further doubling of prices by 1979 created hugh cash balances in the oil-producing countries. Those cash balances constituted a dramatic expansion in world liquidity that ultimately worked its way through the international financial community. In effect, the impetus to generalized inflationary pressure around the world associated with the rapid growth of U.S. dollar balances abroad was compounded by the runup in oil prices in 1974 and again in 1979 that generated much of the liquidity that ultimately became loans to developing countries.

It is one thing to say that the expansion in overall cash balances created inflationary pressures and quite another to assume that rapid inflation will follow in any particular country. Our eariler discussion made it clear that while inflation rates in general did accelerate during the late 1970s, countries differed substantially with respect to inflation rates. The simple fact is that the system of flexible exchange rates created the opportunity for countries to insulate themselves somewhat from global inflationary pressures. Countries such as Japan and West Germany that worked hard to keep inflation rates down were fairly successful even during the late 1970s.

We know that other things being equal, the rate of inflation that a country experiences will respond with a lag to the rate of domestic monetary expansion. Recall that the rate of increase in prices of consumer goods was much greater for the major borrower countries throughout the 1977-1986 period than it was for developing countries in general. Not surprisingly, broad money aggregates grew much more rapidly in the major borrower countries on an annual basis between 1977 and 1984 (71.45 percent) than in indebted developing countries (38.58 percent) or in developing countries in general (36.31 percent). Figure 10 illustrates the fact that monetary expansion in the major borrower countries was consistently well above the expansion rates for other subgroups of developing countries that we have been discussing in this section.

While it is important to call attention to the link between domestic

Figure 10
Changes in Broad Money Aggregates, 1977-1984

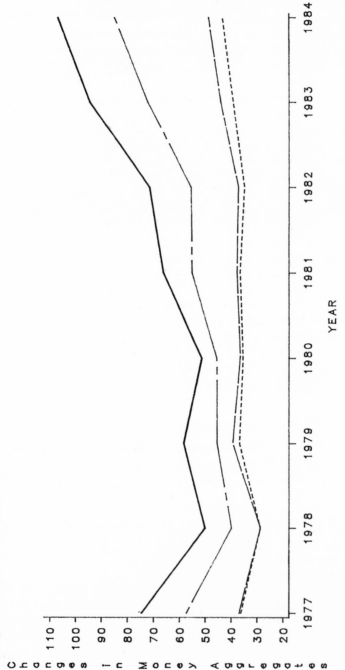

Major Market Borrowers — Wide Solid Line
Indebted Developing Countries — Long Dashed Line   Developing Countries — Short Dashed Line
Countries With Recent Debt Servicing Problems — Broken Line
SOURCE: Adapted from numerical data in IMF, World Economic Outlook,
April 1985, Washington, D.C., Table 17, p. 222.

monetary expansion and consumer goods price inflation, it is also important to avoid too great a rush to judgment. We cannot exclude the possibility that policymakers in major market borrower countries were irresponsible or too myopic in setting domestic policies to control inflation. Perhaps future debt crises could be avoided by simply having brighter bureaucrats running national economies in the future than we have had in the past (presuming that brighter people can be attracted to such jobs). However, there are elements of the current debt problem that would lead one to expect that even bright people in governments had difficulty choosing monetary growth targets correctly.

First, it is worth recalling that the rapid growth in world liquidity after 1973 was closely associated with the rapid rise in crude oil prices and that three of the major market borrower countries are primarily fuel exporters; they are Indonesia, Mexico and Venezuela. They thus experienced tremendous growth in oil export earnings at the same time that banks were looking to lend funds internationally to countries like the fuel-exporting countries that appeared to be on the fast track to industrialization. How could the major market borrowers have anticipated that their average growth of 6.4 percent in 1979 would exceed their total growth over the course of the next four years, 6.1 percent? How could their monetary authorities have anticipated appropriate target rates for monetary expansion under those circumstances?

Countries like Argentina, Brazil and the Phillppines that were not major fuel exporters faced the same energy price pressures as the United States and other developed countries. Like the industrialized countries, developing countries faced with depressed economic conditions in fuel-intensive industries like steel, automobiles and construction found it difficult to resist accelerated monetary expansion to try to avoid the unemployment and slow-growth problems inherent in the rapid runup in energy prices. The problems of the developing countries were compounded by the fact that they depend heavily on the United States and Europe for sales of their exported goods. Slower economic expansion in the industrialized countries translated into less rapid growth in export sales for the primary product exporting countries. Again, the temptation within developing country governments to speed up the growth of the money supply in the hope that it would generate real economic growth and employment expansion at home must have been great.

Fiscal Policy in Developing Countries. One of the curious aspects of foreign lending to developing countries during the late 1970s and early 1980s, apart from the fact that private banks became much more heavily involved in those loans than they had previously, was that many of the loans were made to national governments rather than to specific projects. In effect, banks lent funds to governments on the presumption that governments would not repudiate their debts. Apart from the issue of whether that was a particularly bright assumption, that way of doing business removed an element of control and accountability that we normally associate with lending. In normal circumstances loans are made based on the promise attached to the particular enterprise that is to be funded by the loan and the availability of collateral. While government guarantees for loans might have seemed like acceptable collateral to lenders, it is difficult to understand why banks made loans without some assurance of the potential profitability of the uses to which the funds would be applied.

One possibility that has received very little consideration is that major private banks believed that they had explicit or implicit understandings with their own governments that in a worst case scenario they would not be stuck holding worthless debt. In other words, in the event that loans to developing countries did not get repaid, lending country governments would come to the aid of troubled financial institutions. At the very least it is clear that the industrialized country governments have made substantial efforts to help their own private banks to recoup their losses. In virtually all the major market borrowers the United States would like to see steady economic progress and political stability.

While a great many proposals have been made to resolve the difficulties of developing countries in meeting their payment schedules for foreign loans, there are three worth mentioning here. First, U.S. Senator Bill Bradley of New Jersey has proposed that the developing countries be forgiven part of their external debt obligations. In that event, it is not clear to what extent the private banks would have to absorb their losses. There is the possibility that industrialized country governments would have to make good on the implied losses to the banks. A second alternative associated with former Treasury Secretary James Baker calls for efforts to provide new capital for developing countries through international agencies conditional on internal changes within those countries that would make them better credit risks in the future. The presumption is that banks are on their own to recoup previously invested funds but that they will be encouraged to consider future loans on the basis of fiscally sound internal policies in the developing countries. Finally, in late September 1988, the government of Japan proposed that developing countries sell bonds for the purpose of paying off their already outstanding debt. The bonds would presumably be bought by international agencies or national governments and resold on financial markets. Without more specifics it is unclear whether the proposal represents a bailout for the banks.

What is clear, and all that we intend to suggest here, is that a great deal of effort has gone into defining mechanisms to deal with the external debt problems of the developing countries and that those efforts do not yet exclude the possibility that private lending institutions will get some financial assistance from their governments along the way.

The fact that private bank loans went to central governments resulted in a curious phenomenon in terms of debt financing of government spending in developing countries during the rather depressed period of the early 1980s. As illustrated in Figure 11, central government deficits relative to GDP during the 1977-1984 period tended to be smaller for major market borrowers than for developing countries in general. In fact, central government fiscal deficits relative to GDP were not much different for developing countries with debt servicing problems than for developing countries in general throughout the period. The average annual size of central government deficits relative to GDP for the period 1977-1984 was only 1.94 percent for major borrowers compared to 3.71 percent for indebted developing countries and 3.48 percent for all developing countries. Those figures are consistent with the conjecture that foreign loans were used largely to finance central government projects that would have otherwise generated large fiscal deficits.

INTERNATIONAL MARKET CONDITIONS

One of the lessons that the United States has been relearning in the last twenty years is that domestic economic conditions can be profoundly influenced by international economic conditions. That lesson has had to be relearned because the United States was the dominant influence in international markets and yet relatively unaffected by international economic conditions around the world in the first twenty years after World War II. In contrast, the developing countries have been fairly dependent on external markets to sell their products and to borrow capital throughout the postwar period, and they are always aware, sometimes painfully, of the extent to which their economic fortunes depend upon international economic conditions. Thus, it is not surprising that any discussion of the debt problems faced by developing countries would include consideration of changing economic conditions outside those individual countries.

In general, exports of developing countries grew rapidly throughout the early postwar period. Even during the 1967-1976 period, export volumes for major debtor countries averaged 4.1 percent annual average growth while annual growth rates were 5.5 percent for indebted developing countries and 6.0 percent for all developing countries. However, during the next five years, 1977 through 1981, export volumes increased at an annual rate of 8.04 percent for the major borrowers, 5.66 percent for indebted developing countries and 1.04 percent for developing countries in general. In short, during the period in which our sample countries were

Figure 11
Central Government Fiscal Balances, 1977-1984

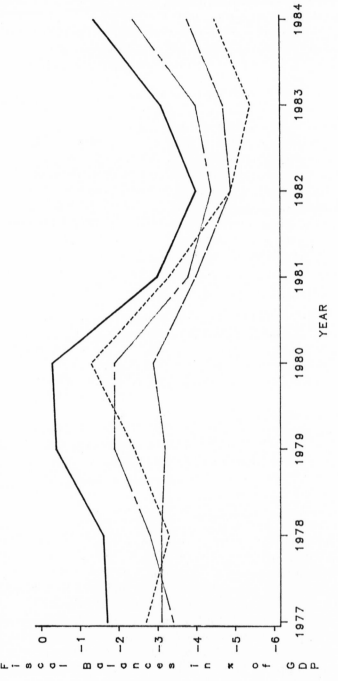

YEAR

Major Market Borrowers — Wide Solid Line
Indebted Developing Countries — Long Dashed Line   Developing Countries — Short Dashed Line
Countries With Recent Debt Servicing Problems — Broken Line

SOURCE: Adapted from numerical data in IMF, World Economic Outlook,
April 1985, Washington, D.C., Table 18, p. 224.

borrowing heavily abroad, their exports were also expanding rapidly. The dramatic slowdown in export growth for developing countries in general should have served as a warning to the debtor nations about the sustainability of their export growth during the late 1970s when they were accumulating external funds. Apparently, neither the borrowing countries nor the banks got the message.

Unfortunately, during the next five years, export volumes increased at an annual rate of only 5.04 percent for the major debtors compared to 5.64 percent for indebted developing countries and 2.6 percent for developing countries as a group. Figure 12 highlights the roller-coaster ride that developing country export volumes took during the 1970s and 1980s.

The explanation for the slowdown in export growth for developing countries in general was the fact that the United States and other industrial countries grew less rapidly after 1967 than during the preceding twenty years. As the United States and other industrial economies grew less rapidly, the demand for exports from developing countries grew less rapidly, too. The crunch in export sales for developing countries was apparent with the mini-recession of 1980 and worsened with the recession of 1982. The fact that export volume grew more rapidly for the major debtor nations between 1978 and 1982 helps to explain why they got the lion's share of foreign loans. Countries like Mexico and Venezuela benefitted particularly from the runup in oil prices effected by the OPEC cartel between 1974 and 1982.

The recession of 1982 dealt a stunning blow to developing countries in two significant respects. First, their export sales dropped dramatically, which reduced their hard currency earnings and undercut their ability to meet foreign loan obligations. Second, the severity of the 1982 recession was at least partially due to the rapid deceleration of inflation in the United States, which in turn implied that international loans defined in terms of nominal interest rates quickly and unexpectedly carried very high rates of real interest.

The first point should be fairly clear while the second is worth explaining a little more fully. If a loan carries a nominal interest rate of 20 percent per year and the rate of inflation is 20 percent, the real rate of interest is zero. The real resources needed to repay the loan after one year carry a price tag that has gone up 20 percent in the last year. Thus, the original loan plus 20 percent interest will buy the same goods and services after one year that the original loan would have bought at the beginning of the period before prices went up 20 percent. The real purchasing power that has to be surrendered to the lender after having the use of the funds throughout that period is no greater than the purchasing power that the lender made available to the borrower.

Now, suppose that the interest rate on a loan is 20 percent for the next year, too. But, unlike the first year, prices go up only 5 percent. The real

Figure 12
Export Volumes, 1967-1986

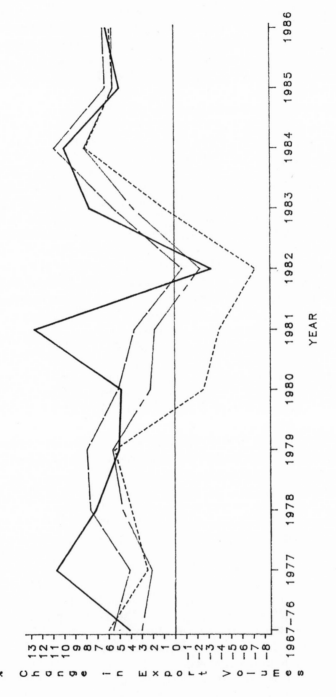

YEAR

Major Market Borrowers — Wide Solid Line
Indebted Developing Countries — Long Dashed Line   Developing Countries — Short Dashed Line
Countries With Recent Debt Servicing Problems — Broken Line
SOURCE: Adapted from numerical data in IMF, World Economic Outlook,
April 1985, Washington, D.C., Table 23, p. 230.

rate of interest on the second one-year loan is 15 percent. That follows from the fact that paying back the loan plus 20 percent interest when prices have gone up only 5 percent means that the lender can buy the same goods and services that would have been obtained with the original loan a year earlier and still have 15 percent of purchasing power left to spend.

The dramatic slowdown in inflation throughout the industrial countries in the early 1980s came as a surprise to developing countries and implied much higher real rates of interest on their outstanding debt than they could have anticipated. Not surprisingly, as rates of inflation diminished in the industrial countries, the prospects for developing countries to meet their external debt obligations dimmed considerably.

Figure 13 illustrates one of the consequences of the increasing real burden of external debt on the developing countries beginning in 1980. On the import side, average annual increases in import volume from 1967 to 1976 were 10.9 percent for the major borrowers, 7.0 percent for the indebted developing countries and 8.4 percent for developing countries in general. During the next ten years, the average annual growth in import volume was 3.52 percent for major borrowers, 4.37 percent for indebted developing countries and 4.23 percent for developing countries in general.

Those figures help to make the point that the worsening of the debt problem beginning in 1980 was not related to a sudden import and consumption binge in developing countries. Rather, the realization of the rising burden of their external debts led developing countries to take action to moderate the rate of growth of imports.

There is another element of the story of the worsening debt problem of developing countries in the early 1980s that deserves mention here. The real cost to a country of external debt will decline as the value of that country's goods rise in international markets. In simple terms, suppose a country can sell grain at $2 per bushel in international markets. In order to use revenues from grain sales to pay an external debt of $2 million, the country would have to sell 1 million bushels of grain abroad. Alternatively, if the country's grain exports are more valuable abroad, selling at a price of $10 per bushel, the country would be able to pay its external debt of $2 million by selling 200,000 bushels of grain in the world market. Because the country's exports are worth five times more in the second case than in the first case, the external debt can be paid off at a real cost in terms of grain that is only one-fifth as great in the second case as in the first case. The price of a country's exports in terms of imported goods is referred to as a country's terms of trade and it reflects the real resource costs of obtaining goods abroad or the cost of settling debts denominated in terms of foreign currency for a given country.

Figure 14 indicates the pattern of changes in the terms of trade of developing countries between 1967 and 1986. Changes in terms of trade

Figure 13
Import Volumes, 1967-1986

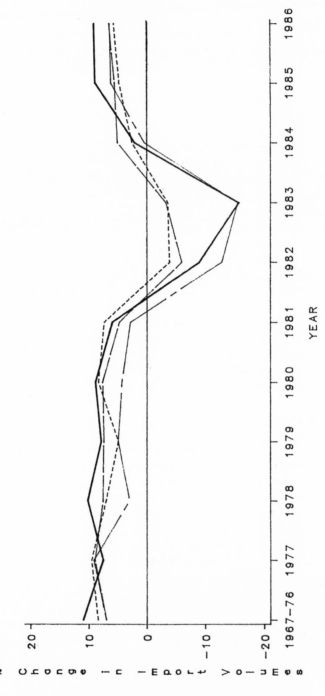

Major Market Borrowers — Wide Solid Line
Indebted Developing Countries — Long Dashed Line   Developing Countries — Short Dashed Line
Countries With Recent Debt Servicing Problems — Broken Line
SOURCE: Adapted from numerical data in IMF, World Economic Outlook,
April 1985, Washington, D.C., Table 24, p. 231.

Figure 14
Terms of Trade, 1967-1986

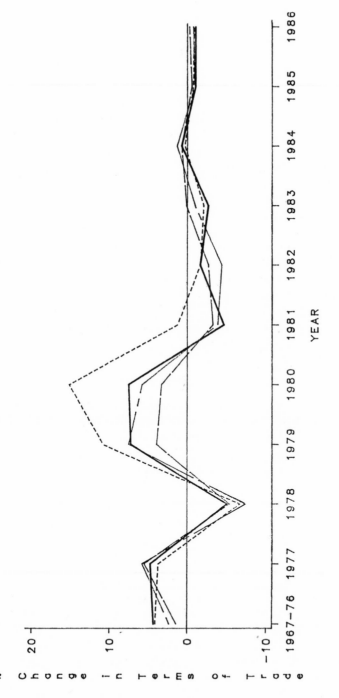
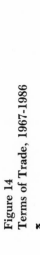

Major Market Borrowers — Wide Solid Line

Indebted Developing Countries — Long Dashed Line   Developing Countries — Short Dashed Line

Countries With Recent Debt Servicing Problems — Broken Line

SOURCE: Adapted from numerical data in IMF, World Economic Outlook,
April 1985, Washington, D.C., Table 27, p. 234.

were in a positive direction for the major borrower countries during 1967-1976 and therefore improved during that period by an average of 4.3 percent per year compared to 4.1 percent for all developing countries and only 1.4 percent for indebted developing countries. However, average annual changes in terms of trade over the next ten years were only 0.4 percent for the major borrowers, 0.1 percent for indebted developing countries and 1.9 percent for all developing countries. In effect, changes in commodity terms of trade in international markets during the 1980s contributed little to offset the rising real burden of the debt faced by the developing countries associated with the decline in inflation rates in the United States and other industrialized nations.

The picture that emerges from this brief review of the data is not consistent with a simple story of external debt problems induced by bad monetary and fiscal policies in debtor nations. It is clear that inflation accelerated in the debtor countries in the last ten years in conjunction with more rapid monetary expansion. However, the economic slowdown and rapid decline in inflation rates in industrialized countries depressed real exports from developing countries during the early 1980s, and terms of trade effects did move adversely for developing countries in general and for the major borrower countries in particular. In short, international market conditions contributed substantially to the financial crisis that the major borrowers face today.

THE RELATIVE BURDEN OF DEBT

While there has been a good deal of discussion concerning the success of major banks in setting aside reserves to write off bad debts by developing countries, there has been less attention paid to the dilemma that those debtor countries face. One measure of the magnitude of the burden of external debts to a country is the ratio of external debt to annual export earnings. The rationale for looking at that ratio is that external debts must be repaid in foreign currency and foreign currency is earned through exporting. The greater the external debt to export revenue ratio is for a country, the greater will be the export effort needed to pay off its debt. Figure 15 illustrates the jump in the external debt to export earnings ratio for developing countries beginning in 1980.

The ratio of external debt to export earnings in percentage terms rose from 110.4 percent for indebted developing countries in 1979 to a peak of 157.9 percent in 1983. Although the figure declined to 141.5 percent in 1986, that still represented a 31 percent increase over the external debt to export earnings ratio faced by indebted developing countries in 1979. For major market borrowers the debt to export earnings ratio rose from 175.2 percent in 1980 to a high mark of 254.6 percent in 1983 before declining to 214.4 percent in 1986. There are two points worth noting here. First,

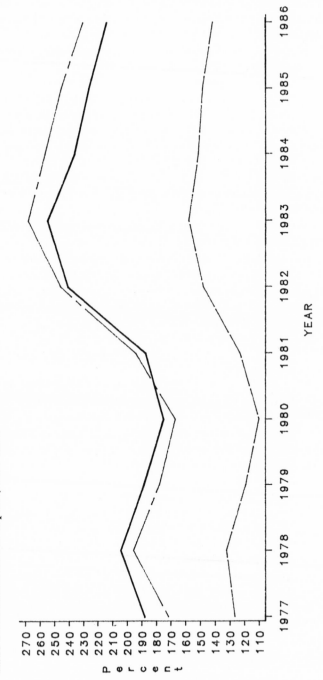

Figure 15
Ratio of External Debt to Exports, 1977-1986

Major Market Borrowers — Wide Solid Line
Indebted Developing Countries — Long Dashed Line
Countries With Recent Debt Servicing Problems — Broken Line

SOURCE: Adapted from numerical data in IMF, World Economic Outlook,
April 1985, Washington, D.C., Table 48, p. 266.

countries that have had problems recently in meeting their debt servicing obligations had an external debt to export earnings ratio of 230.8 percent in 1986. The major market debtors are not under much less of a financial burden with respect to their external debt than countries that in general have been having difficulties in meeting their external debt obligations. In fact, private bankers often use an external debt to export earnings ratio of 300 percent as an indication that a country is a bad credit risk for lenders. The second point is that the external debt to export earnings ratio of 214.4 percent for the major market borrowers in 1986 was above the comparable measure of 187.4 percent in 1981 when the world first took note of the debt problem.

Another measure of the burden of external debts for a country is the ratio of external debt to gross domestic product. The logic behind the measure is that while debt-export earnings ratios can be reduced by vigorously promoting export sales, the ability to do so is ultimately limited by domestic needs and production capabilities. In effect, paying off debts is no different for countries than it is for individuals in the sense that each has to reduce current consumption to pay off debts and the likeliood that either can manage such a transfer is directly related to the magnitude of the debt compared to the resources at the borrower's command. If foreign debt obligations are high relative to total domestic productive capacity, it is difficult to believe that net export growth and therefore forgone domestic consumption could be sufficient to pay off foreign debt obligations.

Figure 16 illustrates the changes during the late 1970s and early 1980s in the external debt to GDP ratio of developing countries. As illustrated, the external debt to GDP ratio for indebted developing countries remained fairly stable between 1977 and 1980 and then rose quickly from 25.7 percent in 1980 to a high point of 36.7 percent in 1985 and 32.5 percent in 1986. In comparison, major market debtors' external debt to GDP ratio increased from 32.9 percent in 1980 to a high mark of 47.3 percent in 1983 before declining to 41.5 percent in 1986.

In short, it is clear that while the major banks have had some success in dealing with potential bad debts in developing countries, the debtor nations themselves face external financial burdens that are comparable to or worse than the burdens that they faced when the international debt crisis first gained public attention. Media coverage of the international debt problem facing developing countries has diminished over time but not because the problem is much less serious today than when it first commanded headlines.

Dealing with the Debt

One of the ongoing methods for dealing with the debt problem that is intended to avoid an international financial crisis has been to bring

Figure 16
Ratio of External Debt to GDP, 1977-1986

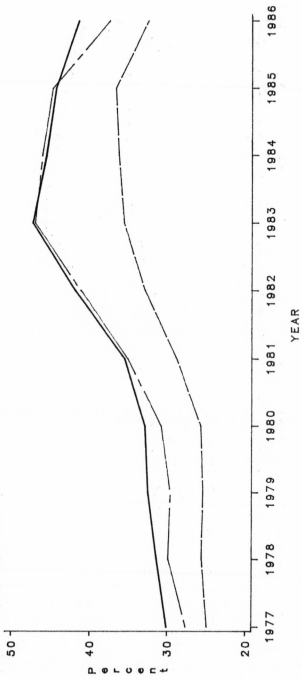

Major Market Borrowers — Wide Solid Line
Indebted Developing Countries — Long Dashed Line
Countries With Recent Debt Servicing Problems — Broken Line
SOURCE: Adapted from numerical data in IMF, World Economic Outlook,
April 1985, Washington, D.C., Table 48, pp. 266—67.

borrowers and lenders together in the hope that they could work out a revised schedule of payments. While national governments and international agencies have encouraged those efforts, the parties involved have had plenty of incentive of their own to pursue the possibility of rescheduling debts. John Maynard Keynes is reported to have observed once that if you owe a bank $1, the bank owns you, but if you owe a bank $1 million, you own the bank. In effect, if you are an important borrower for a bank, the bank's financial success or failure becomes bound up in your success or failure in meeting your loan obligations. Once it is clear to the bank that its own financial survival is tied to your ability to continue to pay your debts, the bank has a strong incentive to try to help you develop a manageable payment schedule. While the sums involved are much greater, that is exactly the kind of action that banks have taken with respect to managing the external debt of the major market borrowers.

Table 7 summarizes the amount of rescheduling that occurred between 1983 and 1986. As indicated, much of the debt rescheduling that has taken place has involved the major market debtor countries that we are focusing on in this study. In 1983 Brazil and Mexico negotiated restructured payment schedules involving $23.252 billion of the $33.803 billion in external debt rescheduled that year (68.8 percent). In 1984 Argentina, Brazil, Mexico, the Philippines and Venezuela together rescheduled $91.443 billion of the total $100.47 billion in debt rescheduled that year (91 percent). In the first three quarters of 1986 Brazil and Mexico negotiated repayment schedules for $50.371 billion in external debt, which corresponded to 90.5 percent of the $55.667 billion in foreign debt rescheduled during the first three quarters of that year.

One aspect of the debt problem that we have not discussed yet is that the same factors that have contributed to the inability of indebted nations to meet their external debt obligations have led domestic businesses and individuals to send their money abroad. The process of sending funds abroad to avoid either confiscation by one's own government or simply a loss in purchasing power as domestic prices rise and the value of a currency declines in international markets is called *capital flight.* Table 8 provides summary data on estimates of capital flight from the Latin American members of our major market borrowing group: Argentina, Brazil, Mexico and Venezuela during the 1976-1985 period. One estimate in the table indicates that capital flight from the four Latin American countries may have totaled almost $120 billion during that period. Obviously, capital flight simply reflects the same loss of confidence in government policies and the value of currencies in major market debtor countries that potential foreign investors experienced as the magnitude of the debt problem became clear. Capital flight compounded the problem of maintaining real investment activity in the major market debtors and contributed to the severity of the economic slowdown that they experi-

Table 7

Amounts of Long-Term Bank Debt Restructured, 1983-Third Quarter 1986

(In billions of U.S. dollars; classified by year of agreement in principle)

	1983	1984	First-third quarter 1985	1986
Argentina	----	14.200	----	----
Brazil	4.452	4.84	----	6.671[1]
Mexico	18.800	48.700[2,3]	----	43.700
Philippines	----	2.660[4]	----	----
Venezuela	----	21.037[2]	----	----
Total (all countries)	33.803	100.47	13.086	55.667

Notes: Amounts include short-term debt converted into long-term debt.

[1] Excluding $9.6 billion in deferments corresponding to maturities due in 1986.

[2] Multiyear restructuring agreement (MYRA).

[3] Agreements signed in March and August 1985. Consists of $5 billion in the form of the syndicated credit raised in 1983, $20.1 billion of public medium- and long-term debt not previously restructured falling due during 1985-1990; $5.8 billion in the form of public medium- and long-term debt previously restructured falling in 1987, and of $17.8 billion in the form of public medium- and long-term debt previously restructured falling due during 1988-90. Excludes $950 million in deferment agreed in October 1985.

[4] Including restructuring of $2,059 million in medium- and long-term public debt, $16 million in medium- and long-term private financial sector debt, and $585 million in medium- and long-term corporate debt.

Source: Maxwell Watson et al., Table 47, p. 123.

Table 8

Studies on Capital Flight in Selected Developing Countries, 1976-1985 (In billions of U.S. dollars)

	1976	1977	1978	1979	1980	1981	1982	1983	1984	1985	1976-1985
Argentina											
Cuddington (1)	0.3	-0.6	1.5	-1.7	2.3	8.7	5.0	...	...	...	———
Cuddington (2)	-0.2	0.9	3.0	1.7	6.7	7.7	-0.4	...	...	...	———
Dooley	...	...	2.0	4.7	-1.1	6.2	9.7	0.2	-0.5	...	———
Morgan	...	...	...	...	...	...	...	...	...	...	26.0[1]
HF	...	...	...	1.6	7.4	8.2	6.9	1.6	-0.2	-1.3	———
IBS	...	...	0.2	3.0	-0.5	1.0	0.4	0.9	-0.2	0.8	———
Brazil											
Cuddington (1)	-0.5	0.6	-0.3	-1.2	0.4	0.4	0.4	...	...	...	———
Cuddington (2)	-1.6	2.4	4.4	1.1	1.8	-0.2	0.2	...	...	...	———
Dooley	...	...	4.8	-4.9	0.4	1.5	-4.5	1.7	6.0	...	———
Morgan	...	...	...	...	...	...	...	...	...	...	10.0[1]
HF	...	...	...	-0.4	0.4	0.7	2.4	3.4	4.0	1.1	———
IBS	...	...	3.9	-1.8	-2.3	0.7	0.3	4.0	0.2	1.5	———

Mexico

Cuddington (1)	3.3	0.9	0.5	1.5	4.8	11.5	7.6	...	...	...	—
Cuddington (2)	3.5	4.3	0.9	2.8	7.1	8.2	6.9	...	...	...	—
Dooley	...	...	-0.1	1.5	6.9	7.9	2.1	11.2	2.1	...	—
Morgan	...	...	...	...	...	...	...	...	...	...	53.0[1]
HF	...	...	5.5	9.2	8.3	12.4	5.6	4.8	...	3.2	—
IBS	...	...	1.0	1.6	1.5	3.8	1.3	2.3	1.7	1.7	—

References and definitions: In John T. Cuddington (*Capital Flight: Issues, Estimates, and Explanations*, Princeton Studies in Intranational Finance, No. 58, Princeton University Press, 1986), two different measures of capital flight are used: (1) as errors and omissions plus certain categories of "other short-term capital, other sector" from International Monetary Fund, *Balance of Payments Yearbook*, and (2) as gross capital outflows defined as changes in external indebtedness plus the net inflow of direct foreign investment minus the current account deficit and the change in total foreign reserve assets less gold plus net foreign assets of commercial banks; in Michael P. Dooley ("Capital Flight: A Response to Differences in Financial Risks," *Staff Papers*, International Monetary Fund, Volume 33, December 1986), capital flight is measured as the diffedrence between the estimated stock of total external claims (defined as sum of capital outflows, excluding direct investment, plus errors and omissions form the balance of payments plus the difference between extrenal debt as calculated by the World Bank and external debt cumulated from the balance of payments) and "interest earning" claims measured as the capitalized value of investment income receipts; in Morgan Guaranty Trust Company ("LDC Capital Flight," *World Financial Markets*, March 1986, pp. 13-15), capital flight is estimated as increases in gross external debt less current account deficits and less the building up of foreign assets by the banking systems and official monetary authorities plus net direct investment flows; in Institute of Intrnational Finance (IIF) ("External Asset Transactions by Residents of Debtor Countries," Working Party on the Future of International Lending; Note by the Staff, June 12, 1986), net private sector asset flow is estimated as debt-creating flows, less the current account balance, and recorded official and monetary sector flows; and in the Fund's international banking statistics (IBS), capital flight is defined as deposit taking from nonbanks in developing countries.

[1]Sum of flows during 1976-1985.

Source: Maxwell Watson et al., Table 523, p. 142.

Table 9
Terms and Conditions of Bank Debt Restructurings and Financial Packages, 1978-September 1986

Country, data of agreement, and type of debt rescheduled	Basis	Amount provided (In millions of U.S. dollars)	Grace period (In years, unless otherwise noted)	Maturity	Interest rate (In percent spread over LIBOR/U.S. prime)
Argentina					
Bridging loan (1982)[1]		1,300[2]	7 months	14 months	$1^5/_8 - 1^1/_2$
New medium-term loan					
(1983)	New financing	1,500	3	$4^1/_2$	$2^1/_4 - 2^1/_8$
Agreement in principle					
(December 3,					
1984), final					
agreement[3] of					
August 27, 1985:					
Refinancing of medium-					
and long-term debt					
Public and publicly					

Country, data of agreement, and type of debt rescheduled	Basis	Amount provided (In millions of U.S. dollars)	Grace period (In years, unless otherwise noted)	Maturity	Interest rate (In percent spread over LIBOR/U.S. prime)
guaranteed debt					
Due in 1982 and 1983	100 percent of principal	14,200	3	10	$1^3/_8$
Due in 1984 and 1985	100 percent of principal		3	12	$1^3/_8$
Private sector					
nonguaranteed debt			3	10	$1^3/_8$
New medium-term loan	New financing	3,700	3	10	$1^5/_8 - 1^1/_4$
New trade credit					
deposit facility		500	----	4	$1^3/_8 - 1$

Table 9 (continued)

Country, data of agreement, and type of debt rescheduled	Basis	Amount provided (In millions of U.S. dollars)	Grace period	Maturity (In years, unless otherwise noted)	Interest rate (In percent spread over LIBOR/U.S. prime)
Trade credit maintenance facility	Banks would make available to the Central Bank on request any amounts outstanding to foreign branches and agencies of Argentine banks on September 30, 1984	1,400	—	—	1/4

Brazil

Agreement of
February 25,
1983:

Country, data of agreement, and type of debt rescheduled	Basis	Amount provided (In millions of U.S. dollars)	Grace period (In years, unless otherwise noted)	Maturity	Interest rate (In percent spread over LIBOR/U.S. prime)
Rescheduling of:					
Medium- and long-term debt due in 1983	100 percent of principal	4,452	$2\frac{1}{2}$ [4]	8	$2\frac{1}{8}-1\frac{7}{8}$ [5] $2\frac{1}{4}-2$ [6]
Short-term debt (1983)	100 percent rollover in 1983	15,175	—		
New loan commitments (1983)	New financing	4,400	$2\frac{1}{2}$	8	$2\frac{1}{8}-1\frac{7}{8}$ [7]

129

Table 9 (continued)

Country, data of agreement, and type of debt rescheduled	Basis	Amount provided (In millions of U.S. dollars)	Grace period (In years, unless otherwise noted)	Maturity	Interest rate (In percent spread over LIBOR/U.S. prime)
Agreement of January 27, 1984:					
Rescheduling of					
Medium- and long-term debt due in 1984	100 percent of principal	4,846[8]	5	9	$2-1^3/_4$
Short-term debt (1984)	100 percent rollover	15,100	—	—	...
New loan commitment (1984)	New financing	6,500	5	9	$2-1^3/_4$
Agreement of September 5, 1986:					
Rescheduling of medium- and long-term debt					
due in 1985	100 percent of principal	6,671	5	7	$1^1/_8$

Country, data of agreement, and type of debt rescheduled	Basis	Amount provided (In millions of U.S. dollars)	Grace period (In years, unless otherwise noted)	Maturity	Interest rate (In percent spread over LIBOR/U.S. prime)
Deferment of medium- and long-term debt due in 1986	100 percent of principal	9,600	---	To March 1987	Original rates
Maintenance of trade credit and interbank credit lines	100 percent rollover	14,750	---	To March 1987	Original rates

Mexico

Agreement of August 27, 1983;[9]

Rescheduling of public sector short-, medium-, and long-term debt[10]

Table 9 (continued)

Country, data of agreement, and type of debt rescheduled	Basis	Amount provided (In millions of U.S. dollars)	Grace period (In years, unless otherwise noted)	Maturity	Interest rate (In percent spread over LIBOR/U.S. prime)
due August 23, 1982–					
December 31, 1984	100 percent				
	of principal	18,800	4	8	$1^{7}/_{8} - 1^{3}/_{4}$
Syndicated loan[11]	New financing	5,000	3	6	$2^{1}/_{4} - 2^{1}/_{8}$
Venezuela					
Agreement with Steering					
Committee					
(September 1984):					
final agreement					
(February 1986):					
Rescheduling of short-,					
medium-, and long-term					
debt falling due during					
1983–1988	Principal	20,037	—	$12^{1}/_{2}$	$1^{1}/_{8}$

132

Country, data of agreement, and type of debt rescheduled	Basis	Amount provided (In millions of U.S. dollars)	Grace period (In years, unless otherwise noted)	Maturity	Interest rate (In percent spread over LIBOR/U.S. prime)
Philippines					
Agreement of May 20, 1985:					
Rescheduling of public and publicly guaranteed debt:					
Due between October 17, 1983 and December 31, 1985	100 percent of principal	1,406	5	10	$1\,5/8$
Due in 1986	100 percent of principal	653	5	10	$1\,5/8$
Short-term debt		1,183	5	10	$1\,5/8$

Table 9 (continued)

Country, data of agreement, and type of debt rescheduled	Basis	Amount provided (In millions of U.S. dollars)	Grace period	Maturity (In years, unless otherwise noted)	Interest rate (In percent spread over LIBOR/U.S. prime)
Rescheduling of					
private financial					
sector debt, medium-					
and long-term:					
Due between					
October 17,					
1983, and					
December 31, 1985	100 percent of principal	10	5	10	$1^5/_8$
Due in 1986	100 percent of principal	6	5	10	$1^5/_8$
Short-term debt		1,594	4	4	Less than 2

134

Country, data of agreement, and type of debt rescheduled	Basis	Amount provided (In millions of U.S. dollars)	Grace period (In years, unless otherwise noted)	Maturity	Interest rate (In percent spread over LIBOR/U.S. prime)
Rescheduling of corporate debt, medium- and long-term, due between October 17, 1983, and December 31, 1985	100 percent of principal	378	5	10	$1\,^5/_8$
Due in 1986	100 percent of principal	207	5	10	$1\,^5/_8$
Short-term debt		448	5	10	$1\,^5/_8$

135

Table 9 (continued)

Country, data of agreement, and type of debt rescheduled	Basis	Amount provided (In millions of U.S. dollars)	Grace period (In years, unless otherwise noted)	Maturity	Interest rate (In percent spread over LIBOR/U.S. prime)
New medium-term loan	New money				
Revolving short-term trade facility	Trade-related outstanding and central bank overdrafts as of October 17, 1983	2,974	annum	Revolving per	$1\frac{1}{4}$

Notes:

[1] An agreement in principle to reschedule arrears at the end of 1982 and public debt falling due in 1983 was reached in January 1983, but the new government requested a renegotiation of this agreement.

[2] The cumulative loan disbursements could never exceed $1.1 billion per annum.

[3] The agreement also provided that the $750 million outstanding under the 1982 bridge loan would be repaid in early 1985 on the date of the first borrowing under the new loan: Argentina would pay at least $750 million before the end of 1985 on the date of the first borrowing under the new loan: Argentina would pay at least $750 million before the end of 1984 to reduce interest arrears on Argentine public sector indebtedness; interest arrears on public sector indebtedness would be brought current during the first half of 1985; and foreign exchange would be made available to private sector borrowers so that interest on Argentine private sector indebtedness could be brought current during the first half of 1985.

[4] First principal payment due 30 months after rescheduling.

[5] The Central Bank stands ready to borrow the committed funds at either 2⅛ percent over LIBOR or 1⅞ percent over U.S. prime rate. For loans to other borrowers, the spreads agreed must be acceptable to the Central Bank, which indicated the following maximums for spreads over LIBOR to be generally acceptable (spreads over U.S. prime rate in parentheses): public sector borrowers with official guarantee as well as Petrobras and CVRD—2⅛ (1⅞ percent); public sector borrowers without official guarantee, private sector borrowers with Development Bank guarantee, and Resolution 63 loans to commercial and investment banks—2¼ percent (2 percent); private sector borrowers, including multinationals—2½ percent (2½ percent). Brazil is also prepared to pay a 0,5 percent commitment fee on undisbursed commitments, payable quarterly in arrears, and a 1.5 percent flat facility fee on amounts disbursed, payable at the time of disbursement.

[6],[7] The spreads over LIBOR/U.S. prime rate are 2⅛ percent/1⅞ percent for amounts on deposit with the Central Bank or—as generally acceptable maximums—for loans to public sector borrowers with official guarantee. Petrobras and Companhia Vale do Rio Doce (CVRD(; 2¼ percent/2 percent as the generally acceptable maximums for public sector borrowers without official guarantee, private sector borrowers with Development Bank guarantee, and for commercial and investment banks under Resolution 63; and 2½ percent/2¼ percent as generally acceptable maximums for private sector borrowers.

[8] Latest estimate of amount subject to rescheduling. Total may be lower, as some of Brazil's debt to banks and suppliers may be eligible for rescheduling through Paris Club. A definitive accounting of Paris Club rescheduling will be available upon termination of bilateral agreements. In addition, trade financing was maintained at approximately $9.8 billion and interbank exposure was restored to $6 billion.

[9] Agreement took effect with disbursement of a new loan in March 1983.

[10] For the purpose of the rescheduling, Mexico's public sector debt (short-, medium-, and long-term) excludes loans made, guaranteed, insured, or subsidized by official agencies in the creditor countries: publicly issued bonds, private placements (including Japanese yen-denominated registered private placements) and floating rate certificates of deposit

Table 9 (continued)

and notes (including floating rate notes); debt to official multilateral entities; forward exchange and precious metal contracts; spot and lease obligations in respect of movable property, short-term import- and export-related trade credits; interbank obligations (including placements) of the foreign agencies and branches of Mexican banks, excluding guarantees on intrbank placements; financing secured by legally recognized security interest in ships, aircraft, and drilling rigs; and the Central Bank's obligations arising from the arrangements to liquidate interest payments in arrears.

[11]The $5 billion loan was raised in the form of a medium-term international syndicated credit in which banks participated on the basis of their pro rata exposure to Mexico as of August 23, 1982. The loan document included a specific reference to a written explanation and confirmation from the Managing Director of the Fund with respect to $2-2.5 billion in financial assistance to be obtained from official creditors (other than the Fund), a requirement to provide information about the implementation of the financial program, a request on the part of the lending syndicate not to object to the final restructuring principles of the contemplated rescheduling opertion, the customary cross-default clause, a specification of events of default (including the failure of Mexico to comply with the performance criteria agreed with the fund in connection with the three-year extended arrangement, and nonmembership), and the implementation of the proposed mechanism to eliminate the interest arrears on the private sector debt. In addition, interbank exposure was restored and would be maintained through the end of 1986 at $5.2 billion.

Source: Maxwell Watson et al., Table 49, pp. 125-39.

enced during the early 1980s. Not surprisingly, the capital flight problem appears to have peaked in 1981 and 1982 when the debt problem first grabbed international headlines and before debt restructuring efforts were undertaken. Table 9 summarizes the terms of debt restructuring negotiated between 1978 and 1986 for Argentina, Brazil, Mexico, Venezuela and the Philippines (five of the seven major market debtors that are the subject of this study). As indicated, negotiations involve grace periods to begin new payment schedules, changes in maturities of loans and changes in interest rates.

If nothing else emerges from the discussion in this chapter, it should be clear that there continues to be a serious international debt problem to resolve and the major market debtors are among the countries most heavily involved in the debt problem. The problem that remains to be solved consists of two related parts. First, how can the debtor nations cope with the burden of their external debt obligations? Second, how can the major debtors attract new capital and deter further capital flight, so that they can promote more rapid development? Clearly, a resumption of rapid export growth would be of great value to developing countries wishing to meet their external debt obligations. The question we turn to next is whether the GSP, which is designed to provide developing countries with preferential access to the U.S. market for their exports, can help them generate the export expansion that they need.

NOTES

1. As indicated in most of the figures in this chapter, the original description of the major market debtors was applied to the seven countries in this study by the International Monetary Fund in its statistical analysis *World Economic Outlook* published in April 1985. In later publications the group was redefined to include a number of other countries. We have kept the original designation because it involves a relatively small group of countries that can be analyzed on an individual basis when we turn to an assessment of the revised GSP in Chapter 6. As the discussion of debt repayment problems later in this chapter will suggest, our group of seven debtor nations includes the major countries affected by the debt problem.

2. Obviously experience with inflation has differed substantially among the major market debtor countries. Argentina and Brazil have had relatively high rates of inflation within the group while Korea has had relatively less inflation.

REFERENCES

Balassa, Bela. "The Impact of the Industrial Countries' Tariff Structure on their Imports of Manufactures from Less Developed Areas." *Economica* 34 (November 1967): 372-83.

———. "The Changing Pattern of Comparative Advantage in Manufactured Goods." *Review of Economics and Statistics* 61, no. 2 (May 1979): 260-66.

_____. "Comparative Advantage in Manufactured Goods: A Reappraisal." *Review of Economics and Statistics* 68, no. 4 (November 1986): 315-19.

Clark, Don P. "Regulation of International Trade: The United States' Caribbean Basin Economic Recovery Act." University of Tennessee (July 1987).

Dornbusch, Rudiger. "International Debt and Economic Instability." *Debt. Financial Stability and Public Policy.* Kansas City, Mo.: Federal Reserve Bank of Kansas City, 1986: 63-86.

Keesing, Donald B. "Linking up to Distant Markets: South to North Exports of Manufactured Consumer Goods." *American Economic Review Papers and Proceedings* 73 (May 1983): 338-42.

Krueger, Anne. "Alternative Trade Strategies and Employment in LDCs." *American Economic Review* 68, no. 2 (May 1978): 270-74.

Ray, Edward John. "Trade Liberalization, Preferential Agreements and Their Impact on U.S. Imports from Latin America," in Michael Connolly and Claudio Gonzalez-Vega, eds., *Economic Reform and Stabilization in Latin America.* New York: Praeger, 1987a: 253-79.

_____. "The Impact of Special Interests on Preferential Tariff Concessions by the United States." *Review of Economics and Statistics* 69, no. 2 (May 1987b): 187-93.

_____. "U.S. Protection and Intraindustry Trade: Evidence and Implications." Ohio State University (May 1987c).

_____. "Protectionism: The Fall in Tariffs and the Rise in NTBs." *Northwestern Journal of International Law and Business* 8, no. 2 (Fall 1987d): 285-325.

Ray, Edward John, and Marvel, Howard P. "The Pattern of Protection in the Industrialized World." *Review of Economics and Statistics* 66, no. 3 (August 1984): 452-58.

Verreydt, Eric, and Waelbroeck, Jean. "European Community Protection Against Manufactured Imports from Developing Countries: A Case Study in the Political Economy of Protection." In Jagdish Bhagwati, ed., *Import Competition and Response.* Chicago: National Bureau of Economic Research, 1982: 362-93.

Watson, Maxwell; Kincaid, Russell; Atkinson, Caroline; Kalter, Eliot; and Folkert-Landau, David. *International Capital Markets: Developments and Prospects.* Washington, D.C.: International Monetary Fund, December 1986.

5

The GSP: 1985

BACKGROUND TO THE REVISIONS IN THE GSP

This chapter begins the process of assessing the role that the revised U.S. preferential trade agreement, called the Generalized System of Preferences, or GSP, adopted in October 1984 and implemented in January 1985 is likely to play in providing major debtor nations with expanded export opportunities. While there are a number of proposals for assisting developing countries in meeting their external debt obligations, it is clear that most of those proposals do not address the related problem of attracting new capital to those countries. To the extent that the current debt problem is solved by simply having the developing countries repudiate their external debt obligations, the message to potential future lenders will be that government loan guarantees are worthless. Stopping somewhat short of that position, debtor nations have announced from time to time that they were suspending their debt payments. No doubt such posturing can have political value domestically, but the message that reaches potential foreign lenders is negative and worth worrying about.

Alternative proposals that have major industrial country governments involved in either forcing their banks to forgive the loans or buying the debt and forcing their taxpayers to pay the bill are not much more helpful in terms of generating future investment capital flows to developing countries. In the first case, the message to the banks would be that their own governments played a role in increasing rather than helping them to cover their losses. In the second case, the message will be that the government bailed them out this time but may not be able to do so in the future. In fact, during the first presidential campaign debate in the United States in September 1988 George Bush indicated that he would not be interested in covering the banks' losses with taxpayer funds. In short, it is unlikely that there is much potential for political gain from bailing out banks facing bad debts abroad this time, much less doing it more than once.

If developing countries are to succeed in meeting their external debt obligations without a heavy reliance on any of the alternatives outlined above, they will have to increase their export earnings substantially. As Chapter 4 pointed out, this study focuses on the seven countries classified by the International Monetary Fund as the major market borrowers. They are countries that obtained at least two thirds of their external borrowings from 1978 to 1982 from commercial creditors, and they have the largest total external indebtedness.

The reason for focusing on the major market borrowers is that they are the countries that by virtue of their ability to borrow from the private sector under favorable economic conditions during the late 1970s and early 1980s, are the best prospects for attracting private capital in the future if favorable economic conditions can be reestablished. One favorable change would be a substantial increase in export earnings from trade with the United States and other industrialized markets. If the GSP, which was first implemented in 1975 and revised in late 1984, cannot be shown to provide much opportunity for export expansion for the seven major market borrowers, it is unlikely that it will make a substantial contribution to the ability of more severely depressed developing countries to avoid repudiating their debts. Obviously, the more dramatically debtor nations fall short of meeting their external debt obligations, the more likely they will have to depend upon one of the alternative assistance programs outlined above. The more the external help looks like a bailout plan for the countries and/or the banks, the harder it will be for the debtor nations to attract foreign capital in the future to reinvigorate their development efforts.

Our focus is on a diverse group of countries. Indonesia, Mexico and Venezuela are considered fuel exporters based on the fact that fuel exports constituted at least 50 percent of their export earnings in 1980. Based on similar export percentages, Argentina, Brazil and the Philippines are classified as primary product exporters, and Korea is an exporter of manufactures. While Balassa (1967, 1979, 1986), Keesing (1983), Krueger (1978) and others have argued that developing countries should have a comparative advantage in exporting manufactured textiles, consumer goods, and agricultural products, it should be clear that such a characterization would hold to varying degrees among the seven countries considered here.

We will be interested in assessing the extent to which the GSP provides positive incentives to exports of each of those categories of manufactures from our sample countries based upon actual export flows from each of those countries to the United States during the first two years that the revised GSP was in effect: 1985 and 1986. In addition to analyzing the relevant data in Chapter 6, we will provide evidence regarding the more general proposition that the GSP provides our sample countries with access to the United States in product categories that would be heavily protected otherwise. In this chapter we will review the text of the revised GSP to compare and contrast the two pieces of legislation. Specifically, we are looking for evidence that the revised bill is or is not more genuinely crafted to provide compensatory, duty-free access to U.S. markets for exports from our sample countries in those product areas that are most promising and/or highly protected.

Recall that in Chapter 3 we noted that the overall thrust of previous studies by Clark (1987), Ray (1987a, 1987b, 1987c, 1987d), Ray and Marvel (1984), Verreydt and Waelbroeck (1982) and others was that protection in the form of tariffs and nontariff trade barriers (NTBs) in the United States and other industrialized nations in the post-Kennedy Round period have been biased against imports of manufactured textiles, processed agricultural products and consumer goods. Recall, too, the evidence that the original GSP legislation not only failed to redress the discriminatory aspects of U.S. trade policy but actually accentuated the disincentives for manufactured exports to the United States faced by the developing countries. The issue at hand is whether the severity of the international debt problem has had any impact on the incentives embodied in the revised GSP program with respect to manufactured exports from developing countries with severe debt problems.

RENT SEEKING AND THE GSP

There is a large and growing literature that documents the role that special interests have played and continue to play in shaping trade policies in the United States and other industrialized nations.[1] For the purposes at hand, it is worth recalling that Ray and Marvel (1984) found consistent evidence that the United States, Canada, Japan and the European Community markets remained highly protected against imports of consumer goods, textiles and manufactured agricultural products even after the Kennedy Round tariff cuts were implemented. In fact they found that nontariff barriers to trade in the United States were used to complement already existing tariff protection in the consumer goods, textile and apparel areas and to provide protection for manufactured agricultural products that had not been protected much in prior years by tariffs.

NTBs were added to the protectionist bundle in the European Community for the benefit of manufactured agricultural products. Canada used NTBs to supplement tariff protection in the textiles area while initiating new protectionist measures in manufactured agricultural products in the form of NTBs. Finally, Japan added NTBs to already substantial tariff protection of processed agricultural products. Those results reenforced earlier general findings for the United States (Marvel and Ray [1983]) that NTBs had been used to substitute for protection that had been lost because of the Kennedy Round tariff cuts and also to provide increased protection for specific industries.[2] Within that context the developing countries complained that the Kennedy Round cuts contributed little to their prospects for expanding exports of manufactured goods to the industrial markets and called for preferential trade concessions by the developed countries in favor of the developing countries.

In response, the Generalized System of Preferences (GSP) was adopted on January 3, 1975, in the United States. Public Law 98-618 authorized the president of the United States to extend duty-free treatment to beneficiary developing countries for any eligible article. One qualification on the president's authority to extend preferential treatment to developing countries was that he should consider the impact on domestic producers of the same or competitive products. That was the opening through which special interests took the opportunity to deflect imports from the developing countries that threatened their domestic markets.

The bill goes on to list articles that are not eligible regardless of where they originate. The "import-sensitive" areas enumerated by the GSP include: textile and apparel articles that are subject to textile agreements, watches, import-sensitive electronic articles, import-sensitive steel articles, various footwear articles, import-sensitive semimanufactured and manufactured glass products, any other article that the president deems to be import-sensitive in the context of the Generalized System of Preferences. Furthermore, Congress limited the eligibility of any beneficiary country based on the success of that country in exporting a product to the United States. Eligibility could be lost if a country accounted for more than 50 percent of the exports of a product to the United States, and there were limits on the maximum value of imports from a beneficiary country that ranged from $25 million in 1975 to approximately $63 million in 1984. The original law required the president to report to Congress on the effects of the GSP within five years and established a ten-year limit for the legislation.

While the language of the GSP legislation adopted in the United States indicated that protectionist interests had some success in limiting the extent to which developing countries would have access to the U.S. economy for exports, there remained the possibility that substantial benefits were realized. The question remains whether the GSP provided developing countries with preferential export opportunities in commodity categories in which they would have been expected to compete for sales in the United States.

The view developed in Marvel and Ray (1983) that international trade agreements represent attempts to reregulate markets in response to changing economic and/or political conditions is useful in attempting to explain the impact of the GSP. Political concerns helped to generate an effort to include the developing countries in the gains from trade liberalization. Unfortunately, changing economic conditions in the United States and other industrialized nations pushed in the opposite direction.

Increased concern over rising unemployment rates, plant closings and slow economic growth in the United States undercut the strength of the national commitment to trade liberalization. As explained in Chapters 1 and 2, the simultaneous deterioration in economic growth and rising unemployment rates in the United States along with a decline in the net export position and rising share of trade in national income in the United States lent credibility to the notion that domestic economic problems were caused by unfair international trade practices abroad beginning in the early 1970s.

The fact that economic conditions in the mid-1970s in the United States did not support vigorous trade liberalization meant that special interest groups played a significant role in shaping the pattern of tariff cuts granted by the GSP. It is difficult to imagine that the same interest groups that were successful in undermining the liberalizing effects of the Kennedy Round cuts would have failed to blunt much of the intended effects of the GSP, since it was targeted at the most vulnerable industries in the United States.

Ray (1987b) provided evidence on the characteristics of GSP imports into the United States in 1984, the last year during which the original GSP law was in effect. While the results of that analysis have already been discussed in detail in Chapter 3, a few of the major points bear repeating here. The likelihood that a product was imported under the conditions of the GSP was negatively related to whether the good was in the textile or processed food category and somewhat positively related to whether or not the good was a consumer good. More generally, the likelihood that goods entered the United States under the terms of the GSP in 1984 was negatively related to post-Kennedy Round tariffs and to the presence of NTB protection for those goods.

The negative association between protectionist measures during the post-Kennedy Round period and GSP imports suggests that the GSP actually biased developing country exports to the United States away from vulnerable industries in the United States.[3]

The eventual bias in GSP-based imports away from the most highly protected areas of the economy is a natural consequence of the fact that the GSP did induce import growth in areas in which developing countries had duty-free access to U.S. markets. Unfortunately, those industries that were most highly protected in the post-Kennedy Round period in the

United States including textiles, processed food manufacturers and producers of manufactured consumer goods successfully avoided GSP status. Therefore, the stimulus to imports from developing countries provided by the original GSP legislation was away from those sectors in which duty-free status would have made the most sense in terms of the export capabilities of the developing nations.

THE NEW GSP AND MAJOR DEBTOR EXPORTS TO THE UNITED STATES

The part of the story of how the GSP worked that is most interesting and significant for policy purposes is what happened when the GSP was revised in 1984. At the time that the original GSP legislation was adopted the debt crisis did not exist. As we have already discussed in some detail in Chapter 4, international debt problems for developing countries did not become general until several years after the first oil shock in 1973. The enormity of the debt problem facing industrializing nations did not gain general recognition until after the second oil shock in 1979 and the subsequent deceleration of inflation in the United States that began in 1981. At the time of the renewal of the GSP in late 1984 the magnitude of the debt problems of countries like Argentina, Brazil, Mexico and Venezuela were well advertised. The fact that export earnings would have to play a substantial role in helping debtor nations meet their external financial obligations was also well understood. Therefore, the question of interest here and in Chapter 6 is whether or not the severity of the world debt problem had any significant influence on the characteristics of the revised GSP legislation in the United States.

There are several ways in which we can assemble evidence regarding the responsiveness of the revised GSP to the need of debtor nations to increase manufactured goods exports to the United States. First, we can look at the revised document itself for evidence that the thrust of the legislation was to reduce concessions to special interests in the United States that played such a significant role in distorting the original legislation away from its advertised objective of providing developing countries with preferential access to U.S. markets in which they had a genuine ability to compete for sales.

A responsive bill would be one that had any number of less restrictive conditions than the original legislation. For example, we might expect to find a more responsive renewal bill in the sense that the revised GSP might have expanded the set of potential beneficiary countries, reduced limitations on how successful beneficiary countries could be in exporting manufactures to the United States without risking a loss of their beneficiary status and an expanded list of articles that would be eligible for GSP status beyond the original possibilities.

A second piece of evidence that we could look at would be the impact of the GSP on the ability of each of the major debtor countries that we are concerned with to export consumer goods, textiles and processed foods to the United States. In fact, in Chapter 6 we will review data for both 1985 and 1986 on the presumption that there should be some adjustment over time. In a more general way the revised GSP should have the effect of expanding exports from each of the major debtor countries in product areas in which protection would be relatively high in the absence of the GSP. Evidence that the revised GSP induced a relative expansion in exports by the major debtor countries to the United States in industries with tariff and/or NTB protection would constitute a major change. The original GSP bill did not provide meaningful compensatory access to the U.S. market for developing country exports in product lines that were largely spared Kennedy Round and Tokyo Round tariff cuts.

Therefore, the issue at hand is whether the revised GSP relaxed some of the constraints of the original bill with respect to exports from developing countries and provided inducements to developing countries to export their most competitive products to the United States. The preamble to the revised law, which is reproduced in Appendix C at the end of this chapter, specifically addresses the export needs of heavily indebted developing countries. Point 6 of Section 501 indicates that the purpose of the revision is in part to "recognize that a large number of developing countries must generate sufficient foreign exchange earnings to meet international debt obligations."

We indicated that the declaration of intent to help developing countries to export competitive products to the United States embodied in the original legislation was undermined by the condition that the president should limit preferential imports that represented a serious threat to domestic producer interests. In a similar vein the revised legislation contains language that makes it clear that politicians did not lose sight of the interests of their constituents. The backsliding is evident in the last point of the same preamble: "(10) address the concerns listed in the preceding paragraphs in a manner that— (A) does not adversely affect United States producers and workers."[4]

With respect to eligible countries, the revised bill indicates that countries can be excluded if domestic workers are not allowed to form unions, bargain collectively or if the United States finds foreign minimum wages, work conditions and/or health and safety standards unacceptable. These conditions for restricting the use of the GSP program by some countries were not present in the original GSP and in that sense represent new hurdles for potential beneficiaries. It may be that the motivation for adding these bases for limiting permissible imports within the revised GSP framework is a genuine concern for the welfare of workers abroad. Maybe it is coincidental that adding such constraints would limit imports in highly unionized and protected sectors of the U.S. economy that are worried about their ability to compete against foreign producers. But the effect of the additional workplace-related conditions on country eligibility is surely to limit imports more severely than did the original GSP.

Furthermore, beneficiary countries can be denied GSP status if the U.S. decides that such countries fail to protect U.S. patents and copyrights, promote freer trade in services and/or if those countries conduct unfair export promotion practices. In the early 1980s the Reagan administration in the United States called for a new round of trade negotiations to liberalize trade beyond the bounds of the Tokyo Round. One of the key features of the set of proposals advanced by the United States was the call for negotiations regarding freer trade in services and protection of patents and copyrights. That effort received little support. Agreement to begin another GATT round took several more years and is the basis for the Uruguay Round in the late 1980s. In effect, the revision of the GSP was used to impose conditions on developing countries with respect to the treatment of copyrights, patents and trade in services that the United States had not been able to get the world community at large to agree to adopt. At the very least that action suggests both that U.S. legislators used the renewal legislation as a vehicle to advance U.S. trade positions that had received little prior support and had little relevance to the problems of the developing countries, and that U.S. legislators were quite willing to restrict countries from gaining beneficiary status on the basis of conditions that were not part of the original legislation.

Finally, there is a requirement at the end of the document that there should be a ruling by appropriate U.S. agencies that a beneficiary country is not promoting exports of agricultural products to the United States "to the detriment of the production of foodstuffs for their citizenry (section 506)." Again, it may be that the agricultural clause was added for noble reasons. Perhaps congressmen in the United States wanted to assure foreign nationals that they would be able to buy "good food at good prices." But this is a condition that had not been present before, and its inclusion in the revised GSP is consistent with increased concern within Congress during the early 1980s with the economic well-being of constituent U.S. farmers.

In the original GSP bill section 503(c) (1) (E) excluded various footwear articles from the list of eligible products. The revised bill expanded that section to exclude footwear, handbags, luggage, flat goods, work gloves, and leather wearing apparel that had not been specified as eligible before April 1, 1984.

On the face of it then, the renewal legislation is less generous to developing countries both in terms of the eligibility of countries for GSP status and with respect to the list of items specifically excluded from consideration for GSP status. On a comparative basis the renewal document does not appear to have been written with a view toward expanding access to preferential trade status with the United States for developing countries with serious international debt problems. In fairness, one might argue that while the renewal legislation has the potential to restrict preferential trade with the United States compared to the original GSP, it may in fact be less restrictive than it would have been in the absence of the debt crisis and in practice it may be no more restrictive than the original GSP.

THE EXPORT STRENGTHS OF THE MAJOR MARKET BORROWERS

The fact that the major market debtor countries are a diverse group makes the inquiry into the impact of the GSP on their exports to the United States more interesting than would otherwise be the case. As we noted earlier, there are three countries that are primarily fuel exporters: Indonesia, Mexico, and Venezuela, three that are primarily primary product exporters: Argentina, Brazil and the Philippines, and one manufactured goods exporter: Korea. Therefore, we would expect those countries to differ in their ability to take advantage of duty-free export opportunities granted through the GSP program. By reviewing the impact of the GSP on the export performances of such a diverse group during 1985 and 1986 in Chapter 6, we should obtain a more informed perspective on whether the success or failure of individual countries to export key manufactured goods and/or otherwise highly protected goods to the United States was the product of their own supply constraints or of the eligibility criteria of the enabling legislation itself.

Before shifting our focus to the evidence on the marginal contribution that the revised GSP has made to the efforts of each of the major market debtors to export products to the United States, it is worth noting the export strengths of each of those countries, with respect to both general exports and exports of manufactured goods to the United States. Tables 10 and 11 summarize the top ten export categories for each of our seven countries with respect to general and manufactured exports to the United States in 1986. With respect to overall export activity in 1986 the dominant role of petroleum and petroleum products in exports to the United States for the fuel-exporting countries is apparent.

The importance of primary-product-based exports to the United States for the primary-product exporting countries is also apparent: Argentina (meat products and packing, canned fruits and vegetables, petroleum refinery products and tanned and finished leather), Brazil (tree nuts, canned fruits and vegetables, candy and other confectionary products, and petroleum refinery products) and the Philippines (tree nuts, canned fruits and vegetables, cane or beet sugar, vegetable oil and byproducts). Finally, South Korea as a manufacturing exporting country did export

Table 10
Top Ten Imports into the United States, 1986 (all industries)

SIC CODE	DESCRIPTION	ARGENTINA	BRAZIL	INDONESIA	MEXICO	SOUTH KOREA	PHILIPPINES	VENEZUELA
0132	Leaf tobacco	19.4 (8) [1]			622.6 (5)			
0161	Vegetables & melons				562.1 (7)			
0173	Tree nuts		675.6 (2)	223.6 (4)			77.9 (6)	47.0 (7)
0189	Horticultural specialties			92.8 (5)				
0912	Finfish							41.1 (9)
0913	Shellfish	32.5 (6)						50.5 (6)
1011	Iron ore							
1311	Crude petroleum & natural gas			1,680.1 (1)	3,261.6 (1)			1,830.4 (2)
2011	Meat products and packing	104.8 (3)						
2033	Canned fruits & vegetables	35.3 (5)	368.7 (4)				97.7 (4)	
2062	Cane or beet sugar	15.8 (9)					85.7 (5)	
2066	Candy & other confectionery							
2076	Vegetable oil & byproducts [2]		238.7 (8)				157.8 (2)	
2099	Food preparations, nspf. [2]	14.8 (10)						
2321	Men's or boy's shirts			53.8 (8)		547.5 (7)	73.1 (7)	
2327	Men's or boy's trousers			30.8 (9)				
2331	Women's or girl's apparel			74.2 (7)		735.3 (4)	55.0 (9)	
2369	Outerwear, nspf.			80.0 (6)			123.4 (3)	
2435	Hardwood, plywood & veneer			259.7 (2)				
2599	Furniture & fixtures, nspf.						58.7 (8)	
2911	Petroleum refinery products	155.7 (1)	406.8 (3)	234.9 (3)				2,474.2 (1)
3111	Tanned and finished leathers	130.9 (2)						
3144	Womens footwear		702.4 (1)			1,093.7 (1)		
3149	Footwear nspf., exc. rubber							
3241	Cement							31.7 (10)
3312	Blast furnaces & steel mills	52.8 (4)	312.1 (6)			491.7 (8)		44.3 (8)
3334	Unwrought aluminum	29.8 (7)	148.5 (10)					75.2 (3)
3339	Nonferrous metals		170.3 (9)					
3354	Rolled & drawn aluminum prod.			28.0 (10)				64.2 (4)
3579	Office machines, nspf.							
3651	Radio & receiving sets				440.2 (9)	548.6 (6)		
3662	Radio & communication equip.				431.7 (10)	968.9 (2)		
3674	Semiconductors etc.						468.1 (1)	
3679	Electronic components				689.7 (4)	584.2 (5)		
3694	Electronic starters & ignit.				595.9 (6)	474.5 (9)		
3711	Motor vehicles & car bodies		254.9 (7)		921.3 (3)	799.0 (3)		
3714	Motor vehicle parts		360.0 (5)		1,072.0 (2)			
3873	Watches, clocks etc.					386.3 (10)	49.4 (10)	
3942	Dolls & stuffed toys							
9100	Scrap and waste							63.0 (5)
9800	U.S. goods returned				454.76 (8)			

[1] Rank in parentheses. [2] Nspf - not specified further.

150

Table 11
Top Ten Imports into the United States, in Manufacturing, 1986

SIC CODE	DESCRIPTION	ARGENTINA	BRAZIL	INDONESIA	MEXICO	SOUTH KOREA	PHILIPPINES	VENEZUELA
2011	Meat products and packing	104.8 (3)[1]	368.7 (3)					
2033	Canned fruits & vegetables	35.3 (5)	15.8 (7)				97.7 (4)	
2062	Cane or beet sugar		238.7 (7)				85.2 (5)	
2066	Candy & other confectionery							
2076	Vegetable oil & byproducts						157.8 (2)	
2091	Canned & cured fish & seafood[2]							13.1 (8)
2099	Food preparations, nspf.	14.7 (8)						
2211	Cotton broadwoven fabrics			25.0 (8)		547.5 (7)		
2321	Men's or boy's shirts			53.8 (5)			73.1 (6)	
2327	Men's or boy's trousers			30.8 (6)			55.0 (8)	
2331	Women's or girl's apparel			74.2 (4)			45.7 (10)	
2342	Corsets & allied garments					735.3 (4)	123.4 (3)	
2369	Outerwear, nspf.							
2386	Leather wearing apparel, nspf.	12.8 (10)		80.0 (3)				
2435	Hardwood, plywood & veneer			259.7 (1)				
2599	Furniture & fixtures, nspf.						68.7 (7)	
2621	Papermill products							15.8 (6)
2819	Industrial inorganic chems.							10.9 (10)
2869	Industrial organic chemicals	13.6 (9)						
2899	Chemicals and chemical prep.			12.1 (10)				
2911	Petroleum refinery products	155.7 (1)	406.8 (2)	234.9 (2)	430.8 (7)			2,474.2 (1)
3111	Tanned and finished leathers	130.9 (2)						
3144	Womens footwear		702.4 (1)					
3149	Footwear nspf., exc. rubber							
3241	Cement					1,093.7 (1)		
3312	Blast furnaces & steel mills	52.8 (4)	312.1 (5)			491.7 (8)		31.7 (5)
3313	Electrometallurgical Prod.							44.3 (4)
3334	Unwrought aluminum	29.8 (6)	148.5 (9)					15.0 (7)
3339	Nonferrous metals		170.3 (8)	28.0 (7)	269.0 (10)			75.2 (2)
3354	Rolled & drawn aluminum prod.							
3357	Drawn & insulated NF metals.				299.8 (9)			
3579	Office machines, nspf.				440.4 (5)	548.6 (6)		64.2 (3)
3651	Radio & receiving sets		144.9 (10)		431.7 (6)	968.9 (2)		11.0 (9)
3662	Radio & communication equip.				355.6 (8)		468.1 (1)	
3674	Semiconductors etc.			13.7 (9)	689.7 (3)	584.2 (5)		
3679	Electronic components					474.5 (9)		
3694	Electronic starters & ignit.				595.9 (4)			
3711	Motor vehicles & car bodies		254.9 (6)		921.5 (2)	799.0 (3)		
3714	Motor vehicle parts		360.0 (4)	1,072.0 (1)				
3873	Watches, clocks etc.					386.3 (10)		
3942	Dolls & stuffed toys						49.4 (9)	

[1]Rank in parentheses.   [2]Nspf - not specified further.

151

significant amounts of manufactured goods to the United States in 1986 (men's and boys' shirts, outerwear, footwear, radios, automobiles, office machines and electronic components).

Once we limit our observations to exports of manufactured goods from each of the major market debtor countries to the United States in 1986, as indicated in Table 11, a somewhat different picture emerges in some cases. With respect to the fuel-exporting countries there is an emphasis on apparel and primary-product-based manufactures in Indonesia (men's or boys' shirts and trousers, women's or girls' apparel, outerwear, hardwood, plywood veneer, and petroleum refinery products), mineral-based manufactures and consumer durables for Mexico (motor vehicles and parts, electronic components, starters and ignitions, radios and other communication equipment, petroleum refinery products and nonferrous metals), and mineral-based manufactures for Venezuela (petroleum refinery products, blast furnaces and steel mills, unwrought aluminum and rolled and drawn aluminum products).

South Korea's manufactured exports to the United States in 1986 were similar in composition to Korea's overall exports that year (apparel, electronic equipment, automobiles and footwear). Argentina's manufac-tured exports to the United States in 1986 were similar to Argentina's overall export strengths in the sense that manufactured exports were also primary-product-based (meat products and packing, canned fruits and vegetables, petroleum refinery products, tanned and finished leather). Brazil's manufactured exports to the United States in 1986 were heavily primary-product-based (canned fruits and vegetables, petroleum refinery products, women's footwear, blast furnaces and steel mills, motor vehicles and motor vehicle parts). Philippine manufactured exports to the United States in 1986, like overall Philippine exports, were primary-product-based for the most part (canned fruits and vegetables, cane or sugar beets, men's shirts and women's apparel). But the Philippines also had relatively substantial exports of semiconductors.

The primary point here as a basis for our assessment of the marginal contribution of the revised GSP on the ability of major market debtors to export products that are generally highly protected in the United States to the United States like processed foods, textiles and consumer goods is that a number of those countries appear to have a general ability to export substantial amounts of each of the three major commodity groups we have identified as important to developing countries generally. For example, Argentina, Brazil and the Philippines appear to have export strength in the area of processed agricultural products. Indonesia, the Philippines and Korea have exporting strength in textiles and apparel, and Brazil, Mexico and Korea have strong export capabilities in the consumer durable goods area.

In the course of the discussion in this chapter, we have suggested that the content of the revised GSP bill does not seem to be conducive to expanded opportunities for the major market debtors to export products on a preferential basis to the United States that are highly protected and in which those countries would be expected to be competitive with U.S. producers. The discussion above indicates that there are at least a few of the major debtor countries who appear to have established their ability to export goods to the United States in product categories that are relatively highly protected. The issue we turn to in Chapter 6 is whether that export strength exists because of or despite the GSP legislation we have been reviewing.

NOTES

1. Examples include Balassa (1967), Baldwin (1976b, 1984, 1986a), Caves (1976), Clark (1987), Deardorff and Stern (1979, 1985), Marvel and Ray (1983), Pincus (1975), Ray (1981, 1987b, 1987c, 1987d), Ray and Marvel (1984), and Verreydt and Waelbroeck (1982).

2. Specifically, Marvel and Ray found that NTBs were added primarily in industries that had surrendered the least amount of protection during the Kennedy Round rather than the industries that had surrendered the most protection. That relationship implies that NTBs were used to complement already high levels of protection in key sectors rather than to compensate or substitute for tariff protection lost due to the Kennedy Round tariff cuts. That use of NTBs to complement already substantial tariff protection rather than simply to compensate for lost tariff protection makes it difficult to assess just how liberalizing the effects of the Kennedy Round were on world product markets.

3. The study also analyzed the impact of the GSP on the pattern of U.S. imports from specific countries including Brazil and Mexico and specific regions like South America and the Caribbean Basin and found the same overall effects of the GSP on U.S. imports. There was no positive stimulus to imports of textiles, processed foods or consumer goods, and there was an induced bias away from industries that would be highly protected in the absence of duty-free status.

4. See "Public Laws," 98th Congress, Second Session, 1984 *United States Statutes at Large*, 3018-3024. Relevant sections also appear in the separate appendix.

REFERENCES

Balassa, Bela. "The Impact of the Industrial Countries' Tariff Structure on Their Imports of Manufactures from Less Developed Areas." *Economica* 34 (November 1967): 372-83.

_____. "The Changing Pattern of Comparative Advantage in Manufactured Goods." *Review of Economics and Statistics* 61, no. 2 (May 1979): 260-66.

_____. "Comparative Advantage in Manufactured Goods: A Reappraisal." *Review of Economics and Statistics* 68, no. 4 (November 1986): 315-19.

Baldwin, Robert E. "The Political Economy of Postwar U.S. Trade Policy."

Bulletin. New York University Graduate School of Business, no. 4 (1976).

———. "The Changing Nature of U.S. Trade Policy since World War II." In Robert Baldwin and Anne Krueger, eds., *The Structure and Evolution of Recent U.S. Trade Policy.* Chicago: National Bureau of Economic Research, 1984: 5-27.

———. "The New Protectionism: A Response to Shifts in National Economic Power." *National Bureau of Economic Research Working Paper*, No. 1823 (January 1986).

Caves, Richard E. "Economic Models of Political Choice: Canada's Tariff Structure." *Canadian Journal of Economics* 9 (May 1976): 278-300.

Clark, Don P. "Regulation of International Trade: The United States' Caribbean Basin Economic Recovery Act." University of Tennessee (July 1987).

Deardorff, Alan V., and Stern, Robert M. "American Labor's Stake in International Trade." In *Tariffs, Quotas and Trade: The Politics of Protectionism.* San Francisco: Institute for Contemporary Studies, 1979: 125-48.

———. "The Structure of Tariff Protection: Effects of Foreign Tariffs and Existing NTB's." *Review of Economics and Statistics* 67 (November 1985): 539-48."

Keesing, Donald B. "Linking Up to Distant Markets: South to North Exports of Manufactured Consumer Goods." *American Economic Review Papers and Proceedings* 73 (May 1983): 338-42.

Krueger, Anne. "Alternative Trade Strategies and Employment in LDC's." *American Economic Review* 68, no. 2 (May 1978): 270-74.

Marvel, Howard P., and Ray, Edward John. "The Kennedy Round: Evidence on the Regulation of International Trade in the United States." *American Economic Review* 73, no. 1 (March 1983): 190-97.

Pincus, J. J. "Pressure Groups and the Pattern of Tariffs." *Journal of Political Economy* 83, no. 4 (August 1975): 757-78.

"Public Laws," 93rd Congress, Second Session, 1974. *United States Statutes at Large*, 88, part 2: 1363-2545.

"Public Laws," 98th Congress, Second Session, 1984. *United States Statutes at Large*, 3018-24.

Ray, Edward John. "The Determinants of Tariff and Nontariff Trade Restrictions in the United States." *Journal of Political Economy* 89 (February 1981): 105-21.

———. "Trade Liberalization, Preferential Agreements and Their Impact on U.S. Imports from Latin America." In Michael Connolly and Claudio Gonzalez-Vega, eds., *Economics Reform and Stabilization in Latin America.* New York; Praeger, 1987a: 253-79.

———. "The Impact of Special Interests on Preferential Tariff Concessions by the United States." *Review of Economics and Statistics* 69, no. 2 (May 1987b): 187-93.

———. "U.S. Protection and Intraindustry Trade: Evidence and Implications." Ohio State University (May 1987c).

———. "Protectionism: The Fall in Tariffs and the Rise in NTBs." *Northwestern Journal of International Law and Business* 8, no. 2 (Fall 1987d): 285-325.

Ray, Edward John, and Marvel, Howard P. "The Pattern of Protection in the Industrialized World." *Review of Economics and Statistics* 66, no. 3 (August 1984): 452-58.

Verreydt, Eric, and Waelbroeck, Jean. "European Community Protection Against Manufactured Imports and Developing Countries: A Case Study in the Political Economy of Protection." in Jagdish Bhagwati, ed., *Import Competition and Response*. Chicago: National Bureau of Economic Research, 1982: 362-93.

Appendix C: Title V—Generalized System of Preferences Renewal

Generalized
System of
Preferences
Renewal Act of
1984.

SECTION 501. SHORT TITLE: STATEMENT OF PURPOSE

(a) This title may be cited as the "Generalized System of Preferences Renewal Act of 1984".

19 USC 2101
note.
19 USC 2461

(b) The purpose of this title is to—

(1) promote the development of developing countries, which often need temporary preferential advantages to compete effectively with industrialized countries;

(2) promote the notion that trade, rather than aid, is a more effective and cost-efficient way of promoting broad-based sustained economic development;

(3) take advantage of the fact that developing countries provide the fastest growing markets for United States exports and that foreign exchange earnings from trade with such countries through the Generalized System of Preferences can further stimulate United States exports;

(4) allow for the consideration of the fact that there are significant differences among developing countries with respect to their general development and international competitiveness;

(5) encourage the providing of increased trade liberalization measures, thereby setting an example to be emulated by other industrialized countries;

(6) recognize that a large number of developing countries must generate sufficient foreign exchange earnings to meet international debt obligations;

(7) promote the creation of additional opportunities for trade among the developing countries;

(8) integrate developing countries into the international trading system with its attendant responsibilities in a manner commensurate with their development;

(9) encourage developing countries—

(A) to eliminate or reduce significant barriers to trade in goods and services and to investment,

(B) to provide effective means under which foreign nationals may secure, exercise, and enforce exclusive intellectual property rights, and

(C) to afford workers internationally recognized worker rights; and

(10) address the concerns listed in the preceding paragraphs in a manner that—

(A) does not adversely affect United States producers and workers, and

(B) conforms to the international obligations of the United States under the General Agreement on Tariffs and Trade.

SEC. 503. AMENDMENTS RELATING TO THE BENEFICIARY DEVELOPING COUNTRY DESIGNATION CRITERIA.

(a) Section 502(a) of the Trade Act of 1974 (19 U.S.C. 2462(a)) is amended by adding at the end thereof the following new paragraph:

"(4) For purposes of this title, the term 'internationally recognized worker rights' includes—

"(A) the right of association;

"(B) the right to organize and bargain collectively;

"(C) a prohibition on the use of any form of forced or compulsory labor;

"(D) a minimum age for the employment of children; and

"(E) acceptable conditions of work with respect to minimum wages, hours of work, and occupational safety and health."

(c) Section 502(c) of the Trade Act of 1974 (19 U.S.C. 2462) is amended—

(2) by striking out the period at the end of the paragraph (4) and of inserting in lieu thereof the following: "and the extent to which such country has assured the United States that it will refrain from engaging in unreasonable export practices," and

(3) by adding at the end thereof the following new paragraphs:

"(5) the extent to which such country is providing adequate and effective means under its laws for foreign nationals to secure, to exercise, and to enforce exclusive rights in intellectual property, including patents, trademarks, and copyright;

"(6) the extent to which such country has taken action to—

"(A) reduce trade distorting investment practices and policies (including export performances requirements); and

"(B) reduce or eliminate barriers to trade in services; and

"(7) whether or not such country has taken or is taking steps to afford to workers in that country (including any designated zone in that country) internationally recognized worker rights."

SEC. 504. REGULATIONS: ARTICLES WHICH MAY NOT BE DESIGNATED AS ELIGIBLE ARTICLES.

(b) Section 503(c)(1)(E) of the Trade Act of 1974 (19 U.S.C. 2463(c)(1)(E) is amended to read as follows:

"(E) footwear, handbags, luggage flat goods, work gloves, and leather wearing apparel which were not eligible articles for purposes of this title on April 1, 1984."

SEC 505. LIMITATIONS ON PREFERENTIAL TREATMENT.

----

(2) by adding at the end thereof the following new paragraph:

President of U.S. Report.

"(2) The President shall, as necessary, advise the Congress and, by no later than January 4, 1988, submit to the Congress a report on the application of sections 501 and 502(c), and the actions the President has taken to withdraw, to suspend, or to limit the application of duty-free treatment with respect to any country which Ante, p. 3019 has failed to adequately take the actions described in section   502(c)."

(b) Section 504 (c) and (d) of the Trade Act of 1974 (19 U.S.C. 2464 (c) and (d) are amended to read as follows:

"(c)(1) Subject to paragraphs (2) through (7) and subsection (d), whenever the President determines that any country—

"(A) has exported (directly or indirectly) to the United States during a calendar year a quantity of an eligible article having an appraised value in excess of an amount which bears the same ratio to $25,000,000 as the gross national product of the United States for the preceding calendar year (as determined by the Department of Commerce) bears to the gross national product of the United States for calendar year 1974; or

"(B) has exported (either directly or indirectly) to the United States a quantity of any eligible article equal to or exceeding 50 percent of the appraised value of the total imports of such article into the United States during any calendar year;

then, not later than July 1 of the next calendar year, such country shall not be treated as a beneficiary developing country with respect to such article.

"(2)(A) Not later than January 4, 1987, and periodically thereafter, the President shall conduct a general review of eligible articles based on the considerations described in section 501 or 502(c).

"(B) If, after any review under subparagraph (A), the President determines that this subparagraph should apply because a beneficiary developing country has demonstrated a sufficient degree of competitiveness (relative to other beneficiary developing countries) with respect to any eligible article, then paragraph (1) shall be applied to such country with respect to such article by substituting—

"(i) '1984' for '1974' in subparagraph (A), and

"(ii) '25 percent' for '50 percent' in subparagraph (B).

"(3)(A) Not earlier than January 4, 1987, the President may waive the application of this subsection with respect to any eligible article of any beneficiary developing country if, before July 1 of the calendar year beginning after the calendar year for which a determination described in paragraph (1) was made with respect to such eligible article, the President—

"(i) receives the advice of the International Trade Commission on whether any industry in the United States is likely to be adversely affected by such waiver,

"(ii) determines, based on the considerations described in sections 501 and 502(c) and the advice described in clause (i), that such waiver is in the national economic interest of the United States, and

Ante, pp. 3018, 3019.

"(iii) publishes the determination des- Federal
cribed in clause (ii) in the Federal Register. Register,
publication.

"(B) in making any determination under subparagraph (A), the President shall give great weight to—

"(i) the extent to which the beneficiary developing country has assured the United States that such country will provide equitable and reasonable access to the markets and basic commodity resources of such country, and

"(ii) the extent to which such country provides adequate and effective means under its law for foreign nationals to secure, to exercise, and to enforce exclusive rights in intellectual property, including patent, trademark, and copyright rights.

"(C) Any waiver granted pursuant to this paragraph shall remain in effect until the President determines that such waiver is no longer warranted due to changed circumstances.

"(D)(i) The President may not exercise the waiver authority provided under subparagraph (A) with respect to a quantity of eligible articles entered in any calendar year which exceeds an aggregate value equal to 30 percent of the total value of all articles which entered duty-free under this title during the preceding year.

"(ii) The President may not exercise the waiver authority provided under subparagraph (A) with respect to a quantity of eligible articles entered from any beneficiary developing country during any calendar year beginning after 1984 which exceeds 15 percent of the total value of all articles that have entered duty-free under this title during the preceding calendar year if for the preceding calendar year such beneficiary developing country—

"(I) had a per capita gross national product (calculated on the basis of the best available information, including that of the World Bank) of $5,000 or more; or

"(II) had exported (either directly or indirectly) to the United States a quantity of articles that was duty-free under this title that had an appraised value of more than 10 percent of the total imports of all articles that entered duty-free under this title during that year.

"(III) There shall be counted against the limitations imposed under clauses (i) and (ii) for any calendar year only that quantity of any eligible article of any country that—

"(I) entered duty-free under this title during such calendar year; and

"(II) is in excess of the quantity of that article that would have been so entered during such calendar year if the 1974 limitation applied under paragraph (1)(A) and the 50 percent limitation applied under paragraph (1)(B).

Federal
Register
publication.

"(4) Except in any case to which paragraph (2)(B) applies, the President may waive the application of this subsection if, before July 1 of the calendar year beginning after the calendar year for which a determination described in paragraph (1) was made, the President determines and publishes in the Federal Register that, with respect to such country—

"(A) there has been an historical preferential trade relationship between the United States and such country,

"(B) there is a treaty or trade agreement in force covering economic relations between such country and the United States, and

"(C)) such country does not discriminate against, or impose unjustifiable or unreasonable barriers to, United States commerce.

"(5) A country which is no longer treated as a beneficiary developing country with respect to an eligible article by reason of this subsection may be redesignated a beneficiary developing country with respect to such article subject to

Ante, pp. 3018
3019.

provisions of sections 501 and 502, if imports of such article from such country did not exceed the limitations in paragraph (1) after application of paragraph (2) during the preceding calendar year.

"(6)(A) This subsection shall not apply to any beneficiary developing country which the President determines, based on the considerations described in sections 501 and 502(c), to be a least-developed beneficiary developing country.

"(B) The President shall—

"(i) make a determination under subparagraph (A) with respect to each beneficiary developing country before July 4, 1985, and periodically thereafter, and

"(ii) notify the Congress at least 60 days before any such determination becomes final.

"(7) For purposes of this subsection, the term 'country' does not include an association of countries which is treated as one country under section 502(a)(3), but does include a country which is a member of any such association.

"(d)(1) Subsection (c)(1)(B) (after application of subsection (c)(2) shall not apply with respect to any eligible article if a like or directly competitive article is not produced in the United States on January 3, 1985.

"(2) The President may disregard subsection (c)(1)(B) with respect to any eligible article if the appraised value of the total imports of such article into the United States during the preceding calendar year is not in excess of an amount which bears the same ratio to $5,000,000 as the gross national product of the United States for that calendar year (as determined by the Department of Commerce) bears to the gross national product of the United States for calendar year 1979."

(c) Section 504 (19 U.S.C. 2464) is amended by adding at the end thereof the following new subsection:

"(f)(1) If the President determines that the per capita gross national product (calculated on the basis of the best available information, including that of the World Bank) of any beneficiary developing country for any calendar year (hereafter in this subsection referred to as the 'determination year') after 1984, exceeds the applicable limit for the determination year—

"(A) subsection (c)(1)(B) shall be applied for the 2-year period beginning on July 1 of the calendar year succeeding the determination year by substituting '25 percent' for '50 percent', and

"(B) such country shall not be treated as a beneficiary developing country under this title after the close of such 2-year period.

"(2)(A) For purposes of this subsection, the term 'applicable limit' means the sum of—

"(i) $8,500, plus

"(ii) 50 percent of the amount determined under subparagraph (B) for the determination year.

"(B) The amount determined under this subparagraph for the determination year is an amount equal to—

"(i) $8,500, multiplied by

"(ii) the percentage determined by dividing—

"(I) the excess if any, of the gross national product of the United States (as determined by the Secretary of Commerce) for the determination year over the gross national product of the United States for 1984, by

"(II) the gross national product for 1984."

SECTION 506. EXTENSION OF THE GENERALIZED SYSTEM OF PREFERENCES AND REPORTS.

(a) Section 505 of the Trade Act of 1974 (19 U.S.C. 2465) is amended to read as follows: "SEC. 505. TERMINATION OF DUTY-FREE TREATMENT AND REPORTS.

"(a) No duty-free treatment provided under this title shall remain in effect after July 4, 1993.

Reports. "(b) On or before January 4, 1990, the President shall submit to the Congress a full and complete report regarding the operation of this title.

"(c) The President shall submit an annual report to the Congress on the status of internationally recognized worker rights within each beneficiary developing country."

(b) CONFORMING AMENDMENT.—The table of contents of the Trade Act of 1974 is amended by striking out the item relating to section 505 and inserting in lieu thereof the following: "Sec. 505. Termination of duty-free treatment and reports."

SEC. 507. AGRICULTURAL EXPORTS OF BENEFICIARY DEVELOPING COUNTRIES.

(a) Title V of the Trade Act of 1974 (19 U.S.C. 2461 et seq.) is further amended by adding at the end thereof the following new section:

19 USC 2466.

SEC. 506. AGRICULTURAL EXPORTS OF BENEFICIARY DEVELOPING COUNTRIES.

"The appropriate agencies of the United States shall assist beneficiary developing countries to develop and implement measures designed to assure that the agricultural sectors of their economies are not directed to export markets to the detriment of the production of foodstuffs for their citizenry.

(b) The table of contents of such Act of 1974 is amended by adding after the item relating to item 505 the following: "Sec. 506. Agricultural exports of beneficiary developing countries".

19 USC 2461 note.

SEC. 508. EFFECTIVE DATE.

The amendments made under this title shall take effect on January 4, 1985.

6

Evidence of Change

GSP IMPORTS INTO THE UNITED STATES IN 1986

In Chapter 5 we indicated that the rhetoric contained in the preamble to the renewal of the GSP in late 1984 suggested that the new GSP might be more responsive to the need for developing countries to obtain duty-free access to U.S. markets for their exports. Again, if deficit countries including the major market debtors are to succeed in meeting their external debt obligations, they will have to increase their export earnings substantially. A more careful reading of the conditions given in Chapter 5 for countries to be classified as beneficiary countries and for products to be included on the list of duty-free goods makes it clear that, if anything, the new GSP is more restrictive than the original legislation. Fortunately, we do not have to restrict ourselves to a simple reading of the enabling legislation to judge the impact of the revised GSP on exports by major market debtors to the United States. We can review the actual pattern of exports for each to the United States in 1985 and 1986.

Table 12 lists the value and rank of the top ten exports from the manufacturing sector of each of our sample countries to the United States for 1986 under the terms of the revised GSP. Recall from Chapter 5 that as a primary-product-exporting country, Argentina's exports of manufactures were biased toward meat products and packing, canned fruits and vegetables, pertroleum refinery products and tanned and finished leather. Those same products were significant among GSP exports to the United States but so were unwrought aluminum and motor vehicle parts.

Brazil's exports of manufactures to the United States in 1986 were

Table 12
GSP Imports into the United States for Manufacturing Industries, 1986

SIC CODE	DESCRIPTION	ARGENTINA	BRAZIL
2011	Meat products & packing	26.6 (1)[1]	
2062	Cane or beet sugar	12.6 (4)	
2066	Candy & other confectionery	5.3 (10)	41.8 (6)
2085	Distilled liquor		
2099	Food preparations, nspf.[2]	6.5 (9)	
2111	Cigarettes		
2371	Fur wearing apparel	8.2 (6)	
2392	Bedding, towels etc.		
2435	Hardwood, plywood & veneer		
2436	Softwood, plywood & veneer		
2499	Wood products nspf.		
2599	Furniture & fixtures, nspf.		
2621	Papermill products		
2647	Sanitary paper products		
2819	Industrial inorganic Chem.		
2821	Plastics mater. & resins.		
2841	Soap & other detergents		
2843	Surface active agents		
2865	Cyclic crudes & intermed.	7.2 (8)	
2869	Industrial organic chemicals	7.3 (7)	85.3 (2)
2899	Chemicals & chemical preps.		
3079	Misc. plastics prods.		30.6 (10)
3111	Tanned & finished leathers	16.5 (3)	
3131	Footwear cut stock		33.6 (9)
3211	Flat glass		
3261	Vitreous plumbing fixtures		
3313	Electrometallurigical prod.		
3331	Primary copper		
3334	Unwrought aluminum	26.0 (2)	147.7 (1)
3354	Rolled & drawn aluminum prod		
3357	Drawn & insulated NF metals		
3499	Fabricated metal prod. nec.		
3519	Internal combustion eng.		57.2 (5)
3531	Construction machinery		40.7 (7)
3537	Ind. trucks & tractors		
3579	Office machines, nspf.		
3585	Refrigeration & heating eq.		66.8 (3)
3651	Radio & receiving sets		
3661	Telephone & telegraph app.		
3662	Radio & communication equip.		
3679	Electronic components		
3714	Motor vehicle parts	8.8 (5)	61.1 (4)
3861	Photographic equip. & sup.		40.1 (8)
3911	Jewelry & precious metals		
3944	Games, toys, etc.		
3949	Sporting & athletic goods		
3961	Costume jewelry		
3999	Manufacturing ind. nec.		

[1]Rank in parentheses.
[2]Nspf - not specified further.

166

INDONESIA	MEXICO	SOUTH KOREA	PHILIPPINES	VENEZUELA
	41.3 (6)			
1.1 (9)				
			4.7 (9)	
4.8 (3)				
7.3 (1)				
6.8 (2)			42.7 (2)	
1.8 (6)	71.0 (2)		67.3 (1)	
				14.8 (2)
				8.7 (6)
			5.3 (8)	
	31.6 (10)			
1.3 (8)			7.3 (6)	
				7.6 (9)
				8.8 (5)
4.5 (4)				
	92.4 (1)	115.5 (4)		
	42.6 (5)			
				8.4 (8)
				13.8 (3)
	43.6 (4)			
				66.0 (1)
				7.2 (10)
				90.0 (4)
		76.4 (9)		
	37.3 (7)			
		53.3 (10)		
		278.1 (1)		
	34.3 (8)			
			7.0 (7)	
		89.2 (5)		
		80.9 (7)		
		182.9 (3)	4.7 (10)	
				8.5 (7)
1.5 (7)	33.8 (9)	78.6 (8)		
	50.7 (3)	85.3 (6)		
2.6 (5)		183.8 (2)	9.5 (4)	
1.1 (10)			10.1 (3)	
			9.1 (5)	

concentrated in canned fruits and vegetables, petroleum refinery products, women's footwear, blast furnaces and steel mills, motor vehicles and motor vehicle parts. However, manufactured GSP exports to the United States from Brazil in 1986 were more heavily concentrated in industrial organic chemicals, unwrought aluminum, and refrigeration and heating equipment.

Indonesian exports to the United States were concentrated in manufactured primary products and apparel (men's or boys' shirts and trousers, women's or girls' apparel, outerwear, hardwood, plywood veneer and petroleum refinery products). Those same categories of manufactured exports along with sporting and athletic goods, chemicals and soaps and detergents were significant among GSP exports to the United States from Indonesia in 1986.

Manufactured exports from Mexico to the United States in 1986 were most significant in mineral-based products and consumer durables (motor vehicles and parts, electronic components, starters and ignitions, radios and other communications equipment, petroleum refinery products and nonferrous metals). Mexican manufactured exports to the United States through the use of the GSP were quite different from manufactured exports in general. GSP exports were biased toward furniture and fixtures, miscellaneous plastic products, flat glass, primary copper and games and toys.

As pointed out in Chapter 5, Korea's exports of manufactures to the United States were concentrated in areas like apparel, electronic equipment, automobiles and footwear in 1986. Leading GSP exports of manufactured goods from Korea to the United States in 1986 included office machines, plastics, telephone and telegraph apparatus, electronic components, radio and communications equipment and sporting and athletic goods. In short, GSP exports to the United States from Korea were quite different from overall manufactured exports from Korea.

Although the Philippines had substantial exports of semiconductors to the United States in 1986, manufactured exports to the United States were largely concentrated in primary products (canned fruits and vegetables, cane or sugar beets, men's shirts and women's apparel). However, GSP exports of manufactures to the United States from the Philippines in 1986 were concentrated in wood products, furniture and fixtures, costume jewelry and sporting and athletic goods.

Manufactured exports to the United States from Venezuela in 1986 were primarily mineral-based manufactured products (petroleum refinery products, blast furnaces and steel mills, unwrought aluminum and rolled and drawn aluminum products). GSP exports from Venezuela to the United States were also mineral-product-based but also included paper mill products, sanitary paper products and motor vehicle parts.

We noted at the end of Chapter 5 that the seven major debtor nations we are focusing on differ in their established strengths with respect to exports of processed foods, textiles and consumer durables to the United States. The preceding summary of strengths under the influence of the GSP indicates some shift away from exports of textiles and processed agricultural goods and toward wood-based and aluminum products. While Argentina had GSP export strength in processed agricultural products, that general export strength did not carry over to GSP export strength for Brazil and the Philippines. Recall that in terms of general export strengths, Indonesia, the Philippines and Korea were strong in textiles and apparel. That general concentration of export capability did not carry over to GSP exports for the Philippines and Korea. Korean and Mexican exports to the United States associated with the GSP in 1986 contained a concentration in consumer goods but with a different mix of products than was evident from their general exports to the United States.

The Relative Importance of GSP Exports

Before proceeding to a more detailed discussion of the composition of GSP exports to the United States for each of the major market debtors, it would be useful to observe whether the GSP program accounts for a major share of U.S. imports in general and from the developing countries we are focusing on in particular. With respect to overall imports into the United States, three observations stand out. First, the percentage of GSP exports in total exports to the United States increased substantially between 1985 and 1986 for the developing countries in general and for our sample countries as well. GSP exports totalling $13.4 billion in 1985 constituted 3.9 percent of U.S. imports. In 1986, GSP exports to the United States accounted for $14.9 billion or 4.0 percent of U.S. imports. Second, except for Indonesia, the share of exports to the United States associated with the GSP program is greater for each of our sample countries than it is for our trading partners in general. Finally, while total U.S. imports increased from $343.6 billion in 1985 to $368.7 billion in 1986, only Korea experienced increased exports to the United States from 1985 to 1986 (from $10 billion to $12.7 billion). The decline in total exports to the United States between 1985 and 1986 was on the order of 25 percent for Argentina, Indonesia and Venezuela. The Indonesian and Venezuelan figures were no doubt influenced by the dramatic fall in world oil prices during the summer of 1986.

In 1986 over $200 million of Argentina's almost $841 million in exports to the United States, 23.8 percent, were associated with the GSP. That export share was slightly above the 21.6 percent GSP export share for Argentina to the United States in 1985. The share of Brazil's exports to the United States associated with the GSP increased from just under 17 percent in 1985 to 19.7 percent in 1986. GSP exports to the United States in 1986 from Brazil accounted for $1.3 billion of Brazil's $6.7 billion in exports to the United States.

GSP exports from Indonesia to the United States grew rapidly between 1985 and 1986 but remained relatively insignificant. The GSP accounted for $40.3 million, or 1.2 percent, of Indonesia's $3.3 billion worth of exports to the United States in 1986 (compared to 0.6 percent in 1985). Mexico's GSP export share to the United States increased from 6.5 percent in 1985 to 8.4 percent in 1986 accounting for almost $1.4 billion of $17.2 billion in total exports to the United States.

Korean exports to the United States in 1986 equaled $12.7 billion, and the total GSP exports of almost $2.3 billion was the highest among our sample countries. Korea's GSP export share to the United States increased from 16.6 percent in 1985 to 18.3 percent in 1986. The Philippines GSP export share to the United States increased from 10.2 percent in 1985 to 11.8 percent in 1986 ($233.6 million out of $2.0 billion in total exports to the United States).

The share of GSP exports to the United States increased dramatically for Venezuela. At 4.2 percent in 1986, Venezuelan GSP exports were twice as significant relative to total Venezuelan exports to the United States than had been the case in 1985 (2.1 percent). The GSP covered $210 million of Venezuela's almost $5 billion in exports to the United States in 1986.

U.S. imports of manufactured goods increased from just over $280 billion in 1985 to $314.1 billion in 1986. Yet, Korea and Mexico were the only two of our sample of seven developing debtor countries that actually expanded their exports of manufactured goods to the United States between 1985 and 1986. In addition, the growth in exports of manufactured goods covered by the GSP program was uniformly more modest than for overall GSP exports from each country. Total U.S. imports of manufactured goods through the GSP program were only $14.6 billion in 1986 and had actually decreased from 4.68 percent to 4.65 percent of total U.S. imports since the previous year.

GSP export shares from each of our sample countries were greater for manufacturing than for trade in general in 1986. However, the share of total GSP imports into the United States accounted for by our seven major debtor countries in 1986 equaled 4.65 percent for manufacturing and 4.04 percent for general GSP imports. So, the overall difference was not great. The value and the share of GSP exports of manufactured goods relative to total exports of manufactured goods to the United States in 1986 for each of the seven major market debtors were as follows: Argentina $191.0 million, or 26.0 percent; Brazil $1.3 billion, or 23.7 percent; Indonesia $38.4 million, or 4.1 percent; Mexico $1.4 billion, or 12.7 percent; Korea $2.3 billion, or 18.6 percent; Phillippines $230.7 million, or 12.7 percent; and Venezuela $200.0 million, or 6.9 percent.

The GSP Share of Major Exports

In the preceding section, we described the overall importance of GSP exports to the United States with respect to general exports and manufactured goods exports to the United States from each of the major market debtor nations. While that kind of evidence is useful, it does not provide a very clear picture of the impact, if any, of the GSP on the success of a country in areas of major export interest. We want to know if the GSP is a major contributor to country exports to the United States in specific industries and if the GSP has fostered exports to the United States in industries that are major export industries for the countries we are analyzing.

Figure 17 provides a picture of the major exporting industries for Argentina in 1986 (the definitions for all of the industry codes in Figures 17-23 are shown in Table 13). The upper half of the figure indicates what the top ten export industries were in trade with the United States and the portion of each industry's trade that was covered by the GSP. The bottom portion of the figure provides the same basic information for the manufacturing sector only.

With respect to general exports from Argentina to the U.S. in 1986, the GSP share of top ten exports to the United States ranged from 87 percent for the seventh leading export, unwrought aluminum (SIC industry 3334), to 0 percent for the leading export sector, petroleum refinery products (SIC industry code 2911). The simple average value of the GSP share for the top ten export sectors for Argentina in 1986 was 25.8 percent. Obviously, the trade-weighted value would be much less.

The GSP share of the top ten manufactured exports from Argentina to the United States also ranged from 87 percent for unwrought aluminum in sixth place to 0 percent for the leading manufactured export industry, petroleum refinery products. The simple average of the GSP share for the top ten manufactured exports from Argentina to the United States in 1986 was 30.4 percent.

Leading general and manufactured export industries for Brazil in trade with the United States during 1986 are depicted in Figure 18. The contribution of the GSP to the four leading export industries for Brazil: women's footwear, tree nuts, petroleum refinery products and canned fruits and vegetables (SIC industry codes 3144, 0173, 2911 and 2933, respectively) was close to 0 percent. But the GSP accounted for 99.4 percent of the tenth leading export from Brazil to the United States in 1986, unwrought aluminum (SIC industry 3334). The same general picture emerges with respect to the leading exports of manufactured goods from Brazil to the United States. Virtually all the exports of unwrought aluminum to the United States were induced by the GSP. The simple average share of the GSP in the top ten export industries for Brazil

Figure 17
Top Ten Imports from Argentina in 1986 (All Goods)

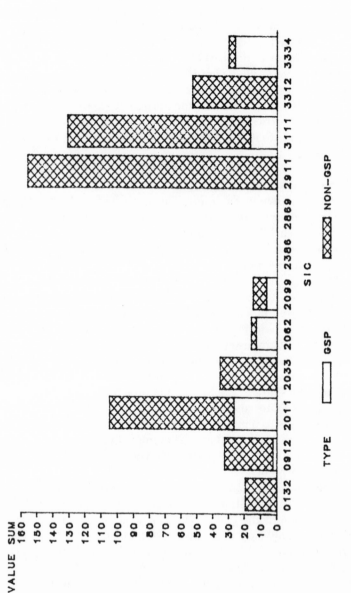

Millions of Dollars

Figure 17 (continued)
Top Ten Imports from Argentina in 1986 (Manuf. Goods)

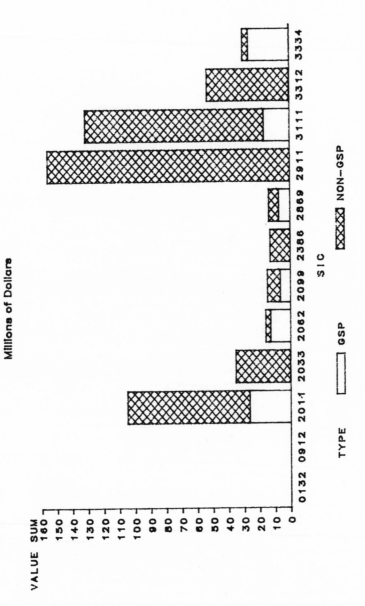

Table 13
Corresponding SIC Codes for Figures 17-23

SIC	Commodity
0132	Tobacco
0161	Vegetables and Melons
0173	Tree Nuts
0189	Horticultural Specialties
08XX	Forestry Products, NEC
0912	Finfish
0913	Shellfish
1011	Iron Ores
1311	Crude Petroleum and Natural Gas
2011	Meat Packing Plants
2033	Canned Fruits and Vegetables
2062	Cane Sugar Refining
2066	Chocolate and Cocoa Products
2076	Vegetable Oil Mills, NEC
2091	Canned & Curred Fish & Seafoods
2099	Food Preparations, NEC
2211	Broadwoven Fabric Mills, Cotton
2321	Men's or Boys' Shirts
2327	Men's or Boys' Shorts, Trousers
2331	Women's & Misses' Blouses & Shirts
2342	Corsets and Allied Garments
2369	Girl's and Children's Outerwear
2386	Leather and Sheep-Lined Clothing
2435	Hardwood Veneer and Plywood
2599	Furniture and Fixtures, NEC
2621	Paper Mills
2819	Industrial Inorganic Chemicals
2869	Industrial Organic Chemicals
2899	Chemical Preparations
2911	Petroleum Refining
3111	Leather Tanning and Finishing
3144	Women's Footwear, Except Athletic
3149	Footwear, NSPF, Except Rubber
3241	Cement, Hydraulic
3312	Blast Furnace and Steel Mills
3313	Electrometalurgical Products
3334	Primary Aluminum
3339	Primary Nonferrous Metals, NEC
3354	Aluminum Extruded Products
3357	Nonferrous Wiredrawing & Insulating
3579	Office Machines, NEC
3651	Household Audio and Video Equipment
3662	Radio & T.V. Communications Equip.
3674	Semiconductors and Related Devices
3679	Electronic Components, NEC
3694	Engine Electrical Equipment
3711	Motor Vehicles and Car Bodies
3714	Motor Vehicle Parts and Accessories
3873	Watches, Clocks, Watchcases & Parts
3942	Dolls and Stuffed Toys
9100	Scrap and Waste
9800	United States Goods Returned

was 14.6 percent, and the simple average GSP share of top ten manufactured exports was 15.3 percent. The trade-weighted value of each measure of GSP shares of exports would, of course, be much less.

Figure 19 illustrates the fact that the GSP was not a dominant factor in any of the general areas of export strength for Indonesia in its trade with the United States in 1986. The lower half of the figure indicates that the same can be said with respect to top ten exports of manufactured goods from Indonesia to the United States. The simple averages for top ten general and manufactured exports from Indonesia to the United States in 1986 were 0.2 percent and 3.9 percent, respectively. The GSP did account for 36.9 percent of the tenth leading manufacturing export area for Indonesia, chemicals and chemical preparations (SIC industry 2899).

U.S. imports and manufactured imports from Mexico in 1986 appear in Figure 20. Among the leading export areas for Mexico in its trade with the United States, the GSP plays no significant role in the top ten export areas, which consist largely of crude petroleum, petroleum and refinery products, motor vehicles and parts, and electronic, radio, TV and communications equipment. In fact, the simple average GSP share of the top ten imports into the U.S. from Mexico in 1986 was 1.0 percent. Manufactured exports are equally unaffected by the GSP. The simple average manufactured goods export share for the top ten manufactured export goods industries in Mexico in 1986 was 0.9 percent.

Except for exports of office machinery and electronic components and accessories (SIC codes 3579 and 3679) the GSP had no major role as a share of the top ten overall and the top ten manufactured exports to the United States from Korea in 1986, as illustrated in Figure 21. Office machines ranked sixth and electronic components eighth in each of the two categories. The GSP shares were 50.7 percent and 38.6 percent for office machines and electronics respectively. The simple average export share for GSP exports for overall exports from Korea to the United States and for manufactured exports in 1986 was 9.4 percent in each case.

Except for furniture and fixtures, ranked eighth overall and seventh among manufactured goods, for which GSP exports accounted for 97.9 percent of total exports from the Philippines to the United States in 1986, the GSP was irrelevant to Philippine exports to the United States. Figure 22 illustrates the dominant role of exports of semiconductors, rectifiers and similar items (SIC industry code 3674). The simple average export shares associated with the GSP for overall exports and manufactured exports from the Philippines to the United States in 1986 were both equal to 10.1 percent.

Figure 23 illustrates the predominance of crude petroleum (SIC code 1311) and petroleum refinery products (SIC code 2911) in general and manufactured exports from Venezuela to the United States in 1986. Among the top ten industries, GSP exports were a significant share of

Figure 18
Top Ten Imports from Brazil in 1986 (All Goods)

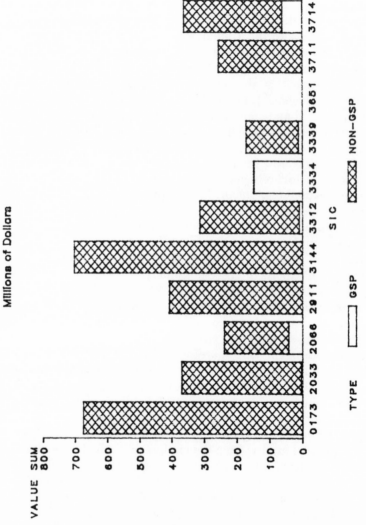

Figure 18 (continued)
Top Ten Imports from Brazil in 1986 (Manuf. Goods)

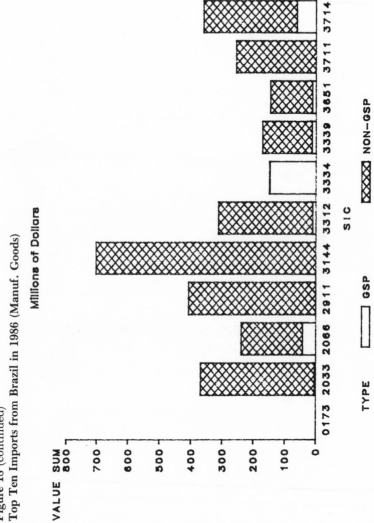

Figure 19
Top Ten Imports from Indonesia in 1986 (All Goods)

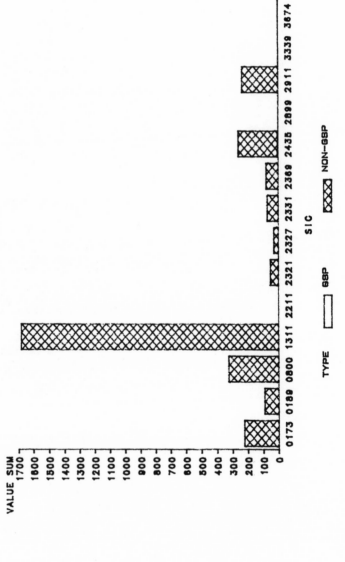

Millions of Dollars

Figure 19 (continued)
Top Ten Imports from Indonesia in 1986 (Manuf. Goods)

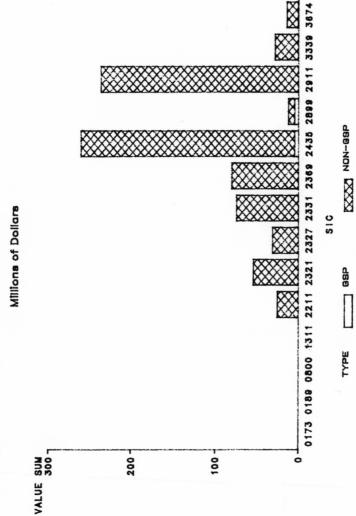

Figure 20
Top Ten Imports from Mexico in 1986 (All Goods)

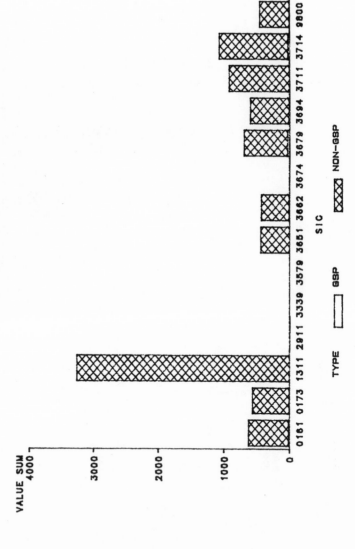

Figure 20 (continued)
Top Ten Imports from Mexico in 1986 (Manuf. Goods)

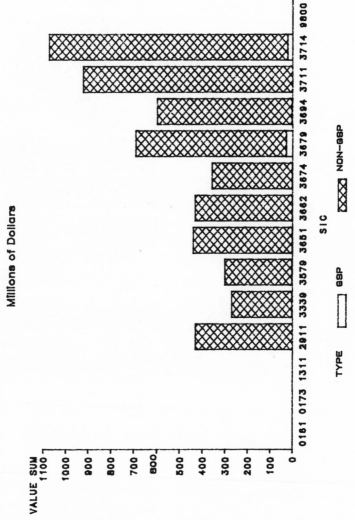

Figure 21
Top Ten Imports from Korea in 1986 (All Goods)

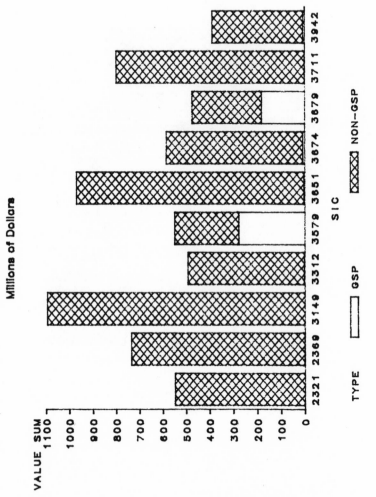

Figure 21 (continued)
Top Ten Imports from Korea in 1986 (Manuf. Goods)

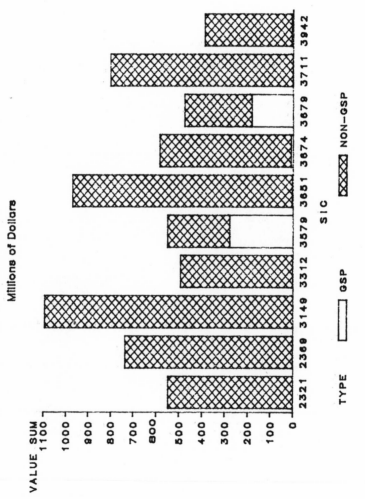

Figure 22
Top Ten Imports from Philippines in 1986 (All Goods)

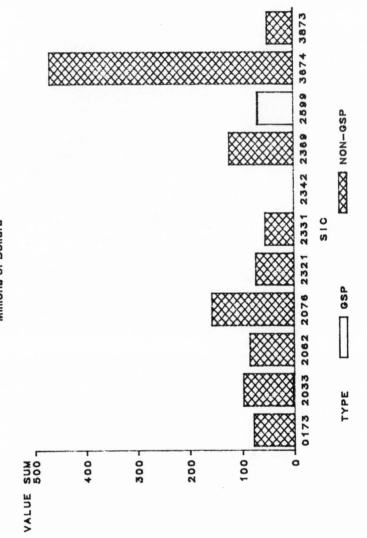

Figure 22 (continued)
Top Ten Imports from Philippines in 1986 (Manuf. Goods)

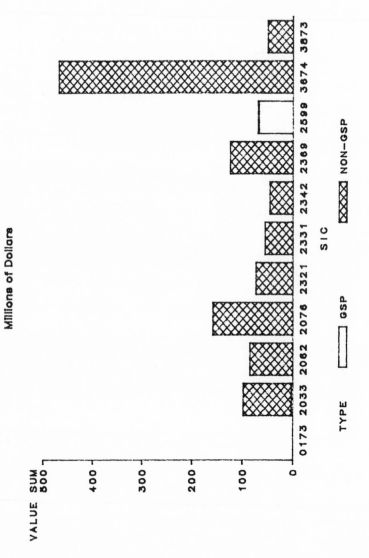

Figure 23
Top Ten Imports from Venezuela in 1986 (All Goods)

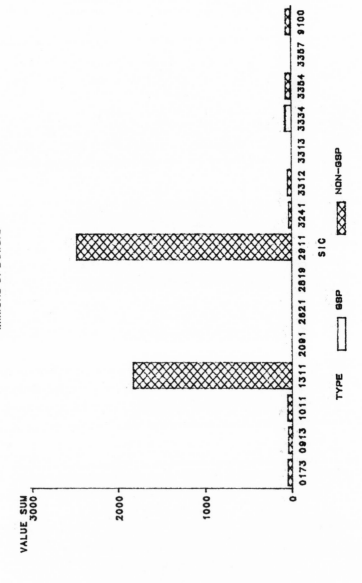

Figure 23 (continued)
Top Ten Imports from Venezuela in 1986 (Manuf. Goods)

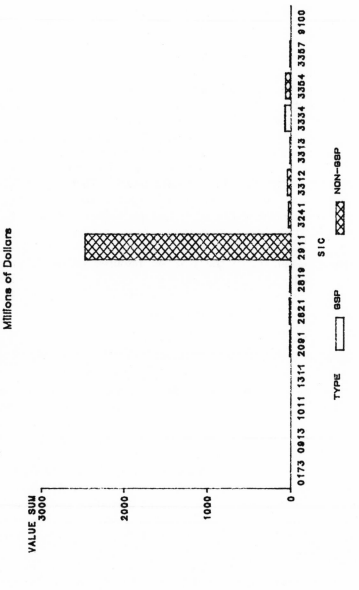

unwrought aluminum (SIC code 3334 and ranked third overall) exports from Venezuela to the United States, 87.7 percent. While it cannot be discerned from the figure, GSP export shares were significant in several manufactured goods areas for Venezuela in its trade with the United States: unwrought aluminum (87.7 percent), papermill products (93.8 percent), electrometallurgical products (92.1 percent) and drawn and insulated nonferrous wire (82.4 percent). However, petroleum refinery product exports to the United States are almost nine times larger than the sum of the value of the other top ten industry exports in manufacturing.

The information that one can glean from this discussion of leading export sectors for each of the seven major market debtor countries includes the facts that GSP export shares are not substantial elements of leading export industry performance for Venezuela, Indonesia, Mexico or the Philippines and are significant in only a few sectors for Argentina, Brazil and Korea. It is somewhat curious that GSP export market shares tend to be either very high or close to zero. That suggests that the GSP program has provided an impetus to substantial export activity in a few key industries for several of our sample debtor countries. The fact that those GSP industries emerge among the top ten export sectors in several of the developing countries we are concerned with here rasies a question about the impact of the GSP on resource allocation in developing countries. Is the GSP encouraging export growth that is consistent with the long-term export potential of the countries affected by the program?

THE POLITICAL ECONOMY OF THE GSP

A more systematic way of assessing the impact of the new GSP on the structure of exports from each of the major debtor countries would be to analyze the characteristics of exports in general and the extent to which the GSP adds incrementally to a given country's strength in proven areas of export capability. For example, none of our seven developing debtor nations has a strong export position in each of the major categories of concern to developing countries: consumer goods, textiles and processed agricultural products. Korea seems particularly strong in textiles and consumer goods but not in processed foods. Brazil and Indonesia also appear to have general export strength in textiles. The Philippines appear to have export strength in consumer goods, too. Export strengths of Argentina, Mexico and Venezuela are not greatly biased toward any of those product areas.

Alternatively, if we look at the production characteristics of exports from the major debtor countries to the United States, we find that Indonesia and Venezuela have export production that is characterized by a high capital-to-labor ratio, no doubt reflecting the capital intensity of refined petroleum production. On the other hand, Korea's export production is labor-intensive, with low capital-to-labor ratios in production, no doubt reflecting the advantage Korea has in producing labor-intensive textiles and consumer goods for export. Given the production advantage of the United States relative to developing nations in the production of R&D-intensive products, it is not surprising that exports to the United States from each of the major market debtor countries are not generally R&D-intensive products.

The next section will provide some evidence regarding the general impact of the revised GSP on U.S. imports from developing countries. In other words, we will analyze whether or not the revised GSP tended to induce increased imports into the United States from developing countries in the consumer goods, textiles and processed foods areas. We will also provide evidence regarding the relationship between overall protection in the United States in the post-Tokyo Round period and the structure of imports from developing countries along the lines developed in Ray (1987) with respect to the initial GSP. We will, however, be most interested in the impact of the new GSP on the characteristics of exports to the United States from each of our major debtor countries both in terms of commodity composition and production characteristics.

Earlier work by Marvel and Ray (1983), Ray (1987) and Ray and Marvel (1984) made it clear that U.S. protection is biased against imports of textiles, processed foods and consumer goods in general. Furthermore, despite substantial tariff cuts in the Kennedy Round and to a lesser extent in the Tokyo Round, those sectors still benefitted from relatively high tariff protection and from additional protection that has emerged over the course of the last thirty years in the form of nontariff trade barriers. Even the original GSP, which was specifically targeted to provide developing countries with compensatory access to U.S. markets by giving them duty-free access to the United States in specific product areas, failed to redress the bias in overall protection against key manufactured export industries in developing countries.

Those findings were explained within the basic analytical framework we have adopted here. Special interests seeking relief from competitors abroad always push for protectionist measures. The success of those groups in recent years in the United States is directly related to the changes in the last three decades in international economic and political conditions. The political effectiveness of protectionist interests in the United States was directly enhanced by the rise in unemployment rates beginning in the late 1960s, the deterioration in the net export position of the United States particularly after 1970, the slowdown in economic growth in the United States during the 1970s and the increase in the size of the trade sector combined with a heightened awareness of the vulnerability of the U.S. economy to OPEC-style collusive behavior abroad.

In terms of our model in Chapters 1 and 2, all those factors influenced politicians to look more favorably upon protectionist demands. Even so, the tilt toward protectionism was not mindless. We find evidence in Marvel and Ray (1983) and elsewhere that the backsliding in surrendering protection in the form of tariffs in the Kennedy Round and the creation of NTBs occurred primarily in slow-growth or declining industries. The political system responded to industry-specific hardship in accepting protectionist arguments. The government acted to minimize losses rather than to create monopoly rents.

The original GSP provided little relief to developing countries from tariff protection in the most highly protected areas including textiles, processed agricultural products and manufactured consumer goods. The failure of the GSP in that regard was the direct result of the conflict between the political system's desire to assist declining industries in the United States and also respond to developing countries' demands for freer trade in manufactured goods of interest to them.

That conflict in objectives resulted in a GSP program that provided duty-free access to U.S. markets that were not terribly vulnerable to competition from developing countries. To the extent that the duty-free access to some U.S. markets induced developing countries to redirect resources to take advantage of the preferential import program, those countries necessarily shifted productive resources away from their areas of export strength and/or potential. That phenomenon was what Ray (1987) pinpointed by showing that GSP imports were biased away from manufactured textiles, consumer goods and processed agricultural products for developing countries in general. In different terms, GSP exports to the United States were biased away from industries with substantial tariff and NTB protection.

The political cross currents associated with the revised GSP were, if anything, even more intense than those accompanying debate over the original GSP. On the one hand, the United States experienced the worst recession since the 1930s in 1981 and 1982 and the rapid appreciation of the U.S. dollar, by 60 percent between 1980 and 1985, generated unprecedented trade deficits. Those forces added substantial strength to the call by protectionist interest groups for tighter controls on competitive imports. On the other hand, the enormity of the world debt problem made the call for access to U.S. markets for manufactured exports from developing countries more urgent and economically significant for both the United States and its trading partners.

Against that backdrop we focus on the content of the revised GSP. The language of the revised document seemed more rather than less restrictive in granting access to U.S. markets compared to the original law as indicated in Chapter 5. The relative importance of GSP exports in key sectors for the major market debtor countries that we discussed in the previous section did not encourage one to believe that the new GSP augmented export capabilities in competitive areas. The remaining issue that we turn to in the next section is whether or not the new GSP had the effect of distorting developing country export efforts away from established strengths. That issue is nowhere more important than in the case of the most heavily indebted nations of the world. Our analysis reminds us that both protectionist and freer trade interests were intensified during the decade following adoption of the GSP. The empirical question is: Which way did the political balance tilt?

THE NEW GSP AND MAJOR DEBTOR EXPORTS TO THE UNITED STATES

Now that we have discussed the characteristics of major export items for each of the seven countries in which we are interested, we now pursue that inquiry in a broader, more systematic way. In particular, we present a summary picture of the product characteristics and production techniques that are representative of our seven countries' exports of manufactured goods to the United States for 1985 and 1986.[1] The picture that emerges, based on regression analyses of trade flows between the United States and each of the seven countries involving samples of 243 four-digit SIC manufacturing industries, is that among the seven countries U.S. import shares are weighted toward consumer goods for Korea and the Philippines. Processed foods are important in Brazilian exports to the United States and quite negatively related to Korean exports. Textiles are somewhat important in the export shares of Brazil, Indonesia and Korea.

Footloose industries are those in which geographic location is often tied to labor costs rather than the availability of raw materials. They tend to locate near the markets for products rather than where raw materials are located. Footlose industries are somewhat important in the manufactured goods export performance of Brazil, Mexico and Venezuela.

Manufactured exports to the United States from the seven developing countries in this study do not tend to be particularly R&D-intensive. That finding is not particularly surprising given the strongly competitive export position of the United States with respect to R&D-intensive goods. However, manufactured exports to the United States from Indonesia and Venezuela tend to be capital-intensive, no doubt reflecting the importance of capital-intensive crude oil and refined petroleum products. Korea has a competitive advantage in exporting manufactured goods to the United States that require relatively intense use of low-skill, low-wage labor. Thus, it is not surprising that Korean manufactured exports to the United States tend to be fairly labor-intensive.

With that general information in mind, it is interesting to inquire about the product characteristics that explain import shares into the United

States from each of the seven major debtor countries as a result of their having access to GSP status in 1985 and 1986. At the margin, we would expect the revised legislation to reinforce the patterns observed in the general data regarding imports of consumer goods, processed foods and textiles into the United States if the bill served the advertised goal of expanding export opportunities for the debtor nations in key product lines. In fact, just the opposite is true. Consumer goods imports are not induced from any of the debtor countries. Recall that Korea and the Philippines are strong exporters of consumer goods to the United States. The GSP has no positive effect on Philippine exports of consumer goods to the United States, and consumer goods exports are actually discouraged from Korea. Processed foods exports are somewhat discouraged from Brazil and provided no inducement for any of the other countries in our study. Textile exports as a share of exports to the United States are discouraged by the GSP for all seven countries including Brazil, Indonesia and Korea, all of which have some overall presence in those markets. There is no inducement for exports of footloose industry goods from Brazil, Mexico or Venezuela, where some general export potential already appears to exist, but there is such an inducement effect for exports from the Philippines.

Before exploring the general impact of the revised GSP on the relative export performance of the major market debtor countries with respect to goods that are highly protected in the United States, it is worth considering whether the major market debtors are treated any differently from other developing nations. Estimates can be generated of the likelihood that GSP imports into the United States from all developing countries in 1985 and 1986 were related to the product characteristics we have been discussing. The evidence demonstrates clearly that the revised GSP did not substantially enhance the likelihood that developing countries would export consumer goods, processed agricultural products, textiles or footloose industry products to the United States.

As an alternative, one can address the issue of whether the revised GSP enhanced the likelihood that developing countries in general would export manufactured goods that were highly protected after the Tokyo Round.[2] In discussing the results, it is worth noting that most of the recent protection provided to manufacturing in the United States and other industrialized countries has been in the form of NTBs and that the most highly protected sectors enjoy both tariff and NTB protection.[3] Therefore, significant evidence that the revised GSP provided the kind of compensatory access to U.S. markets that it was advertised to provide to developing countries would be a positive and significant relationship between GSP status for a product and the presence of both tariff and NTB protection for that product in the United States. In fact, the evidence suggests that the revised GSP actually reduced the likelihood of developing country exports to the United States for the most highly protected sectors of the U.S. economy as indicated by a negative and significant relationship between the joint tariff-NTB measure and duty-free status for commodities in both 1985 and 1986.

It is also possible to find evidence regarding the relationship between U.S. import shares of products from each of the seven major market debtors in both 1985 and 1986 and the structure of tariff and NTB protection in the United States. The first point is that there is not one single case in which GSP import shares from one of the seven countries is positively related to tariff and/or NTB protection in the United States with any reasonable degree of significance. In fact, contrary to the advertised compensatory intent of the GSP legislation, there are a number of cases for which the inducement effects of the GSP have been away from highly protected industries in the United States.

GSP exports to the United States are biased away from products protected by nominal tariffs and NTBs for Argentina, Brazil and Korea. GSP exports to the United States from Mexico are biased away from industries with high tariffs. With respect to Indonesia, the Philippines and Venezuela, there is no positive evidence that the revised GSP provided any stimulus to U.S. imports from any of those countries of goods with high U.S. tariff and/or NTB protection. In short, the best that can be said in reviewing the country-by-country evidence is that while the revised GSP provided no compensatory access to U.S. markets for manufactured exports from Indonesia, the Philippines or Venezuela, there is at least no evidence of the counterproductive effects observed with respect to the other four major market borrowers.

Given the media attention often focused on the regional effects of the world debt problem, it is instructive to review evidence on the relationship between GSP import shares into the United States from the four Latin American countries as a group and the product characteristics of those imports. While import shares from Latin American members of the major market debt group are positively related to the footloose industry category and to some extent processed agricultural products as well, the same is not true of GSP import shares. The revised GSP discouraged Latin American exports of textiles to the United States and reduced the likelihood of processed food and textile exports.

When one investigates the relationship beteen GSP imports into the United States and U.S. protectionism, it is clear that the revised GSP discouraged exports of goods with high tariffs from Latin America and decreased the likelihood of positive export shares in industries with NTBs and in industries with joint tariff and NTB protection, in other words, the most highly protected manufacturing sectors in the United States.

Finally, it is worthwhile to inquire about the impact of the GSP on trade relations of the United States with all seven major market debtors considered as a group. While import shares from the group as a whole are biased toward consumer goods and to some extent textiles, the revised GSP tends to reduce consumer goods and textile import shares from the group of seven major market debtors into the United States. The revised GSP also reduces the likelihood that the group would export processed foods or textiles to the United States. GSP import shares from the group of major market debtor countries into the U.S. are biased away from industries with high nominal tariff rates or NTB protection. Furthermore, the revised GSP actually reduces the likelihood that the group will export manufactured products to the United States that are protected with NTBs or have joint tariff and NTB protection, which again are the most highly protected manufacturing sectors in the United States.

CONCLUSION

The evidence regarding the impact of the revised GSP on the ability of the seven major market debtor countries to export manufactured goods to the United States is quite clear. There is no evidence that the revised GSP provided any of the compensatory access to U.S. markets for manufactured exports from developing countries that it was advertised to provide. In fact, there is evidence that in some cases the legislation appears to have induced export expansion by developing countries in general and the major market debtor countries in particular away from products in which those countries might be expected to be competitive for sales in the U.S. market.

Any success that may be realized in expanding exports of manufactured goods to the United States by the major market debtors as part of a strategy to meet their external debt obligations is likely to be accomplished despite rather than because of the revised GSP bill. In its original and revised form the GSP in the United States stands as an unholy tribute to the ability of special interest groups in the United States to preserve whatever rents they enjoy.

NOTES

1. The empirical work referred to in this section is contained in Ray (1989) in the form of regression analyses of trade flows for the United States and its trading partners for 1985 and 1986.

2. The nominal tariff data referred to in our discussion below are actual average tariff duties collected in percentage terms for 1985 and 1986. Therefore, the nominal tariff data reflect post-Tokyo Round tariff rates. The NTB data and the effective protection rate data are from the post-Kennedy Round period. Unfortunately, four-digit SIC effective protection data are not available for the post-Tokyo Round period. Updates of both the NTB data and the effective protective rate data would not be expected to change the empirical results

substantially. The NTB changes that have occurred in recent years have tended to extend protection in already protected areas such as textiles, steel and so on.

3. The interactive tariff and NTB effects we describe in the text were represented by a joint tariff and NTB variable in the underlying regression analysis, tariff × NTB. That tariff × NTB term captures the effect first noted in Ray (1981) and Marvel and Ray (1983) that NTBs have been used primarily to augment tariff protection in the most highly protected industries.

REFERENCES

Marvel, Howard P., and Ray, Edward John. "The Kennedy Round: Evidence on the Regulation of International Trade in the United States." *American Economic Review* 73, no. 1 (March 1983): 190-97.

"Public Laws," 98th Congress, Second Session, 1984. *United States Statutes at Large*, 3018-24.

Ray, Edward John. "The Impact of Special Interests on Preferential Tariff Concessions by the United States." *Review of Economics and Statistics* 69, no. 2 (May 1987): 187-93.

_____. "The Impact of Rent Seeking Activity on U.S. Preferential Trade and World Debt." *Weltwirtschaftliches Archiv* (forthcoming 1989).

Ray, Edward John, and Marvel, Howard P. "The Pattern of Protection in the Industrialized World." *Review of Economics and Statistics* 66, no. 3 (August 1984): 452-58.

7

The Caribbean Basin Initiative

SPECIAL INTERESTS AND GLOBAL POLITICS

The GSP was a response to developing countries' complaints about what they perceived as a lack of access to U.S. markets for their exports of manufactured products. In contrast, the Caribbean Basin initiative (CBI) had its origins within the Reagan administration. The basic idea behind the legislation, which itself was ignored for several years, was to provide economic assistance to the Caribbean area in order to blunt political and military actions by leftist movements that were contributing to political instability in a number of countries in the region. El Salvador, Nicaragua, Grenada, Haiti, Jamaica and a number of other countries were facing varying degrees of domestic turmoil.

One component of the legislation, adopted on August 5,1983, and known more formally as the Caribbean Basin Economic Recovery Act (CBERA), was to provide eligible countries, primarily those that did not have communist governments and had not expropriated property of United States citizens, with duty-free access to the United States for exports of manufactured goods. Obviously, special interest groups associated with the production of importable goods in the United States opposed such special access to U.S. markets by means of the CBI just as they had opposed efforts to open U.S. markets to exports of developing countries in general. The political impetus that got the legislation off the shelf and enacted into law was the invasion of Grenada by U.S. troops. The consideration and adoption of the CBI in the form of the Caribbean Basin Economic Recovery Act followed directly and quickly from the political capital the Reagan administration acquired domestically following the action in Grenada.[1]

Given the unusual circumstances surrounding the adoption of the CBI on August 5, 1983, it is worth asking whether or not the CBI was more successful than the GSP in providing countries in the Caribbean region with duty-free access to markets in the United States for some of their key export products. In the sections that follow we will consider the relative impact of the GSP and the CBI programs on exports from the Caribbean to the United States. Since the CBI preceded the revised GSP, we will assess the extent to which the tightening of conditions of eligibility both for beneficiary countries and for commodities under the revised GSP were signaled by the eligibility requirements of the CBI.

Eligible Countries and Eligible Commodities

The discussions in Chapters 5 and 6 indicated that the revised GSP is more restrictive than the original legislation. One piece of evidence we reviewed was the change in language from the original GSP bill to the revised bill concerning country and product eligibility for duty-free access to U.S. markets. Excerpts from the CBI bill appear in Appendix D at the end of the chapter.[2] Some of those sections of the Caribbean Basin Economic Recovery Act help indicate whether the tightening of eligibility criteria in the revised GSP at the end of 1984 were predictable from the language of the CBI legislation.

With respect to potential beneficiary countries, the CBI explicitly excludes communist countries and countries that have expropriated property with majority ownership by United States citizens. But there are some new wrinkles, too. Perhaps in response to the decline in the U.S. net export position at the time, the bill requires that beneficiary countries not be involved in preferential trade agreements with other developed countries that work to the detriment of U.S. economic interests by providing other industrialized countries with favored access to Caribbean markets. There is also a broader requirement that beneficiary countries are expected to provide the United States with equitable and reasonable access to the markets and commodity resources of the beneficiary countries.

There are several conditions that could bar a country from obtaining beneficiary status that find their way into the later GSP legislation. For example, the language of the bill suggests that country eligibility will be down-graded if the country subsidizes exports, if workplace conditions are judged to be poor and workers do not have a right to organize and bargain collectively and if U.S. patents and copyright restrictions are not honored.

The product eligibility restrictions are quite explicit and include most of the major exports from the Caribbean region to the United States. Excluded items include: textile and apparel articles that are subject to textile agreements, footwear, handbags, luggage, flat goods, work gloves, some forms of leather wearing apparel, tuna prepared or preserved in any manner, crude petroleum and many petroleum products and watches and watch parts. Clearly, protectionist interest groups in a number of product areas made sure that duty-free access to U.S. markets did not include their industries.

Furthermore, the CBI requires annual reports to the Congress by the United States International Trade Commission (USITC) regarding the impact of the CBI on U.S. producers of commodities that compete with articles imported under the duty-free status of the CBI. The reports include consideration of the impact of imports from the Caribbean on employment, profits, capacity utilization, prices, wages, sales, inventories, patterns of demand, capital investment, obsolescence of equipment and product diversification among affected firms in the United States. The secretary of labor is also required to provide a report to Congress on the impact on U.S. labor of CBI imports. Finally, the CBI duty-free treatment will automatically expire on September 30, 1995.

There are two issues involving duty-free access to U.S. markets under the auspices of the CBI that should be considered, given the evidence from the language of the bill itself that special interest groups were influential in shaping the legislation. The first issue is whether the bill made any difference at all with respect to the ability of Caribbean countries to export manufactured goods to the United States. The second issue is whether the CBI had misallocative effects on resources used in export industries from the Caribbean Basin region.

Recall our earlier discussions of the apparent perverse resource allocative effects of the original and revised GSP with respect to developing countries exports to the United States. If protectionist special interest groups in the United States succeeded in shaping the legislation to provide duty-free access to the United States in product areas in which the Caribbean countries are not competitive, they will have succeeded in minimizing the threat to themselves from competitive imports. But they also will have created an incentive for the developing countries of the region to misallocate economic resources toward the production of exports that the developing countries are not particularly good at producing.

THE COMPOSITION OF CARIBBEAN EXPORTS
TO THE UNITED STATES

If one simply looked at the total value of imports into the United States from the Caribbean countries, it would be hard to imagine that much benefit derived from adoption of the CBERA. U.S. imports from the region fell from $9 billion in 1983, the year before the bill went into effect, to $8.9 billion in 1984, $6.8 billion in 1985 and $6.2 billion in 1986

(U.S. imports from the Caribbean were $6.1 billion in 1987). However, the decline in the value of U.S. imports from the Caribbean was primarily due to rapidly falling prices for crude oil and petroleum products.

Since most of the decline in U.S. imports from the Caribbean occurred in the 1983-1985 period, it is worth noting that imports from the area, excluding oil-exporting countries, actually increased somewhat. Specifically, nonoil imports into the United States from the Central American, Central Caribbean and Eastern Caribbean regions increased 13.4 percent, 15.9 percent and 19 percent, respectively. Even those increases were substantially below the overall increase of 33.8 percent in U.S. imports from the world between 1983 and 1985. In addition to the decline in the value of oil imports into the United States from the region during the mid-1980s, there were substantial declines in U.S. imports of sugar, bauxite and alumina.

The impact of the bill on the overall employment and economic conditions in the United States has been minimal. Imports from the Caribbean constitute about 2.5 percent of U.S. imports, and less than 6 percent of those imports in 1986 achieved new duty-free status as a result of the Caribbean Basin Economic Recovery Act. The principal beneficiary countries appear to have been the Dominican Republic and Costa Rica, which accounted for 45 percent of U.S. imports under the provisions of the CBERA.

The composition of U.S. imports from the CBERA countries has changed substantially over the last few years. Petroleum imports from the region fell 73 percent between 1983 and 1986, and coffee replaced petroleum as the leading import into the United States from the region in 1986. The share of petroleum products in CBERA exports to the United States declined from 57 percent in 1983 to 23 percent in both 1986 and 1987. At the same time, nontraditional export growth was led by textiles and apparel, which increased from 4.5 percent of CBERA exports to the United States in 1983 to 19 percent in 1987. Textiles and apparel are specifically excluded from duty-free status under the CBERA, but other bilateral agreements and provisions of the U.S tariff schedules have guaranteed access to the United States for cut and finished products from the region, using fabrics made in the United States.

Figures 24 illustrates the composition of imports into the United States from the CBERA countries in 1985 and 1986. The figure also indicates the extent to which duty-free status under the provisions of the CBERA has affected the leading export sectors for the Caribbean countries. Among the leading sectors, only sugar, syrup and molasses (code number 155.20) imports into the United States have substantially benefitted from duty-free status in 1985. Duty-free imports of those goods accounted for $97.8 million of the total U.S. imports of $163 million of sugar, syrups and molasses from the CBERA countries. Unfortunately for the region, tightening of U.S. sugar import quotas undercut the benefit gained through access to the duty-free status of the CBERA for imports of sugar-based products.

By 1986, duty-free status was associated with $124.9 million of the $201.6 million in U.S. imports of sugar, syrup and molasses from the Caribbean. Duty-free status was also associated with $121.1 million of the $128.5 million of U.S. imports of fresh and chilled beef and veal and $51 million of $138 million of U.S. imports of analgesics from the Caribbean region.

Key exports from the Caribbean region to the United States that are specifically excluded from eligibility for duty-free status include apparel, footwear, handbags, luggage, textiles and petroleum products. Together those products represented $5.4 billion (60 percent) in Caribbean exports to the United States in 1983, $4.8 billion (53.9 percent) in 1984, $3.1 billion (45.6 percent) in 1985 and $2.3 billion (37.1 percent) in 1986. Again, the dominant influence on export values to the United States from the CBERA-eligible countries was the decline in the value of petroleum product exports from $5 billion in 1983 to $1.4 billion in 1986 that accompanied the overall decline from $9 billion to $6.2 billion for exports from the region.

Figure 25 provides another perspective on the relative importance of the duty-free status granted to exports from Caribbean countries designated as beneficiaries to the United States under the CBERA. As indicated, duty-free exports to the United States under the provisions of the CBERA increased from $577.7 million (6.59 percent) in 1984 to $689.8 million (11.37 percent) in 1986. At the same time, GSP exports declined from $593.9 million in 1984 to $476.2 million in 1986. Therefore, the combined value of CBERA plus GSP exports to the United States remained fairly constant between 1984 and 1986, falling from $1.172 billion in 1984 to $1.166 billion in 1986. Given the overall decline in CBERA eligible country exports to the United States between 1984 and 1986, the combined share of CBERA and GSP exports from the region actually increased from 13.7 percent to 19.23 percent.

What emerges from this brief summary of trade relations between the United States and the Caribbean Basin countries is a sense that to date, the CBERA has not dramatically influenced trade flows. The overall trend in trade has been downward, and trade has been dominated by changes in petroleum and coffee prices. CBERA duty-free exports have offset declines in GSP exports to the United States. A number of the major export products from the region to the United States have been explicitly excluded from duty-free eligibility provisions of the program. Nontraditional export growth has been fairly strong in textiles due to bilateral agreements and other U.S. trade provisions outside the scope of the CBERA. Even so, the issue remains of whether the CBERA duty-free pro-

Figure 24
Top Ten Imports from Caribbean Basin and CBI Shares, 1985

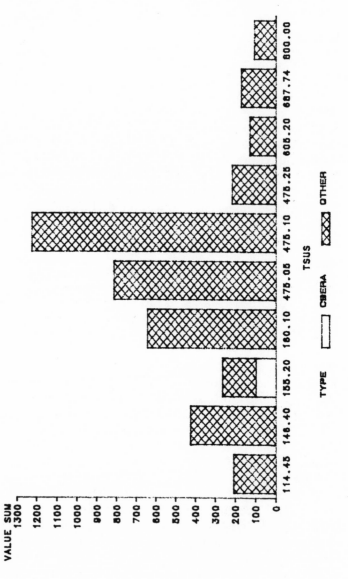

Millions of Dollars

Figure 24 (continued)
Top Ten Imports from Caribbean Basin and CBI Shares, 1986

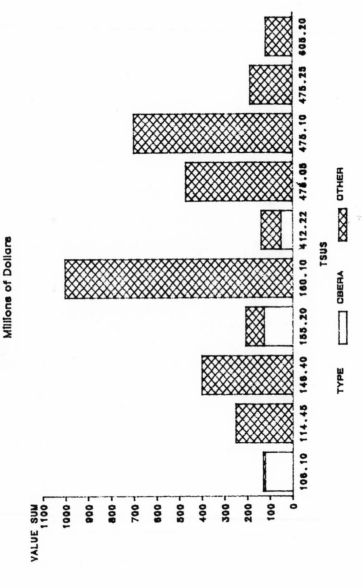

Figure 24 (continued)
TSUS Codes for 1985 and 1986

106.10 Beef and veal, fresh, chilled

114.45 Shellfish, other than clams, crabs

146.40 Bananas, fresh

155.20 Sugars, syrups, and molasses

160.10 Coffee, crude, roasted or ground

412.22 Analgesics, antipyretics

475.05 Crude petroleum, under 25 degrees A.P.I.

475.10 Crude petroleum, 25 degrees A.P.I. or more

475.25 Motor fuel

605.20 Gold or silver bullion/ore

687.74 Monolithic integrated circuits

800.00 U.S. goods returned

Figure 25
U.S. Imports from the Caribbean Basin Countries, 1983-1986

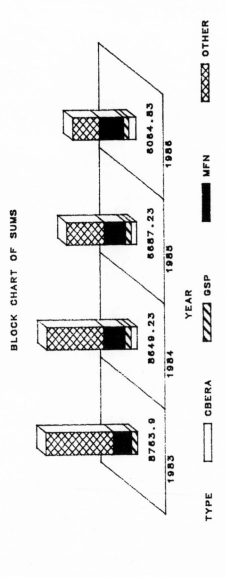

Millions of Dollars

BLOCK CHART OF SUMS

Item	1983	1984	1985	1986
CBERA	0	577.704	497.645	689.776
GSP	567.138	593.949	533.507	476.151
MFN	1746.962	2009.448	2033.327	2298.274
OTHER	6449.800	5468.134	3622.747	2600.633

Millions of Dollars

visions induced a reallocation of resources to export industries within the affected region contrary to the competitive capabilities of the CBERA region countries.

THE RESOURCE ALLOCATIVE EFFECTS OF THE CBERA

Previous studies by Clark (1987) and Ray (1987a, 1987b) have attempted to provide some information about the general commodity characteristics of duty-free exports from the Caribbean to the United States under the auspices of the CBERA. The study is made somewhat more complicated by the fact that the countries of the region have duty-free access to U.S. markets for some goods through both the GSP and the CBERA. Thus, a certain amount of substitution and simultaneous use of the programs is inevitable.

The first question we want to address following the work of Marvel and Ray (1983) and Ray and Marvel (1984) is whether the CBERA stimulated exports of goods highly protected in the United States like consumer goods, textiles and processed agricultural products. The second issue is whether in a more general sense duty-free access to U.S. markets through the provisions of the CBERA are biased toward or away from industries in which the United States has maintained high tariff and/or NTB restrictions on trade. Finally, given the substitution possibilities between the CBERA and the GSP, we are interested in assessing the extent to which the duty-free provisions of the CBERA have a more or less distortionary impact on Caribbean region exports to the United States than does the GSP program.

Ray (1987) analyzed U.S. trade flows with the Caribbean region in 1983 using a sample of 201 manufacturing industries. In general, Caribbean exports to the United States were not particularly strong in textiles or consumer goods, but they were significantly associated with processed agricultural products. Evidence from that study indicated that the GSP program strongly discouraged textile and, to a lesser extent, consumer goods exports from the Caribbean to the United States in 1983. Furthermore, the GSP provided no positive stimulus to the already potentially strong export trade in processed agricultural products from the Caribbean to the United States, and it did not provide duty-free access to U.S. markets for Caribbean exports that faced high tariffs in the United States. It discouraged Caribbean exports of products protected by NTBs in the United States in 1983.

Using Caribbean exports to the United States in 1983 as a base case, an effort was made to determine if eligibility for duty-free access to the United States under the terms of the CBERA would be likely to stimulate exports to the United States of any of the three general commodity groups referred to above. The answer was no.

By 1984 it as apparent that Caribbean region exports to the United States were significantly associated with all three of the major commodity groups we have been discussing: consumer goods, textiles and manufactured agricultural products (Ray [1987b]). At the same time, GSP export shares to the United States from the Caribbean in 1984 were, if anything, negatively related to those three commodity classifications. Furthermore, GSP export shares to the United States continued to be negatively related to the presence of NTBs in an industry and therefore to the locus of concentration of protection in the United States. As we found in our discussion of the GSP and the major debtor countries, the GSP encouraged duty-free exports to the United States from the Caribbean region in product areas that were least protected in the first place.

With respect to commodity characteristics, duty-free exports from the CBERA countries during the first year of the program, 1984, were positively related to exports of manufactured agricultural products. However, the duty-free provisions of the CBERA provided no stimulus to Caribbean exports of consumer goods and discouraged Caribbean exports of textiles to the United States. Furthermore, duty-free CBERA exports to the United States were systematically biased away from industries in the United States that otherwise enjoyed the protection of both tariffs and NTBs.

In short, the structural characteristics of exports to the United States from the Caribbean Basin under the duty-free provisions of the GSP and the CBERA reflect the same general biases as the export flows to the United States from the major debtor countries and from developing countries in general under the provisions of the original and the revised GSP. Apparently, special interest groups in the United States were effective in influencing the eligibility criteria of the CBERA with respect to duty-free import access to U.S. markets in the direction of minimizing the exposure of domestic producers to foreign competition. Duty-free access to markets was biased toward areas of export in which the initial barriers were small and in areas in which competitive threats from potential beneficiary countries were minimal.

The evidence in this section suggests that both the GSP and the CBERA provide duty-free access to U.S. markets for exports from Caribbean countries that would not face substantial protection in the absence of these programs. That supplements the earlier observation that the CBERA explicitly excludes many of the leading export sectors for the Caribbean region from access to the duty-free provisions of the bill. To the extent that inducement effects are embodied in the legislation, they are not compatible with the likely competitive opportunities facing the region in international trade.

NOTES

1. It is important to note that the original CBERA legislation contains other provisions besides the duty-free access to U.S. markets for particular commodities and countries that the discussion in this chapter highlights. In particular, there are also incentives to investment in the Caribbean region that are potentially important at least in the longer run.

2. Since the focus of this chapter is on the trade preference aspects of the CBERA, only those sections have been included in the appendix and only to the extent necessary to provide a clear sense of the thrust of the legislation. The interested reader is referred to the reference list at the end of the chapter, which includes the source of the full text of Public Law 98-67. The United States International Trade Commission annual reports on the impact of the CBERA that are called for in the legislation provide a much more detailed discussion of many of the points we can only touch on in a single chapter. Those reports are listed in the end-of-chapter reference list.

REFERENCES

Clark, Don P. "Regulation of International Trade: The United States' Caribbean Basin Economic Recovery Act." University of Tennessee (July 1987).

Marvel, Howard P., and Ray, Edward John. "The Kennedy Round: Evidence on the Regulation of International Trade in the United States." *American Economic Review* 73, no. 1 (March 1983): 190-97.

"Public Laws," 98th Congress, First Session, 1983. *United States Statutes at Large*, 5060-74.

"Public Laws," 98th Congress, Second Session, 1984. *United States Statutes at Large*, 3018-24.

Ray, Edward John. "Trade Liberalization, Preferential Argreements and Their Impact on U.S. Imports from Latin America." In Michael Connolly and Claudio Gonzalez-Vega, eds., *Economics Reform and Stabilization in Latin America*. New York: Praeger, 1987a: 253-79.

———. "The Impact of Special Interests on Preferential Tariff Concessions by the United States." *Review of Economics and Statistics* 69, no. 2 (May 1987b): 187-93.

Ray, Edward John, and Marvel, Howard P. "The Pattern of Protection in the Industrialized World." *Review of Economics and Statistics* 66, no. 3 (August 1984): 452-58.

USITC. *Annual Report on the Impact of the Caribbean Basin Economic Recovery Act on U.S. Industries and Consumers*. First Report 1984-85. USITC Publication 1897 (September 1986).

———. *Annual Report on the Impact of the Caribbean Basin Economic Recovery Act on U.S. Industries and Consumers*. Second Report 1986. USITC Publication 2024 (September 1987).

———. *Operations of the Trade Agreements Program*, 39th Report, 1987 (July 1988).

———. *International Economic Review* (July 1988).

Appendix D: Caribbean Basin Economic Recovery Act (Public Law 98-67, August 5, 1983)

. . . the President shall not designate any country a beneficiary country under this title—

(1) if such country is a Communist country;
Seizure of U.S. property.
(2) If such country—

(A) has nationalized, expropriated or otherwise seized ownership or control of property owned by a United States citizen or by a corporation, partnership, or association which is 50 per centum or more beneficially owned by United States citizens,

(B) has taken steps to repudiate or nullify—

(i) any existing contract or agreement with, or

(ii) any patent, trademark, or other intellectual property of,

a United States citizen or a corporation, partnership, or association which is 50 per centum or more beneficially owned by United States citizens, the effect of which is to nationalize, expropriate, or otherwise seize ownership or control of property so owned, or

(C) has imposed or enforced taxes or other exactions, restrictive maintenance or operational conditions, or other measures with respect to property so owned, the effect of which is to nationalize, expropriate, or otherwise seize ownership or control of such property, unless the President determines that—

(i) prompt, adequate, and effective compensation has been or is being made to such citizen, corporation, partnership, or association,

(ii) good-faith negotiations to provide prompt, adequate, and effective compensation under the applicable provisions of international law are in progress, or such country is otherwise taking steps to discharge its obligations under international law with respect to such citizen, corporation, partnership, or association, or

(iii) a dispute involving such citizen, corporation, partnership, or association, over compensation for such a seizure has been submitted to arbitration under the provisions of the Convention for the Settlement of Investment Disputes, or in another mutually agreed upon forum, and

Determination submittal to Congress.

promptly furnishes a copy of such determination to the Senate and House of Representatives;

(3) If such country fails to act in good faith in recognizing as binding or in enforcing arbitral awards in favor of United States citizens or a corporation, partnership or association which is 50 per centum or more beneficially owned by United States citizens, which have been made by arbitrators appointed for each case or by permanent arbitral bodies to which the parties involved have submitted their dispute.

(4) If such country affords preferential treatment to the products of a developed country, other than the United States, which has, or is likely to have, a significant adverse effect on United States commerce, unless the President has received assurances satisfactory to him that such preferential treatment will be eliminated or that action will be taken to assure that there will be no such significant adverse effect, and he reports those assurances to the Congress;

(5) If a government-owned entity in such country engages in the broadcast of copyrighted material, including films or television material, belonging to United States copyright owners without their express consent;

(6) If such country does not take adequate steps to cooperate with the United States to prevent narcotic drugs and other controlled substances (as listed in the schedules in section 202 of the Comprehensive Drug Abuse Prevention and Control Act of 1970 (21 U.S.C. 812)) produced, processed, or transported in such country from entering the United States unlawfully; and

(7) unless such country is a signatory to a treaty; convention, protocol, or other agreement regarding the extradition of United States citizens.

Determinations based on U.S. national interest, report to Congress.

Paragraphs (1), (2), (3), and (5) shall not prevent the designation of any country as a beneficiary country under this Act if the President determines that such designation will be in the national economic or security interest of the United States and reports such determination to the Congress with his reasons therefore.

Designation criteria.

(c) In determining whether to designate any country a beneficiary country under this title, the President shall take into account—

An expression by such country of its desire to be so designated;

(2) an expression by such country, the living standards of its inhabitants, and any other economic factors which he deems appropriate;

(3) the extent to which such country has assured the United States it will provide equitable and reasonable access to the markets and basic commodity resources of such country;

19 USC 2503.

(4) the degree to which such country follows the accepted rules of international trade provided for under the General Agreement on Tariffs and Trade, as well as applicable trade agreements approved under section 2(a) of the Trade Agreements Act of 1979;

(5) the degree to which such country uses export subsidies or imposes

export performance requirements or local content requirements which distort international trade;

(6) the degree to which the trade policies of such country as they relate to other beneficiary countries are contributing to the revitalization of the region;

(7) the degree to which such country is undertaking self-help measures to promote its own economic development;

(8) the degree to which workers in such country are afforded reasonable workplace conditions and enjoy the right to organize and bargain collectively;

(9) the extent to which such country provides under its law adequate and effective means for foreign nationals to secure, exercise, and enforce exclusive rights in intellectual property, including patent, trademark, and copyright rights;

(10) the extent to which such country prohibits its nationals from engaging in the broadcast of copyrighted material, including films or television material, belonging to United States copyright owners without their express consent; and

(11) the extent to which such country is prepared to cooperate with the United States in the administration of the provisions of this title.

U.S. insular possessions.   19 USC 1202.

(d) General headnote 3(a) of the TSUS (relating to products of the insular possessions) is amended by adding at the end thereof the following paragraph:

"(iv) Subject to the provisions in section 213 of the Caribbean Basin Economic Recovery Act, articles which are imported from insular possessions of the United States shall receive duty treatment no less favorable than the treatment afforded such articles when they are imported from a beneficiary country under such Act."

Withdrawal or suspension.   19 USC 2702.

(e) The President shall, after complying with the requirements of subsection (a)(2), withdraw or suspend the designation of any country as a beneficiary country if, after such designation, he determines that as the result of changed circumstances such country would be barred from designation as a beneficiary country under subsection (b).

SEC. 213.   ELIGIBLE ARTICLES.

Exceptions.

(b) The duty-free treatment provided under this title shall not apply to—

(1) textile and apparel articles which are subject to textile agreements;

19 USC 2461.

(2) footwear, handbags, luggage, flat goods, work gloves, and leather wearing apparel not designated at the time of the effective date of this title as eligible articles for the purpose of the generalized system of preferences under title V of the Trade Act of 1974;

(3) tuna, prepared or preserved in any manner, in airtight containers;

19 USC 1202.

(4) petroleum, or any product derived from petroleum, provided for in part 10 of schedule 4 of the TSUS; or

(5) watches and watch parts (including cases, bracelets and straps), of whatever type including, but not limited to mechanical, quartz digital or quartz analog, if such watches or watch parts contain any material which is the product of any country with respect to which TSUS column 2 rates of duty apply.

(c) (1) As used in this subsection—

19 USC 2704.   Sec. 215.   INTERNATIONAL TRADE COMMISSION REPORTS ON IMPACT OF THIS ACT.

Submitted to Congress and President.

(a) The United States International Trade Commission (hereinafter in this section referred to as the "Commission") shall prepare, and submit to the Congress and to the President, a report regarding the economic impact of this Act on United States industries and consumers during—

(1) the twenty-four-month period beginning with the date of enactment of this Act; and

Infra.

(2) each calendar year occurring thereafter until duty-free treatment under this title is terminated under section 216(b).

For purposes of this section, industries in the Commonwealth of Puerto Rico and the insular possessions of the United States shall be considered to be United States industries.

Assessment.

(b)(1) Each report required under subsection (a) shall include, but not be limited to, an assessment by the Commission, regarding—

(A) the actual effect, during the period covered by the report, of this Act on the United States economy generally as well as on those specific domestic industries which produce articles that are like, or directly competitive with, articles being imported into the United States from beneficiary countries; and

(B) the probable future effect which this Act will have on the United States economy generally as well as on such domestic industries, before the provisions of this Act terminate.

(2) in preparing the assessments required under paragraph (1), the Commission shall, to the extent practicable—

(A) analyze the production, trade and consumption of United States products affected by this Act, taking into consideration employment, profit levels, and use of productive facilities with respect to the domestic industries concerned, and such other economic factors in such industries as it considers relevant, including prices, wages, sales, inventories, patterns of demand capital investment, obsolescence of equipment, and diversification of production; and

(B) describe the nature and extent of any significant change in employment, profit levels, and use of productive facilities, and such other conditions as it deems relevant in the domestic industries concerned, which it believes are attributable to this Act.

Submittal period.

(c)(1) Each report required under subsection (a) shall be submitted to the

Congress and to the President before the close of the nine-month period beginning on the day after the last day of the period covered by the report.

(2) The Commission shall provide opportunity for the submission by the public, either orally or in writing, or both, of information relating to matters that will be addressed in the reports.

Report to Congress

19 USC 2705.

SEC. 216.   IMPACT STUDY BY SECRETARY OF LABOR.

The Secretary of Labor, in consultation with other appropriate Federal agencies, shall undertake a continuing review and analysis of the impact which the implementation of the provisions of this title have with respect to United States labor; and shall make an annual written report to Congress on the results of such review and analysis.

Suspension.

19 USC 2253.

19 USC 1862.

(e)(1) The President may by proclamation suspend the duty-free treatment provided by this title with respect to any eligible article and may proclaim a duty rate for such article if such action is proclaimed pursuant to section 203 of the Trade Act of 1974 or section 232 of the Trade Expansion Act of 1962.

19 USC. 2251.

(2) In any report by the International Trade Commission to the President under section 201(d)(1) of the Trade Act of 1974 regarding any article for which duty-free treatment has been proclaimed by the President pursuant to this title, the Commission shall state whether and to what extent its findings and recommendations apply to such article when imported from beneficiary countries.

19 USC 2253.

(3) For purposes of subsections (a) and (c) of section 203 of the Trade Act of 1974, the suspension of the duty-free treatment provided by this title shall be treated as an increase in duty.

19 USC 2251.

(4) No proclamation which provides solely for a suspension referred to in paragraph (3) of this subsection with respect to any article shall be made under subsections (a) and (c) of section 203 of the Trade Act of 1974 unless the United States International Trade Commission, in addition to making an affirmative determination with respect to such article under section 201(b) of the Trade Act of 1974, determines in the course of its investigation under section 201(b) of such Act that the serious injury (or threat thereof) substantially caused by imports to the domestic industry producing a like or directly competitive article results from the duty-free treatment provided by this title.

19 USC 2253.

(5)(A) Any proclamation issued pursuant to section 203 of the Trade Act of 1974 that is in effect when duty-free treatment pursuant to section 101 of this title is proclaimed shall remain in effect until modified or terminated.

Ante, p. 384.

(B) If any article is subject to import relief at the time duty-free treatment is proclaimed pursuant to section 211, the President may reduce or terminate the application of such import relief to the importation of such article from beneficiary countries prior to the otherwise scheduled date on which such reduction or termination would occur pursuant to the criteria and procedures of subsections (h) and (i) of section 203 of the Trade Act of 1974.

19 USC 2253.
Emergency relief, petition filing.
19 USC 2251

(f)(1) If a petition is filed with the International Trade Commission pursuant to the provisions of section 201 of the Trade Act of 1974 regarding a perishable product and alleging injury from imports from beneficiary countries, then the petition may also be filed with the Secretary of Agriculture with a request that emergency relief be granted pursuant to paragraph (3) of this subsection with respect to such article.

19 USC 2706.
SEC. 218.   EFFECTIVE DATE OF SUBTITLE AND TERMINATION OF DUTY. FREE TREATMENT.

(a) EFFECTIVE DATE.—This subtitle shall take effect on the date of the enactment of this Act.

(b) TERMINATION OF DUTY-FREE TREATMENT.—No duty-free treatment extended to beneficiary countries under this subtitle shall remain in effect after September 30, 1995.

ELIGIBLE BENEFICIARY COUNTRIES UNDER THE TERMS OF THE CARIBBEAN BASIN INITIATIVE (August 5, 1983)

Anguilla	Jamaica
Antigua and Barbudo	Nicaragua
Bahamas, the	Panama
Barbados	Saint Lucia
Belize	Saint Vincent and the Grenadines
Costa Rica	Suriname
Dominica	Trinidad and Tobago
Dominican Republic	Cayman Islands
El Salvador	Montserrat
Grenada	Netherlands Antilles
Guatamala	Saint Christopher-Nevis
Guyana	Turks and Caicos Islands
Haiti	Virgin Islands, British
Honduras	

8

Summing Up and Alternative Futures

THE LESSONS FROM PREFERENTIAL TRADE AGREEMENTS

The discussions regarding both the original and revised versions of the GSP and the CBERA in Chapters 5 through 7 should make it clear that there is nothing magical about preferential trade agreements. Such agreements do represent opportunities to deal directly with any unintended inequities in multilateral trade arrangements. In fact, the motivation for adoption of the original GSP legislation was to deal with the charge by the developing countries that the Kennedy Round tariff cuts provided little stimulus to developing country exports of manufactured goods to the United States. There is substantial evidence that the structure of protection in the United States, Canada, Japan and the EC in the post-Kennedy Round years remained biased against imports of manufactured consumer goods, textiles and processed agricultural goods, which are key manufactured goods exports for developing countries.

The analysis of the impact of the original GSP legislation on U.S. trade with developing countries did not support the view that the bill provided the kind of compensatory access to U.S. markets that had been promised. In fact, we cited evidence that the overall impact of the bill may have been counterproductive. Our model of U.S. trade policy in Chapters 1 through 3 made it clear that the political and economic conditions that prevailed in the United States in 1975 when the GSP was adopted were not conducive to genuine trade liberalization relative to the developing countries. The same political and economic realities that made it possible for protectionist special interest groups to blunt the trade liberalizing effects of the Kennedy Round made it possible for them to take the compensatory element out of the GSP.

In the final analysis, the GSP provided duty-free access to the United States for manufactured exports from the developing countries that were least threatening to U.S. protectionist interests. Obviously, the sectors involved tended to be those in which protection was already at a minimum and therefore did not include textiles, processed agricultural goods and consumer durables. In essence, the same protectionist forces shaped the Kennedy Round and the GSP to the disadvantage of the developing countries. Protectionist interest groups within the United States were not about to let special legislation within the confines of the American political process do what protectionist forces had prevented a global round of trade talks from accomplishing.

In two respects the adoption of the original GSP may have been worse than no preferential concessions at all. First, by granting tariff concessions in commodity groups in which the developing countries are least likely to have long-term competitive capabilities, the GSP induced some shift in resource allocations within the developing countries toward the wrong kinds of exports. The inducement to expand production and export of goods facing zero tariff barriers in the United States discouraged expansion in relatively highly protected areas in which the developing countries have the greatest export potential.

Second, the illusion of gains in trade concessions through preferential trade arrangements contributed to the belief among policymakers in the developing countries that they could cut a better deal with the industrialized nations by negotiating bilateral trade agreements with them rather than by going through the GATT. As a result, it took eight years after the completion of the Tokyo Round negotiations for the current Uruguay Round to begin in earnest.

The revised GSP was adopted well after the severity of the international debt crisis had been established. The preamble to the bill acknowledges the need for developing countries to expand exports to the United States in order to obtain the dollars needed to service their debt payments. Given the magnitude of the debt problem and the potential political problems that could arise from failed efforts to service external debts, one might expect to find evidence that the revised GSP provided greater access to U.S. markets for exports of developing countries than had been provided by the original legislation.

If the discussions about the content of the revised GSP in Chapters 5 and 6 and the CBERA in Chapter 7 illustrate anything, it is the strength of special interest groups favoring protectionist legislation in the United States. One might expect the revised GSP to be more genuinely compensatory toward the developing countries than the original bill given the severity of the international debt crisis and the fairly rapid expansion in the U.S. economy beginning in 1983. Yet, the revised GSP appears to be more restrictive with respect to the definitions of commodity and country eligibility than the original GSP and the locus of concentration of trade concessions is not compatible with the needs of the developing countries in general or the major market debtor countries in particular.

The Caribbean Basin Economic Recovery Act was adopted following U.S. military intervention in Grenada. In that context, one might expect to find legislation that was geared to help an economically small but politically significant area to be quite generous. Yet, a reading of the actual legislation and an analysis of the likely stimulus that the act would give to Caribbean exports to the United States makes it clear that special interests with protectionist motives were not thrown off balance by the suddenness with which the legislation was adopted. The CBERA appears to offer little impetus for exports of manufactured goods from the Caribbean to the United States.

The results of both GSP agreements and the CBERA indicate that the gains to the developing countries through bilateral agreements are small. The lesson of the bilateral preferential trade agreements that may have come too late is that they may yield little in the way of positive trade liberalization and they may undermine the multilateral system of the last forty-five years.

Despite the fact that the United States led the call for the Uruguay Round, the United States proceeded to negotiate bilateral free trade arrangements with Israel and Canada and suggested that similar negotiations might be possible with Mexico. The United States also negotiated agreements with Japan to limit Japanese exports of automobiles and semiconductors to the United States. Representative Gephardt gained a prominent position in the U.S. presidential campaign in 1988 by calling for bilateral retaliation against individual countries with persistent balance-of-trade surpluses with the United States.

There is no guarantee that the same forces pushing for protection in the United States will not be working in other countries, too. But the diversity of the international marketplace provides some hope that special interests within the United States would be less likely to dictate trade relations embodied in international agreements than they would the terms of bilateral arrangements. If that assumption is correct, the best prospects for continued trade liberalization will be found in multilateral negotiations like the current Uruguay Round. If the developing countries want to make continued progress in gaining access to industrialized countries' markets for their exports of manufactured goods, they may have to give up claims for special treatment and start acting like full participants in the GATT.[1]

One can only hope that the lesson has been learned and that the opportunity for further multilateral progress still exists. At present, there is little evidence of a strong commitment to substantial trade liberalization in the Uruguay Round.[2] The United States has been focusing most of its attention on the free trade agreement with Canada and both overall and bilateral trade deficits. The European Community has become preoccupied with the problem of harmonizing its constituent markets by 1992. Thus, it is not clear where one would look to find a driving force for substantial progress toward freer trade agreements during the Uruguay Round.

To the extent that U.S. attention can be focused on the broader issue of multilateral trade relations either within the context of the Uruguay Round or beyond, there is still the question of what position the United States will take with respect to world trade. There are several kinds of evidence that we can look at to get some sense of any changes in course that might be developing in U.S. trade policy. In the next section, we will review some of the key characteristics of the Canada-United States Free Trade Agreement to uncover clues regarding the future course of U.S. trade policies. The following section will summarize some of the key features of the Omnibus Trade and Competitiveness Act of 1988 in the search for additional clues regarding U.S. trade policy.

Before turning to recent legislation for clues regarding possible shifts in U.S. trade policies, we will review current economic conditions and assess their impact on international trade relations. That assessment is possible based upon the analysis developed in Chapters 1 and 2. Recall our argument that the govenment is an active participant in the process of defining international trade policy. Government policy decisions are responsive to the demands of special interest groups particularly if what those groups want can be expressed in terms of fairness and a reliance on competitive market forces.

Protectionist pressures are greatest and most effective when the economy is declining or stagnant as it was in the 1980-1982 period (growth in GNP average − 0.08 percent per year from 1980 to 1982 compared to 2.7 percent per year from 1970 to 1979) and unemployment rates are high as they were during that same period (averaging 8.5 percent from 1980 to 1983 compared to 6.2 percent during 1970-1979). Beginning in 1983, the U.S. economy expanded steadily. The real rate of growth in GNP averaged about 2.8 percent per year for 1987-1988 and the unemployment rate, which declined steadily after 1982, averaged 6.2 percent for 1987 and 5.5 percent for 1988. It is not surprising, then, that the political debate over trade policy lost much of its intensity after 1983 and shifted away from general protectionist demands to the consideration of the overall trade balance deficit and bilateral commodity trade imbalances.[3]

U.S. trade deficits for 1987 and 1988 of almost $160 billion and $145 billion, respectively, were close in value to overall federal spending deficits for those same years. The trade balance deficit with Japan accounted for over one-third of the total U.S. balance-of-trade deficit in

1987. Yet, the issue of protectionism played a much less significant role in the presidential primary races and the election campaign in 1988 than it did in the 1984 campaigns. Clearly, negative net export positions alone are not enough to rally public support for protectionist legislation. As long as the U.S. economy continues to expand at a modest pace and unemployment does not jump toward double digit rates, there is little likelihood of a dramatic shift toward protectionism within the United States. The election of George Bush as president of the United States by a comfortable margin in 1988 in part reflected the fact that the public did not want any dramatic shifts in national economic policies, including trade policies. Although most observers have been surprised by the persistence of the balance-of-trade deficits despite substantial declines in the foreign value of the U.S. dollar between 1985 and 1988, there is no reason to believe that the trade deficits will increase dramatically in the near future.

Obviously, a dramatic turn of events comparable to the oil shocks of 1974 and 1980 could change the economic prospects facing the United States enough to rekindle public support for protectionist programs. Absent such an unanticipated turn of events, the basic economic conditions that currently prevail in the United States do not support any dramatic shifts toward protectionism. There remains some possibility that the United States will become embroiled in trade conflicts with particular trading partners. Two-thirds of the U.S. balance-of-trade deficit of almost $160 billion in 1987 was associated with trade with Japan and the newly industrialized countries (NICs). The NICs include Brazil, Hong Kong, Mexico, Singapore, South Korea and Taiwan. Virtually all of that deficit was associated with trade imbalances in manufactured goods.[4] The fact that Brazil, Mexico and Korea are three of the seven major market debtor countries we discussed in Chapters 4-6 reminds us that protectionist legislation targeted to reduce bilateral trade deficits could have a direct and harmful impact on efforts to solve the world debt problem.

THE CANADA-UNITED STATES FREE TRADE AGREEMENT

The basic language of the Canada-U.S. Free Trade Agreement was finalized on October 4, 1987. The process referred to as "fast-track" calls for a straight up or down decision by the national government of each party without any changes in the document by December 31, 1988. (Appendix E summarizes many of the key features of the legislation.) The United States completed the approval process during the summer of 1988. Final Canadian approval awaited the outcome of the national elections on November 21, 1988, which represented a referendum on the free trade agreement. There is a ten-year transition period for phasing in the provisions of the agreement, and either party can withdraw from the agreement with six months' notice. Canadian voters retained Brian Mulroney as prime minister and effectively ratified the free trade agreement in time for the deadline for ratification of December 31, 1988.

The trade agreement is worth reviewing for two purposes. First, we would like to know how protectionist special interest groups affected the terms of the agreement, if at all. The fact that annotated text from which the appendix has been drawn exceeds 300 pages suggests that the agreement is a complicated document that had to address many special interest group demands. In a sense we want to examine how free of restrictions the free trade agreement is once all of the qualifying language is considered. The second important issue for this study is the likely impact, if any, of the Canada-U.S. Free Trade Agreement on the ability of the developing countries to export manufactured goods to both the United States and Canada. As indicated elsewhere (Ray and Marvel [1984]), trade restrictions in the United States and Canada are biased against imports of processed agricultural products, consumer durables and textiles, which are key export categories for developing countries in general. To varying degrees, those are important export categories, too, for our sample of major market debtors.

One aspect of a bilateral trade agreement that rarely gets mentioned is the impact of the arrangement on third party trading partners. To the extent that the agreement provides Canadian and U.S. producers with competitive advantages in selling consumer durables, textiles and processed foods in each other's markets, those gains will come at the expense of third parties. So, one effect of the agreement may be to decrease the ability of developing countries in general and the major market debtors in particular to export manufactured goods to both the United States and Canada.

Addressing Special Interest Group Demands

As noted earlier, the fact that the annotated document proclaiming free trade between Canada and the United States is more than 300 pages long is testimony to the care that must be taken in addressing the concerns of constituent special interests in the participating countries. One way of addressing special interest anxieties is to provide for a phasing-in of free trade conditions with some assurance that the whole package can be scrapped if the political heat is too great. Two conditions that assure special interests that nothing dramatic will occur are the ten-year timetable for the elimination of trade restrictions and the sourcing requirement for goods to qualify for duty-free access to both markets.

Sectors that are described as ready to compete now face immediate elimination of tariff protection and include: computers and equipment, vending machines and parts, paper-making machinery, whiskey and some other items. A number of other goods have a five-year timetable for the elimination of tariffs on the presumption that they are not quite ready to compete. Those items include: most machinery, paper and paper products, chemicals, furniture and others. Finally there are a number of industries that are even less ready to compete freely, including: most agricultural products, textiles, steel, appliances and so on. It requires little imagination to appreciate that the industries that are less ready to compete are the ones in which interest groups have provided strong pressure to avoid foreign competition.

In addition to the phased timetable for the elimination of tariffs, there are possibilities of additional delays for specific sectors. For example, Canada is allowed to restore temporarily tariffs on fresh fruits and vegetables for a twenty-year period under depressed price conditions. Both countries can impose grain import restrictions if imports threaten to undercut the effectiveness of domestic support programs. Canada can restrict chicken, turkey and egg imports. The United States is obligated not to impose quantitative restrictions on imports from Canada containing sugar only if the sugar content is less than 10 percent by dry weight. Specific quantitative restrictions are applied to imports of woolen and nonwoolen textiles into each country, and there is an open-ended requirement to review those restrictions in 1990-1991. Both countries maintain export restrictions on logs.

The agreement is modified with respect to automobile trade to permit a five-year phase-in of the elimination of Canadian restrictions on the sale of used cars from the United States in Canada. Waivers of customs duties for Canadian automobile dealers are only gradually phased out over a ten-year period.

The country-of-origin conditions for duty-free access to each market require 50 percent U.S. or Canadian cost content for many goods, particularly in footwear and apparel. Cost content is defined to include production costs and specifically excludes advertising, retailing and other marketing costs. Furthermore, goods that are finished in third countries such as U.S. shirts stitched together in Mexico are specifically excluded from the agreement regardless of the percentage of U.S. cost content. It is clear that the domestic content condition is intended to keep products that could be partially sourced in third countries to take advantage of the cost savings associated with the use of cheap labor from being imported under the terms of the agreement.

Nevertheless, the Canada-U.S. Free Trade Agreement is a substantial step forward in the effort to liberalize international trade, but special interest demands on the specific terms of the agreement are still relevant.

Clearly, the domestic content condition will have a relatively adverse effect on products that originate in developing countries and would otherwise be exported from the United States to Canada or vice versa. Such products will be placed at a competitive disadvantage compared to goods that are finished within the participating countries or otherwise are eligible for duty-free treatment.

The immediate phase-in of duty-free status for commodities like computer equipment, unwrought aluminum, and ferro alloys may result in lost export sales in the United States and Canada for countries like Argentina, Mexico, Brazil and Korea. However, most of the significant trade-diverting effects of the Canada-U.S. agreement will occur over a much longer time horizon. Both Canada and the United States have maintained relatively high protection on agricultural products, steel, appliances and textiles in response to powerful protectionist interests within their own borders. Therefore, it is not surprising that protection will decline most slowly in those areas for U.S.-Canada trade. Since protectionism in the industrialized countries is product-specific rather than targeted at specific trading partners, we find that the most dramatic trade-diverting effects of the free trade agreement are likely to be slow to emerge. Neither country has been eager to let competitive imports enter their markets regardless of where those imports come from.

Canada-U.S. Trade and Developing Country Interests

As indicated in the previous section, there are bound to be some trade diversion effects of the Canada-U.S. trade agreement. Export gains by U.S. and Canadian producers that arise from the duty-free access to each other's markets under the domestic content cost conditions will surely displace some developing countries' export sales to each country. What we have not discussed is the magnitude and significance of the trade flows involved for Canada and the United States. Some perspective on the quantitative dimensions of U.S.-Canada trade may provide a better perspective on the potential trade-diverting impact of the agreement.

U.S. merchandise exports to Canada in 1987 were equal to $59.8 billion and accounted for 23.6 percent of total U.S. exports. U.S. imports from Canada in 1987 were equal to $72.7 billion and represented 17.9 percent of total U.S. imports. U.S. exports to Canada equaled 1.3 percent of GNP in the United States in 1987.

Canadian exports to the United States represented 73.1 percent of total Canadian exports in 1987, and Canadian imports from the United States represented 67.1 percent of total Canadian imports. Finally, Canadian exports to the United States in 1987 were equal to 18.5 percent of GNP in Canada.[5]

Apart from the fact that Canada and the United States are important trading partners for each other, it is worth noting that the overall potential for trade diversion is much greater with respect to U.S. imports from third parties than for Canadian imports from third parties. Major areas for expansion of Canadian imports from the United States as a result of the free trade agreement are expected to include machinery, electrical machinery, chemicals, fabricated metals and transportation equipment. Major areas for expansion of U.S. imports from Canada as a result of the agreement are expected to include machinery, primary metals, electrical machinery, rubber, chemicals and transportation equipment.[6] Therefore, the trade-diverting effects on U.S. imports as a result of the free trade agreement with Canada are most likely to be concentrated in areas that would affect exports to the United States from newly industrialized countries like Brazil, Mexico and Korea, which are among the major market debtors that we discussed in Chapter 4.

The assurance that the agreement provided to both parties that they could not be locked into trade relationships that were not tenable in terms of domestic politics is embodied in the escape clause. Either country could suspend the free trade agreement after giving six months' notice. In the televised debate in early November 1988, Prime Minister Brian Mulroney responded to the charge that he had negotiated away Canada's national identity by asserting that the agreement could be scrapped with six months' notice. Unfortunately, that fact was seen as damaging to his argument that the free trade agreement was of the utmost importance to Canada's future. It is hard to argue credibly that an agreement that can be scrapped so easily is vital to a country's national interests.

The two primary objections to the agreement that appear to have been convincing to Canadian voters were that closer ties to the United States threatened Canada's cultural identity and that freer trade with the United States would undermine Canada's more generous social welfare programs. With respect to the first point it is odd that one would believe that a country's cultural identity rests upon the fact that trade restrictions keep imported goods prices higher than they would be otherwise. With respect to the second argument, Canadians need not be forced to decide if they preferred to maintain a more benevolent welfare system than the United States *or* to buy consumer goods at lower prices. Domestic taxes could certainly be used to maintain social welfare programs without distorting the prices of imported goods.

If nothing else, the Canadian vote on the free trade agreement issue, embodied in the elections on November 21, 1988, reflected the role that nationalistic fervor can play in shaping trade relations. To the extent that international negotiations remove artificial barriers to the exchange of goods and services and financial assets and technological advances in communications and transportation reduce the costs of moving people and resources across the world, the issue of group identity will take on an increasingly important role in debates regarding further liberalization.

THE OMNIBUS TRADE AND COMPETITIVENESS ACT OF 1988

One could easily write a book trying to explain the various components of the U.S. trade legislation adopted in August 1988 after almost five years of continuing debate over trade issues in Congress. The Omnibus Trade and Competitiveness Act of 1988 takes up almost 470 pages of fine print. However there are several key features of the bill that are worth noting, given the thrust of our analysis.

Perhaps the most reassuring aspect of the bill is that it does not implement specific protectionist measures that signal a U.S. retreat from the role of leader in the battle to liberalize world trade. In fact, the bill specifically provides support for expanded efforts by the president to negotiate bilateral trade agreements with Mexico and multilateral agreements through the GATT.

There are, however, several aspects of the bill that raise concerns. First, it repeatedly addresses the bilateral trade position of the United States with Japan and calls for investigations and actions, if necessary, to force Japan to provide freer access to its markets for manufactured goods from the United States. More generally, the bill calls for the executive branch to negotiate with the Japanese regarding ways to reduce Japan's bilateral surplus with the United States.

The bill also calls for efforts by the executive to negotiate reciprocal trade liberalization agreements with the developing countries on the condition that the developing countries provide more equal access to their markets for U.S. goods than has historically been the case. The obvious concern should be that such calls for fair trade relations might be used later as smoke screens by protectionist interest groups hoping to reduce competitive import pressure from developing countries in U.S. markets.

Finally, the bill increases the demands on the U.S. special trade representative to investigate possible unfair trade practices and to propose retaliatory measures. It is also explicit about the requirement that the special trade representative testify before Congress on a regular basis about active efforts to identify and redress any unfair trade practices by U.S. trading partners.

The shift toward greater accountability to Congress on the part of the special trade representative has suggested the possibility to some observers that Congress will use the new arrangement to push more directly than it has in the past for retaliatory actions in specific trade disputes. Whether or not that concern is appropriate, it is a far cry from the more direct controls of trade relations that Congress called for at the end of the 1970s.

NOTES

1. A more detailed discussion of the strategic interests of developing countries with respect to preferential treatment can be found in Martin Wolf, "Differential and More Favorable Treatment of Developing Countries and the International Trading System," *The World Bank Economic Review* 1, no. 4 (September 1987): 647-68.

2. The World Bank has published papers from a symposium that focused on the multilateral trade negotiations and developing country issues in volume 1, no. 4 of *The World Bank Economic Review* (September 1987). The papers by Hindley, Sathirathal and Siamwalla, Wolf and Valdes listed in the References are most directly related to issues we have discussed.

3. The basic data source for the discussion of contemporary economic conditions is the IMF *World Economic Outlook* for October 1988, listed more fully in the References.

4. The basic data on trade balances can be found in the USITC *International Economic Review* (March 1988), cited more fully in the References.

5. See Tables 1.1 and 1.2 on pages 9 and 10 of Jeffrey J. Schott, "The Free Trade Agreement: A US Assessment," in Jeffrey Schott and Murray G. Smith, eds., *The Canada-United States Free Trade Agreement: The Global Impact*, which appears in the References.

6. See Tables 1.4 and 1.5, pages 14 and 15, of Schott, "The Free Trade Agreement."

REFERENCES

Diebold, William, Jr. *Bilateral, Multilateralism and Canada in U.S. Trade Policy*. Cambridge, Mass.: Ballinger, 1988.

Hindley, Brian. "GATT Safeguards and Voluntary Export Restraints: What Are the Interests of the Developing Countries?" *The World Bank Economic Review* 1, no. 4 (September 1987): 689-706.

International Monetary Fund. *World Economic Outlook*. Washington, D.C. October 1988.

International Trade Communications Group. *The Canada-U.S. Free Trade Agreement*. The Department of External Affairs, Ottawa, Ontario, Canada. October 1987.

Office of Economics, USITC. "Composition of the U.S. Merchandise Trade Deficit: 1983-1987." *International Economic Review* (March 1988).

Public Laws, 100th Congress, Second Session. "The Omnibus Trade and Competitiveness Act of 1988." *United States Statutes at Large* (August 23, 1988): 1107-574.

Ray, Edward John, and Marvel, Howard P. "The Pattern of Protection in the Industrialized World." *Review of Economics and Statistics* 66, no. 3 (August 1984): 452-58.

Sathirathal, Surakiart, and Siamwalla, Ammar. "GATT Law, Agricultural Trade, and Developing Countries: Lessons from Two Case Studies." *World Bank Economic Review* 1, no. 4 (September 1987): 595-618.

Schott, Jeffrey J., and Smith, Murray G., eds. *The Canada-United States Free Trade Agreement: The Global Impact*. Institute for International Economics, Washington, D.C., and the Institute for Research on Public Policy, Ottawa, Canada, 1988.

Smith, Murray G., and Stone, Frank, eds. *Assessing the Canada-U.S. Free Trade Agreement*. Institute for Research on Public Policy, Ottawa, Canada, 1987.

Valdes, Alberto. "Agriculture in the Uruguay Round: Interests of Developing Countries" 1, no. 4 (September 1987): 571-94.

Wolf, Martin. "Differential and More Favorable Treatment of Developing Countries and the International Trading System." *The World Bank Economic Review* 1, no. 4 (September 1987): 647-68.

Appendix E: The Canada-U.S. Free Trade Agreement

CHAPTER THREE: RULES OF ORIGIN FOR GOODS

The Agreement will eliminate all tariffs on trade between Canada and the United States over a ten-year period. However, both countries will continue to apply their existing tariffs to imports from other countries. Rules of origin are, therefore, needed to define those goods which are entitled to duty-free, or "free-trade area" treatment when exported from one country to the other.

Since the Agreement is intended to benefit the producers of both countries and generate employment and income for Canadians and Americans, origin rules require that goods traded under the Agreement be produced in either country or both. The origin rules establish the general principle that goods that are wholly produced or obtained in either Canada or the United States or both will qualify for area treatment. Goods incorporating offshore raw materials or components will also qualify for area treatment if they have been sufficiently changed in either Canada or the United States, or both, to be classified differently from the raw materials or components from which they are made. In certain cases, goods, in addition to being classified differently, will also need to incur a certain percentage of manufacturing cost in either or both countries, in most cases 50 percent. This is particularly important for assembly operations.

Apparel made from fabrics woven in Canada or in the United States will qualify for duty-free treatment whereas apparel made from offshore fabrics will qualify for duty-free treatment only up to the following levels:

	Non-Woolen Apparel	Woolen Apparel
	(in million square yard equivalent)	
Imports from Canada	50	6
Imports from the United States	10.5	1.1

Above these levels, apparel made from offshore fabrics will be considered, for tariff purposes, as products of the country from which the fabrics were obtained. The levels established for imports from Canada are well above current trade levels. Canadian clothing manufacturers, including manufacturers of fine suits, coats, snowsuits and parkas, can, for all practical purposes, continue to buy their fabric from the most competitive suppliers around the world and still benefit from duty-free access to the United States. In addition, should their exports to the United States consume more than 56 million square yards of imported fabric they will pay the US tariff but be able to benefit from the drawback of Canadian duties paid on such fabric.

There is a similar quantitative limit governing duty-free exports to the United States of non-woolen fabrics or textile articles woven or knitted in Canada from yarn imported from a third country. Such exports, otherwise meeting the origin rules, will benefit from area treatment up to a maximum annual quantity. The level has initially been set at 30 million square yards for the first four years. The two governments will revisit this issue in 1990-1991 to work out a mutually satisfactory revision of this arrangement.

The rules of interpretation in Annex 301 make clear that goods that are further processed in a third country before being shipped to their final destination would not qualify for area treatment even if they meet the rule of origin. For example, cloth woven from U.S. fibres, cut in the United States but sewn into a shirt in Mexico, would qualify for duty-free re-entry into the United States under its outward-processing program, but would not qualify for duty-free entry into Canada under the Agreement.

Article 304: Definitions

For purposes of this Chapter:
direct cost of processing or direct cost of assembling means the costs directly incurred in, or that can reasonably be allocated to, the production of goods, including:

    a) the cost of all labour, including benefits and on-the-job training, labour provided in connection with supervision, quality control, shipping, receiving, storage, packaging, management at the location of the process or assembly, and other like labour, whether provided by employees or independent contractors;

    b) the cost of inspecting and testing the goods;

    c) the cost of energy fuel dies molds, tooling, and the depreciation and maintenance of machinery and equipment, without regard to whether they originate within the territory of a Party;

    d) development, design, and engineering costs;

    e) rent, mortgage interest, depreciation on buildings, property insurance premiums, maintenance, taxes and the cost of utilities for real property used in the production of the goods; and

    f) royalty, licensing, or other like payments for the right to the goods;
but not including:

g) costs relating to the general expense of doing business, such as the cost of providing executive, financial, sales, advertising, marketing, accounting and legal services, and insurance;

h) brokerage charges relating to the importation and exportation of goods;

i) costs for telephone, mail and other means of communication;

j) packing costs for exporting the goods;

k) royalty payments related to a licensing agreement to distribute or sell the goods;

l) rent, mortgage interest, depreciation on buildings, property insurance premiums, maintenance, taxes and the cost of utilities for real property used by personnel charged with administrative functions; or

m) profit on the goods;

materials means goods, other than those included as part of the direct cost of processing or assembling, used or consumed in the production of other goods;

TARIFFS

The tariff has been an important but waning import policy instrument in Canada for many decades. More than 75 percent of Canada-United States trade now moves free of duty. This figure, however, fails to take account of the trade which could take place but for tariffs. High U.S. tariffs—15 percent and more on petro-chemicals, metal alloys, clothing and many other products—continue to pose serious barriers to the U.S. market and prevent Canadian firms from achieving the economies of scale on which increased competitiveness and employment in Canadian industry depend. In addition to high tariffs, escalating tariffs on resource-based products discourage the development of more sophisticated manufacturing in Canada. While a 1.7 cent per kilo tariff on zinc ore may not impose a significant barrier, a 19 percent tariff on zinc alloy has effectively retarded the establishment of a zinc metal fabricating industry in Canada. Additionally, the existence of Canadian tariffs on imports from the United States is often costly to Canadian consumers and producers.

This chapter eliminates all remaining tariffs over a ten-year period in order to allow companies to adjust to the new competitive circumstances. The cuts will begin January 1, 1989 and after that date, no existing tariff may be increased unless specifically provided elsewhere in the agreement (for example, in Chapter Eleven providing for temporary emergency safeguards). Tariffs will be eliminated by January 1, 1998 on the basis of three formulas:

for those sectors ready to compete now, tariffs will be eliminated on the Agreement entering into force on January 1, 1989, for example:

computers and equipment	some pork
some unprocessed fish	fur & fur garments
leather	whiskey
yeast	animal feeds
unwrought aluminum	ferro alloys
vending machines and parts	needles
airbrakes for railroad cars	skis
skates	warranty repairs
some paper-making machinery	motorcycles

for other sectors, tariffs will be eliminated in five equal steps, starting on January 1, 1989, for example:

subway cars	chemicals including resins
printed matter	(excluding drugs and
paper and paper products	cosmetics)
paints	furniture
explosives	hardwood plywood
after market auto parts	most machinery

all other tariffs will be eliminated in ten steps, most starting on January 1, 1989, for example:

most agricultural products	steel
textiles and apparel	appliances
softwood plywood	pleasure craft
railcars	tires

Both countries refund the customs duty levied on imported materials and components when these are incorporated into exported goods. This is called duty drawback. In the U.S., for example, foreign trade zones are often used as a means for U.S. exporters to avoid having to pay U.S. duties on imported components. Some of the advantages of the free-trade area, however, would be eroded if a U.S. producer could source some components from a third country, manufacture a final product in a U.S. foreign trade zone without paying any duty on these components and compete in Canada with a manufacturer who has paid Canadian duties on the same components. Accordingly, the agreement provides for duty drawbacks on third-country materials and similar programs to be eliminated for bilateral trade after January 1, 1994.

There are two exceptions to the general drawback obligation. Drawbacks will continue to be permitted on citrus products. As well, duties paid on fabric imported and made up into apparel and subsequently exported to the other country can be recovered if the apparel does not qualify for duty-free treatment. Chapter Three establishes quotas for duty-free treatment for apparel made up from imported fabrics. Should trade rise above these levels, Canadian manufacturers using imported fabric will be able to apply for drawback of Canadian duties paid on fabric incorporated into apparel exported to the United States.

Import and Export Restrictions

Import or export quotas can be severely damaging to international trade by limiting the quantity which may be traded. In Article 407, Canada and the United States affirm their GATT obligations not to prohibit or restrict imports or exports of goods in bilateral trade except under strictly defined circumstances. Nothing in the Agreement, for example, in any way prevents Canada from prohibiting the import of pornographic materials (see Chapter Twelve). Outside of such special circumstances, these obligations provide a guarantee that the benefits of tariff elimination will not be eroded by quotas or other restrictions. Unless specifically allowed by the agreement, e.g., "grandfathered" or permitted under the GATT, existing quantitative restrictions will be eliminated, either immediately or according to a timetable.

Among those restrictions eliminated are the Canadian embargoes on used aircraft and used automobiles (provided in Chapter Ten) and the U.S. embargo on lottery materials. Canada and the United States will retain their right to control log exports while the United States will retain marine transportation restrictions under the Jones Act (provided for in Chapter Twelve). For shipbuilders, Canada has reserved the right to apply quantitative restrictions on U.S. vessels until such time as the United States removes the prohibitions under the Jones Act on Canadian vessels. Provincial laws governing the export of unprocessed fish caught off the East Coast have been safeguarded (also provided for in Chapter Twelve). Both countries will continue to be able to apply import restrictions to agricultural goods where these are necessary to ensure the operation of a domestic supply management or support program.

Where either Canada or the United States applies restrictions on trade with other countries, it may limit or prohibit the pass-through of imports from those other countries into its own territory. It may also require that its exports to the other be consumed within the other's territory. Controls on exports to third countries for strategic reasons will thus continue to be enforced.

Export Taxes

Neither country applies export taxes as a matter of general policy. These taxes render exports less competitive and are highly disruptive of production and investment. Article 408 confirms existing practice by specifically prohibiting export taxes or duties on bilateral trade unless the same tax is applied on the same goods consumed domestically.

The 1986 Softwood Lumber Understanding, which requires Canada to collect an export tax on Canadian softwood exports to the United States until such time as the provincial governments have adjusted certain stumpage practices, is specifically grandfathered by Article 1910.

ANNEX 407.6
ELIMINATION OF QUANTITATIVE RESTRICTIONS

1. Canada shall eliminate, as of January 1, 1989, the embargo (set out in Tariff Item 99216-1 of Schedule C of the Customs Tariff, or its successor) on used or second-hand aeroplanes and aircraft of all kinds.

2. The United States of America shall eliminate, as of January 1, 1993, the embargo set out in 19 U.S.C. 1305 of any

   (a) lottery ticket,

   (b) printed paper that may be used as a lottery ticket, or

   (c) advertisement,

for a United States lottery, printed in Canada.

The principal trade liberalizing elements agreed in agriculture are:

Article 701: prohibition of export subsidies on bilateral trade. This marks the first time that any two governments have agreed to prohibitions on export subsidies in the agricultural sector and marks an important signal to others around the world; Article 701: elimination of Canadian Western Grain Transportation rail subsidies on exports to the United States shipped through Canadian west coast ports; the provision does not affect shipments through Thunder Bay or exports to third countries through west coast ports;

Articles 401 and 702: the phased elimination of all tariffs over a period of ten years (Canada is allowed to restore temporarily tariffs on fresh fruits and vegetables for a 20-year period under depressed price conditions in order to give Canada's horticultural industry an opportunity to adjust to more open trading conditions). This snapback provision applies only if the average acreage under cultivation for that product is constant or declining. Acreage converted from wine-grape cultivation is not included in this calculation;

Article 702: Special Provisions for Fresh Fruits and Vegetables

1. (a) Notwithstanding Article 401, for a period of 20 years from the entry into force of this Agreement, each Party reserves the right to apply a temporary duty on fresh fruits or vegetables originating in the territory of the other Party and imported into its territory, when
   (i) for each of five consecutive working days the import price of such fruit or vegetable for each such day is below 90 percent of the average monthly import price, for the month in which that day falls, over the preceding five years, excluding the years with the highest and lowest average monthly import price; and
   (ii) the planted acreage in the importing Party for the particular fruit or vegetable is no higher than the average acreage over the preceding five years, excluding the years with the highest and lowest acreage.

5. Each Party shall, for purposes of restricting the importation of a grain or of a grain product due to its content of that grain, retain the right, to the extent consistent with other provisions of this Agreement, to introduce or, where they have been eliminated, reintroduce quantitative import restrictions or import fees on imports of such grain or grain products originating in the territory of the other Party if such imports increase significantly as a result of a substantial change in either Party's support programs for that grain. For purposes of this paragraph, grain means wheat, oats, barley, rye, corn, triticale and sorghum.

Article 706: Market Access for Poultry and Eggs

If Canada maintains or introduces quantitative import restrictions on any of the following goods, Canada shall permit the importation of such goods as follows:
   (a) the level of global import quota on chicken and chicken products, as defined in Annex 706, for any given year shall be no less than 7.5 percent of the previous year's domestic production of chicken in Canada;
   (b) the level of global import quota on turkey and turkey products, as defined in Annex 706, for any given year shall be no less than 3.5 percent of that year's Canadian domestic turkey production quota; and

   (c) the level of global import quotas on eggs and egg products for any given year shall be no less than the following percentages of the previous year's Canadian domestic shell egg production:

     (i) 1.647 percent for shell eggs;

     (ii) 0.714 percent for frozen, liquid and further processed eggs; and

     (iii) 0.627 percent for powdered eggs.

Article 707: Market Access for Sugar-Containing Products

The United States of America shall not introduce or maintain any quantitative import restriction or import fee on any good originating in Canada containing ten percent or less sugar by dry weight for purposes of restricting the sugar content of such good.

Article 804: Distribution

1. Any measure related to distribution of wine or distilled spirits of the other Party shall conform with Chapter Five.

2. Notwithstanding paragraph 1, and provided that distribution measures otherwise ensure conformity with Chapter Five, a Party may:

   (a) maintain or introduce a measure limiting on-premise sales by a winery or distillery to those wines or distilled spirits produced on its premises; or

   (b) maintain a measure requiring private wine store outlets in existence on October 4, 1987 in the provinces of Ontario and British Columbia to discriminate in favour of wine of those provinces to a degree no greater than the discrimination required by such existing measure.

3. Nothing in this Agreement shall prohibit the Province of Quebec from requiring that any wine sold in grocery stores in Quebec be bottled in Quebec, provided that alternative outlets are provided in Quebec for the sale of wine of the United States of America, whether or not such wine is bottled in Quebec.

ANNEX 902.5

Import Measures

1. The United States of America shall exempt Canada from any restriction on the enrichment of foreign uranium under section 161v of the Atomic Energy Act.

Export Measures

2. Canada shall exempt the United States of America from the Canadian Uranium Upgrading Policy as announced by the Minister of State for Mines on October 18, 1985.

3. The United States of America shall exempt Canada from the prohibition on the exportation of Alaskan oil under section 7(d) of the Export Administration Act of 1979, as amended, up to a maximum volume of 50 thousand barrels per day on an annual average basis, subject to the condition that such oil be transported to Canada from a suitable location within the lower 48 states.

TRADE IN AUTOMOTIVE GOODS

Article 1002: Waiver of Customs Duties

1. Neither Party shall grant a waiver of otherwise applicable customs duties to a recipient other than those recipients listed in Annex 1002.1, nor shall either Party expand the extent or application of, or extend the duration of, any waiver granted to any such recipient with respect to:
  (a) automotive goods imported into its territory from any country where such waiver is conditioned, explicitly or implicitly, upon the fulfillment of performance requirements applicable to any goods; or
  (b) any goods imported from any country where such waiver is conditioned, explicitly or implicitly, upon the fulfillment of performance requirements applicable to automotive goods.

2. Waivers of customs duties granted to the recipients listed in Part Two of Annex 1002.1, where the amount of duty waived depends on exports, shall:
  (a) after January 1, 1989 exclude exports to the territory of the other Party in calculating the duty waived; and
  (b) terminate on or before January 1, 1998.

3. Waivers of customs duties granted to the recipients listed in Part Three of Annex 1002.1, where the amount of duty waived depends on Canadian value added contained in production in Canada, shall terminate not later than:
  (a) January 1, 1996; or
  (b) such earlier date specified in existing agreements between Canada and the recipient of the waiver.

Article 1003: Import Restrictions

Canada shall phase out the import restriction on used automobiles set out in tariff item 99215-1 of Schedule C to the Customs Tariff, or its successor, in five annual stages commencing on January 1, 1989 in accordance with the following schedule:
  (a) in the first year, used automobiles that are eight years old or older;
  (b) in the second year, used automobiles that are six years old or older;
  (c) in the third year, used automobiles that are four years old or older;
  (d) in the fourth year, used automobiles that are two years old or older; and
  (e) in the fifth year and thereafter, no restrictions.

Index

Agricultural products. *See* Processed foods

Aluminum, 171, 175, 188

Analytical framework, 19-22, 33, 189-90

Apparel, 85, 143, 148, 149, 152, 198-99, 201, 221. *See also* Textiles; *name of specific nation*

Argentina: and the Canada-United States Free Trade Agreement, 222; and capital flight, 122; economic conditions in, 109; exports to the U.S. in 1986 of, 165; export strenghts of, 188; and the GSP, 89, 149, 152, 165, 169-70, 171, 188-93; and the leather industry, 165; as a major debtor nation, 5-6, 68-69, 90-91, 99, 146; and manufactured goods, 165, 171; and NTBs, 193; and petroleum products, 165; as a primary product exporter, 100, 142, 149, 152; and processed foods, 89, 149, 152, 165, 169; production characteristics of exports in, 188-89; and restructuring of debt, 122, 139; and tariffs, 193; and textiles, 89, 192; top industries in, 171. *See also* Major debtor nations

Arms talks, 76-79

Automobile industry, 24, 36, 221. *See also name of specific nation*

Baack, Bennett D., 9, 10, 21-22, 39

Baker, James, 110

Balance of trade, 34, 51, 60, 103, 105-6, 217, 219

Baldwin, Robert E., 12

Banks, 109-11, 120, 122, 141-42

Becker, Gary, 5, 15-16, 17

Bilateral agreements, 14-15, 26, 45-46, 53, 201, 216, 217, 224. *See also name of specific agreement*

Bradley, Bill, 110

Brazil: and the Canada-United States Free Trade Agreement, 222; and capital flight, 122; and consumer goods, 149, 152; economic conditions in, 109; exports to the U.S. in 1986 of, 165, 168; and the footloose industries, 191, 192; and the footwear industry, 165, 168, 171; and the GSP, 88-89, 149, 152, 165, 168, 169-70, 171, 175, 188-93; and intraindustry trade, 47-48; as a major debtor nation, 5-6, 68-69, 90-91, 99, 146; and manufactured

NTBs, 46, 81-82, 144; and the
Omnibus Trade and Competitiveness
Act (1988), 224; and processed
foods, 80-82, 143, 144, 215; proposal for debt reduction by, 110;
and research and development,
81-82; semiconductor agreement between U.S. and, 14; and tariffs, 46,
82; and textiles, 80-82, 143, 215;
U.S. bilateral agreement with, 217;
as a U.S. competitor, 14; U.S. trade
deficit with, 218-19; and VERs, 12,
26,
Kennedy Round: analysis of the, 12-13;
bad-faith component of the, 76-77;
and consumer goods, 22, 74, 80-83;
and the developing nations, 80-83,
144; and domestic concerns, 74; and
employment, 79; and the 50 percent
rule, 74, 77; and the GSP, 73-74,
80-83, 144; and low-skill, labor-
intensive products, 12-13; and
NTBs, 11, 18, 22, 24, 25, 74, 75-76,
77, 80-83, 144; and the pattern of
tariff protection, 77; and special
interest groups, 74, 76-77, 79, 145;
and tariff cuts, 11, 18, 22, 40,
46-47, 73-74, 75-76, 77, 79-80, 143,
144, 189, 190, 215; and trade
liberalization, 10-11, 25, 79, 215;
U.S. legislation concerned with the,
12. *See also name of specific goods*
Keynes, John Maynard, 122
Kissinger, Henry, 14
Korea: and the apparel industry, 168,
169; and the automobile industry,
168; and the Canada-United States
Free Trade Agreement, 222; and
consumer goods, 149, 152, 169, 188,
189, 191, 192; exports to the U.S. in
1986 of, 168; and the footwear
industry, 168, and the GSP, 149,
152, 168, 169-70, 175, 188-93; as a
major debtor nation, 5-6, 68-69, 99;
as a manufacturing exporter, 100,
142, 149, 152, 170, 175, 191; and
NTBs, 193; and processed foods,
188; production characteristics of

exports in, 188-89; and tariffs, 193;
and textiles, 149, 152, 169, 188,
189, 191, 192; top industries in,
175; U.S. trade deficit with, 219.
See also Major debtor nations
Krugman, Paul, 47

Labor, 36, 147-48, 199, 200. *See
also* Employment
Latin American, 193. *See also* Carib-
bean; *name of specific nation*
Leather industry, 86, 148, 198-99,
201. *See also name of specific
nation*
Lome Convention, 73, 84, 86
Long Term Agreement (LTA) on
Tariffs and Trade (1962), 12

Major debtor nations: allocation of
resources in, 188; and the banks,
120, 122, 139; and the burden of
debt, 115, 118-39; and capital
flight, 122, 139; and consumer
goods, 100, 149, 152, 168-69,
188-91, 193-94; credibility of, 6;
and currency stability, 6; definition
of, 99, 142; diversity in, 100, 149;
economic conditions among, 101-11,
113, 115; export earnings of, 118,
120, 146, 169-70; exports of the,
111, 113, 149-53; and fiscal policy,
118; and foreign investments, 6;
GDP in, 101, 111, 120; and the
GSP, 99-100, 146-49, 165, 168-70,
188-94; importance of, 142; and
inflation, 103, 107, 109; and international market conditions,
111-18; and monetary policy, 118;
and processed foods, 100, 149, 152,
168-69, 188-91, 193-94; and terms
of trade, 115, 118; and textiles, 100,
149, 152, 168-69, 188-91, 193-94.
See also Argentina; Brazil;
Indonesia; Korea; Mexico; Philippines; Venezuela
Manufactured goods: and the Canada-
United States Free Trade Agreement, 220-23; and the Caribbean,

trade sector, 43, 45; and special interest groups, 13, 22-23, 45; and textiles, 100, 143, 189; in the U.S., 10-16. *See also* Tariff cuts; Tariff rates; *name of specific nation*
Taussig, Frank, 9-10
Terms of trade, 115, 118
Textiles: and the Canada-United States Free Trade Agreement, 220-23; and the Caribbean, 87; and the CBI, 47, 198-99, 200, 201, 206-7; and developing nations, 142; and the European Community, 80-82; and the GSP, 47, 80-91, 100, 144-47, 149, 152, 165-69, 188-93, 198-99, 216; and the history of protectionism in the U.S., 36; and intraindustry trade, 47-48; and the Kennedy Round, 25, 46, 80-83; and the major debtor nations, 100, 149, 152, 168-69, 188-91, 193-94; and NTBs, 80-82, 100, 143-44, 189; and political parties, 36; tariffs, 100, 143, 189; and VERs, 12. *See also name of specific nation*
Tokyo Round, 10-11, 12, 14, 24, 79, 189, 192
Trade Act (1974), 12
Trade deficits, 60, 61, 190, 217-18
Trade Expansion Act (1962), 12
Trade liberalization: and bilateral agreements, 217; and the current transition in U.S. trade policy, 54, 56; and economic conditions, 145; and emerging patterns of protectionism, 61, 68; and employment, 87; and the executive branch, 20; and the GSP, 79-80, 215; and the history of U.S. trade policy, 33-39; and the Kennedy Round, 79, 215; and multilateral agreements, 217-18; and NTBs, 68; and the Omnibus Trade and Competitiveness Act (1988), 224; and patterns of protectionism in the U.S., 9-16; and special interest groups, 46-48; and the Tokyo Round, 79; and twentieth-century U.S. trade policy, 39-48

Trade policy: elements in the formation of, 7-8; literature review of postwar, 8; micro-/macroviews of decisionmaking, 16-18. *See also name of specific nation*
Trade regulation, 23-26, 79-80
Trade sector, 43. 45, 48, 51, 54, 56

Underwood-Simmons Tariff Act (1913), 9
Unions, labor, 147-48
United Kingdom, 12, 103, 105, 106
United States: current transition in trade policy of the, 48-56; future course of trade policies in the, 218-24; GSP exports of developing nations to the, 83-91; history of protectionism in the, 33-39; patterns of protectionism in the, 9-16, 74; twentieth-century trade policy of the, 39-48. *See also name of specific topic*
United States-Canada Free Trade Agreement, 7
United States International Trade Commission, 199
Uruguay Round, 7, 11, 60, 79, 148, 216, 217-18
USSR, 85

Venezuela: and capital flight, 122; and export earnings, 142; exports to the U.S. in 1986 of, 168; export strengths of, 188; and the footloose industries, 191, 192; as a fuel exporter, 100, 109, 142, 149, 152; and the GSP, 89, 149, 152, 168, 169-70, 175, 188-93; as a major debtor nation, 5-6, 68-69, 90-91, 99, 146; and manufactured goods, 168, 188; and NTBs, 193; and oil prices, 113; and petroleum products, 168, 175, 188, 191; production characteristics of exports in, 188-89; and restructuring of debt, 122, 139; and the steel industry, 168; and tariffs, 193; and textiles, 192; top industries in, 175, 188. *See also* Major debtor nations

VERs (voluntary export restrictions), 12, 14, 26, 45-46, 78-79

West Germany, 14, 103, 105, 106, 107

Wheat sales, 14

Workers, as a special interest group, 19

Workplace conditions, 147-48, 198

World Bank, 56, 68

About the Author

EDWARD JOHN RAY is Professor and Chairperson of the Department of Economics at Ohio State University. Ray is coauthoring a book on the history of financing of the federal government in the United States as well as revising a principles text. He has had research support from the Department of Labor, Department of Commerce, U.S.A.I.D., and the Office of Technology Assessment. Ray's research has been published in a number of leading economics journals including: *The American Economic Review, The Journal of Political Economy, The Quarterly Journal of Economics, The Review of Economic Studies, The Review of Economics and Statistics, The Journal of Law and Economics,* and the *Journal of Economic History.*